Cracking the TExES

FRITZ STEWART AND RENÉE HUMPHREYS

FIRST EDITION

RANDOM HOUSE, INC.
NEW YORK

www.PrincetonReview.com

Princeton Review Publishing, L. L. C.
2315 Broadway
New York, NY 10024
E-mail: booksupport@review.com

ISBN 0-375-76457-7

Editor: Allegra Burton
Production Editor: Patricia Dublin
Production Coordinator: Jennifer Arias

Manufactured in the United States of America.

10 9 8 7 6 5 4 3 2 1

First Edition

ACKNOWLEDGMENTS

Thanks to Randal Ford of the University of Texas at Arlington and Stuart Bammert, both of whom answered important questions in the course of my research. Thanks also to Ellen Mendlow and Allegra Viner for their constructive criticism, their unfailing good humor, and their patience.

CONTENTS

Introduction

The Princeton Review was started in 1981 by a couple of college graduates helping 19 students prepare for the SAT, and over the past twenty years we have grown into the country's leading test-preparation company. We work with students at all levels to prepare them for college entrance exams, graduate school tests, and professional development exams. Now our goal is to help you pass the TExES. And we can help you, because our methods work.

ABOUT THE TExES

WHAT IS IT AND WHO WROTE IT?

Anyone who wishes to become a certified public school teacher in the state of Texas will have to take an exam from the battery of tests known as the TExES. Before we get started, there are three acronyms that you should know:

TEKS—Texas Essential Knowledge and Skills

The TEKS is state-required curriculum for students in Texas. It's an all-encompassing curriculum that is supposed to ensure a seamless educational experience from kindergarten through college for all students throughout the state.

SBEC—Texas State Board for Educator Certification

The SBEC developed standards for teachers designed to match the TEKS curriculum. These standards are the lists of things that the SBEC believes that every new teacher in Texas should know.

TExES—Texas Examination of Educator Standards

Once the SBEC decided on the standards, it wrote a test to measure whether a teacher possessed enough professional knowledge to meet those standards. The result is the TExES test. It's actually written and administered by a company called NES, which stands for National Educational Services.

WHY AM I TAKING THE TExES?

If you're not already certified to teach in the Texas public school system, you will need to pass some combination of the TExES exams, according to which field you want to teach in. Usually you will need to pass at least one test that demonstrates you are an expert in your field (math, biology, chemistry, English, for example) and a TExES PPR, which stands for Pedagogy and Professional Responsibilities exam, for the specific set of grade levels you want to teach in, which are listed on the following page:

Early Childhood (EC)–4

4–8

8–12

EC–12

Trade and Industrial Education 8–12

This book is designed to prepare you for the first four of these (the PPR EC–4, PPR 4–8, PPR 8–12, and PPR EC–12 examinations) so other TExES exams will not be discussed anywhere else in this book. This is not to say that you won't need to pass other parts of the TExES in order to be certified. For information about exactly which tests are required, contact the SBEC at its website— www.sbec.state.tx.us/SBECOnline/certinfo/becometeacher.asp—and be sure to ask your advisor or the certification officer of your educator preparation program for more information.

WHAT ARE THE REQUIREMENTS TO TAKE THE TExES?

You are required to take the TExES test if you fall into one of the following five categories:

- You are fulfilling the program requirements of an approved Texas educator preparation program.

- You are fully certified to teach in a state other than Texas or a country other than the United States, and you are seeking a Texas standard teacher certificate.

- You hold a valid Texas standard or lifetime teacher certificate and you are seeking an additional certificate or endorsement.

- You are seeking to demonstrate content mastery as a charter school teacher.

- You are seeking a temporary 8–12 teaching certificate.

WHICH TExES PPR EXAM SHOULD I TAKE?

That depends. You are probably interested in taking a TExES PPR exam to fulfill the requirements of an educator preparation program. If this is the case, talk to your advisor or program director to help determine which of the PPR tests you should be taking.

Starting in the 2004–2005 school year, recent college graduates can also apply to teach in their field of expertise at the 8 through 12 grade levels if they pass two TExES tests (a content exam and PPR exam). Teachers who fall into this category will be asked to complete 80 hours of training before school starts and another 300 hours during the first two-year teaching period.

You may also need to take the TExES PPR exam if you are certified to teach in another state or country and wish to obtain a Texas standard teacher certificate. The SBEC has compiled a list of certification tests from other states and countries that they deem acceptable substitutes for the TExES. The list gets updated frequently, and the most recent information can be found at the SBEC website: www. sbec.state.tx.us. If you find that you need to take a TExES PPR exam for this reason, call the SBEC at 1-888-863-5880 for special information about registering.

If you already hold a Texas standard or lifetime certificate in your age range, you don't need to take a TExES PPR exam at all.

How Often Is the Test Administered?

The TExES is administered in October, December, February (or early March), April, May, and June, for a total of six administrations per school year. You can find the exact dates of each administration on the SBEC website.

Two of these administrations (those in April and June) offer testing only at a limited number of sites, which include the following:

> Abilene area
>
> Austin area
>
> Dallas-Central area
>
> Edinburg/McAllen area
>
> El Paso area
>
> Fort Worth/Arlington area
>
> Houston-Southwest area
>
> Houston-West area
>
> Lubbock area
>
> Lufkin/Nacogdoches area
>
> San Antonio area
>
> Waco area

How Do I Sign Up?

The first thing you will need to do is get an authorization-to-test bar code label from your advisor or certification officer at your educator preparation program, or through the SBEC if you're trying to get a temporary teaching certificate. You won't be able to register without it.

There are three possible registration deadlines: Regular Registration, Late Registration, and Emergency Registration. The Regular Registration deadline is always about five weeks earlier than the test date. The Late Registration deadline is about three weeks before the test date, and you'll be charged an additional $30 fee if you wait that long. (For some reason, Late Registration is not available for the limited-site exam test dates.) At many sites, you can even register up to one week before the test. That's called Emergency Registration, and if you wait that long you'll be gouged for an additional $70.

You can register by web or by mail. You can also register by telephone, but only for Emergency Registration.

To register on the web, you'll need an email address, your social security number, and a credit card (MasterCard or VISA) for payment. Log on to the website at: www.texes.nesinc.com.

To register by mail, request a copy of the registration form by calling NES (National Evaluation Systems, the company that actually administers and scores the exam) at 1-800-423-7088. You can't do Emergency Registration by mail. You must register by Internet or by phone if you're past the Late Registration deadline.

To register by phone (for Emergency Registration only), call 1-512-927-5151, from 8:00 A.M. to 5:00 P.M. Central Time, Monday through Friday (excluding holidays).

HOW MUCH DOES IT COST TO TAKE THE TExES?

It costs $82 per test to take the TExES. If you need to take three tests for your certification, you'll need to shell out $246.

ABOUT THE COMPUTER-ADMINISTERED TESTS

Recently, the SBEC began offering computer versions of some TExES examinations, and we expect that eventually all TExES exams will be offered in computer-based format. As of this writing, the only PPR exam that is offered on computer is the PPR EC–4 exam. The content tested on the computer version is identical to that tested on the paper-and-pencil version, and the time given to complete the exam is the same, too.

In our view, here are the advantages and disadvantages of the computer-administered tests:

Advantages

- You find out your score immediately.

- The test is offered several times per month.

- The test is offered in more locations than the paper-and-pencil version.

Disadvantages

- Taking an exam on a computer is disconcerting for many people.

- There is a $28 surcharge, so the test costs $110.

For information about how to register for the computer-administered version, call 1-800-523-7088.

HOW ARE THE TESTS SCORED?

All TExES exams are scored on a scale of 100–300, and the passing score for each exam is 240. The exams aren't graded on a curve, so you don't have to worry about your performance relative to other test takers. If you get enough questions right, then you pass.

One important point: There is no penalty for getting a question wrong, so you should never leave a question blank.

WHAT IS THE FORMAT OF A PPR EXAM?

The PPR exams consist of approximately 90 multiple-choice questions; 80 of these will count toward your score. The other 10 or so are experimental questions that the SBEC is trying out on you before they're used on a test as questions that count. You won't know which questions are experimental though, so you'll have to assume that every question counts toward your score.

The questions can come singly, in small groups known as clusters, or in larger groups called decision sets. But they're all still multiple-choice questions. There are no essays or short-answer questions.

Each PPR test is supposed to take less than two-and-a-half hours to complete. However, if you're only taking one test during a testing session, you are allowed to spend up to five hours working on it.

WHAT IS THIS BOOK FOR?

Our book will help you understand the following:

- The content that will be tested on the PPR exam you choose to take

- How that content will be tested on the exam

Each of these aspects of the test is important. Understanding the content will do you no good unless you understand how your knowledge of the content will be tested on the exam. On the other hand, understanding the structure of the exam will not help you unless you have a basic grasp of pedagogy, educational psychology, and the legal requirements of teachers in Texas.

The next chapter will show you the basic approach you should take to answer each question on the TExES. The following chapters will review the content that appears on the test and show you how to apply it to the questions using the basic approach.

Ready? Let's get started.

PART I

Orientation

1

General TExES Strategies

GENERAL TEXES STRATEGIES

Consider the following question (which you would *never* see on the TExES):

> 1. You have a Saturday afternoon free. What activity should you perform?

One of the reasons the test writers would never ask a question like this (aside from the fact that it has nothing to do with education) is that virtually anything could be a plausible answer. You could say, "Sleep," or you could say, "Write a book," and, while both of those are activities you could perform on a Saturday afternoon, you'd have no idea whether either one was the answer that they are looking for. Why is it important for you to give them what they're looking for? Because they're the ones who decide what the right answer is. It's important to know now that what *you* think doesn't matter. This exam is all about giving the test writers what they want.

The good news is that they give you clues.

In fact, they go so far as to give you the right answer. Unfortunately, they give you three wrong ones, too. Let's take a look at the same question with some answer choices.

> 1. You have a Saturday afternoon free. Which of the following activities should you perform?
>
> A. Read a good book.
>
> B. Play a round of golf.
>
> C. Eat a quart of your favorite ice cream.
>
> D. Run three miles.

There are only four answer choices, so your chances of getting the problem right just jumped from practically 0 percent to 25 percent. Now, there are merits to all of the above choices, and your answer at this point should be something like, "Heck, I don't know. They all seem like pretty good ideas to me!" or "It depends." And you're right. It does depend. Fortunately, the test writers also give you more clues in the questions you will see on the exam. Often the writers tell you, right in the questions, what your goals are. Try answering the question now:

> 2. You have a Saturday afternoon free. Which of the following activities should you perform if you wish to burn calories and best improve your cardiovascular health?
>
> A. Read a good book.
>
> B. Play a round of golf.
>
> C. Eat a quart of your favorite ice cream.
>
> D. Run three miles.

Aha! Now you've got a basis for judgment.

The way to answer these questions is to use process of elimination, or POE. All of a sudden, you know a couple of answer choices are wrong. Reading a book and eating ice cream, though reasonable Saturday afternoon activities, do nothing to burn calories or improve your cardiovascular health. Which means you can cross out answer choices A and C.

Now you have a slightly tougher problem. Playing golf and running both would burn calories, and probably improve your cardiovascular health, too. So, reread the question. The question asks which activity would *best* improve your health. Perhaps you've never played golf, and perhaps you've never run, but maybe you've met a few runners and golfers and maybe you've seen professionals on TV. Which group tends to be in better shape overall? That's right, runners.

You might be thinking, "Yeah, but what about really overweight people? They shouldn't go running without talking to a doctor first, and they might actually do themselves more damage by running than by golfing!" Or, you might be saying to yourself, "What if the golf course is really long—longer than three miles? Then, if the golfer walks the whole way, the golfer will be burning more calories than the runner!" If you're thinking along these lines, then you're overthinking the problem. If the test writers wanted you to consider the exceptional cases, they'd have said so somewhere in the question itself. They give you clues, remember?

The *best* answer to this question is D.

THE STRATEGY

Believe it or not, you can use similar methods of reasoning on TExES PPR questions. The process works like this:

> Step 1: **Identify the scenario.**
>
> Step 2: **Use POE to narrow down the answer choices.**
>
> Step 3: **Choose from among the remaining answer choices. (We'll call this step "Make a final decision" for short.)**

Let's break down each of these steps:

Step 1: Identify the scenario.
There are two important things to look for here:

- Age range of students (if applicable)

- Goal of scenario (if applicable)

Not every question will include these details, but if a question does, the right answer will hinge on correctly identifying them.

Step 2: Use POE to narrow down the answer choices.
There will probably be one or two answer choices that are obviously incorrect. Use process of elimination to identify the incorrect answer choices as well as the one or two that could be correct. Cross out the ones that can't be right.

Step 3: Make a final decision.
This is obviously the tricky part, but with a combination of common sense, a working knowledge of the fundamental educational concepts being tested, and an understanding of what the test writers are looking for, you will be able to accurately choose the correct answer.

Let's try the process with a question similar to one you might see on the actual exam:

2. A first-grade teacher wants her class to understand how a flapadillo works. Which of the following technologies would be most appropriate for her class?

    A.   video

    B.   simulation

    C.   word processor

    D.   spreadsheet

Step 1: Identify the scenario.

- The age range is specific, and quite young: first graders.

- The goal is to use technology to get students to understand how a flapadillo works.

Step 2: Use POE to narrow down the answer choices.

I don't know whether you know how a flapadillo works. I don't care if you know what a flapadillo *is*. It doesn't matter. This is a first-grade class. It is extremely unlikely that first graders will benefit from the use of a spreadsheet or a word processor, because those technologies involve math and verbal skills that most first graders do not yet possess. So we can immediately cross off answer choices C and D. That leaves A and B.

Step 3: Make a final decision.

Both videos and simulations can be used effectively as teaching tools under various circumstances. And, in the absence of any other information, it's difficult to tell what the right answer is. So, let's add a new rule that can help you make a final decision:

If you're down to two answer choices that both seem plausible, pick the one that involves *more* **work for the teacher.**

Why? Think about what this test is designed to do. This test is supposed to weed out unfit teachers, according to the criteria laid out by the SBEC. Do you think that the SBEC would prefer to certify a hard-working teacher or a lazy teacher? It would prefer a hard-working teacher, of course.

So, which requires more work on the part of the teacher: popping a video into the VCR, or planning and demonstrating an effective simulation? Naturally, planning and demonstrating an effective simulation is going to take more time and effort, and therefore B is the right answer.

If we asked the SBEC to explain why this is the right answer to the question, it would probably start off like this:

This question addresses PPR Competency 009:

The teacher incorporates the effective use of technology to plan, organize, deliver, and evaluate instruction for all students.

It would probably eliminate choices B and C for pretty much the same reasons we did. But then it would likely go into some long discussion about how educational researchers have proved that passive learning systems (such as videos) are less helpful to students than active ones (such as simulations). You might have known that from having taken education courses. Or you might simply consider that common sense. And the more you know about such things, the easier you will find many of these questions to be. But even if you didn't have any knowledge about this aspect of educational theory, you could still get the question right simply by knowing that using simulations requires more work for teachers than turning on the TV and watching a video. And we still don't know what a flapadillo is. (Don't worry about it. We made it up.)

THE CRITERIA

You're probably saying to yourself, "The questions can't all be that easy." And you're right; they're not. But process of elimination is an extraordinarily powerful tool, especially when used in conjunction with a few key criteria. Incorrect answers on the TExES are actually very predictable.

You should always cross out answers that do any of the following:

Answer the wrong question

If you identify the scenario, you should be able to eliminate answers that are reasonable and make good educational sense—but fail to meet the stated goal of the question. Misreading the problem is the single greatest source of errors, so be careful.

Contradict accepted educational theories and practices or Texas state law

Occasionally, you'll be faced with a down-to-two-choices situation (or even more rarely, a question that tests nothing but educational theory content) that will be easier to answer if you're familiar with some basic educational pedagogy and the Texas laws regulating education. We'll review the important concepts and legalities in later chapters.

Make things easy for the teacher

We already discussed this one: when in doubt, pick the answer choice that involves more work for the teacher.

Use extreme language

It's difficult to justify an answer choice that includes words like *only* and *always*. (Questions dealing with ethics or Texas state law can be exceptions to this rule.) Teaching is both an art and a science, and consequently there are very few absolutes.

Upset parents / caregivers, other teachers, or the school administration

This may seem like common sense, but you can bet the SBEC would prefer not to certify people who are likely to inflame potentially difficult situations and turn them into crises. Always pick the answer that stresses polite, respectful behavior between teachers and other adults.

Let's try some more problems:

3. A first-year middle school history teacher is starting to plan lessons for a unit on the colonization of New England. Which of the following initial approaches is most likely to result in an effective lesson plan for the unit?

    A. Review the curriculum guidelines and TEKS standards.

    B. Try to anticipate every question a student could ask and formulate responses.

    C. Brainstorm a list of related activities.

    D. Plan an introductory lesson explaining the reasons why New England was colonized.

Step 1: Identify the scenario.

- We're in middle school.

- The goal is an effective lesson plan.

Step 2: Use POE to narrow down the answer choices.

Answer choice A looks pretty good, but seems very general. B is incorrect for several reasons: "every" is an example of extreme language, and it would be impossible to anticipate every question. Further, anticipating every possible question wouldn't accomplish the goal of an effective lesson plan, because the plan would lack structure. Get rid of B. Choice C is a good secondary step, but wouldn't make a good first step. Get rid of it, too. Choice D is a good initial lesson idea, so let's leave it in.

Step 3: Make a final decision.

Choice D is a specific, good idea for creating the first lesson, and A is a general idea that could be applied almost anywhere. Is that a criterion for judgment? No. What was the question asking? "Which of the following initial approaches is most likely to result in an effective lesson plan for the unit?" Would the planning of the first lesson guarantee that all the others are effective, too? Probably not. Would reviewing curriculum guidelines help to plan a whole unit? Probably. The best answer is A.

Try another one:

4. Which one of the following questions would most likely stimulate students' divergent thinking?

    A. Is 23 a prime number?

    B. How many different ways can you think of to clear a clogged drainpipe?

    C. What is the capital of North Dakota?

    D. What are the two chemical elements that make up water?

Step 1: Identify the scenario.

- There's no age range mentioned, so that must not be important for this question.

- There's not much of a scenario here, but we're clearly being asked something about divergent thinking.

Step 2: Use POE to narrow down the answer choices.

Let's assume that you have no idea what divergent thinking is. Because three of these answer choices don't stimulate it, they must have something in common. One must stick out somehow. Let's look at the answer choices:

A.   Is 23 a prime number?

That's not a particularly hard question. The answer happens to be yes.

B.   How many different ways can you think of to clear a clogged drainpipe?

That's tougher. There are lots of ways: chemical products, one of those snake things, calling a plumber, taking the pipe apart, for example.

C.   What is the capital of North Dakota?

Ooh! I know this one! It's Pierre, or Bismarck, or something. OK, so maybe I don't know it, but I know I could go look it up.

D.   What are the two chemical elements that make up water?

Hydrogen and oxygen, right? But even if you didn't know that, you knew there were only two. It said so in the question.

Step 3: Make a final decision.

Take a look at our responses. Three of these answer choices have concrete, game-show–style answers that could be labeled right or wrong. Only one answer choice posed a question that could have more than one right answer. That may or may not be the definition of divergent thinking (in fact, it's pretty close), but it's the only reason that one of the answer choices sticks out from all the others. It must therefore be the right answer to this question, even if you're not sure why. The correct answer is B.

Okay. At this point you should have a good idea about how to approach questions you see on the TExES. The next chapters will cover the actual content that could appear on the exam.

2

Format and Pacing

FORMAT AND PACING

As we mentioned in an earlier chapter, every TExES PPR exam consists of approximately 90 multiple-choice questions. Given the exam's two-and-a-half-hour time limit, that comes to about one minute and forty seconds per question. So, although you don't want to rush through the exam, you don't have time to dawdle either.

In this chapter, we'll discuss the three different question styles (single items, clustered items, and decision sets) as well as how you can adjust your pacing strategy to meet your specific needs.

SINGLE ITEMS

Most of the questions that you'll see will include all of the pertinent information in the question itself. A typical example looks like this:

> A teacher is planning to have students use the Internet as a research tool for a certain assignment. Before the assignment is given, it is most important that the teacher take which of the following steps?
>
> A. Ensure that adequate computer time is available for each student.
>
> B. Ensure that all students are familiar with browser software.
>
> C. Ensure that software is in place that blocks access to inappropriate sites.
>
> D. Ensure that students from lower socioeconomic backgrounds are given extra time to familiarize themselves with computer equipment they are less likely to have at home.

Answering these questions involves working through the process exactly the way we did in the last chapter. Let's review the process:

Step 1: Identify the scenario.

- Age range: not given

- Goal: not given

That's odd. There's no age range, and there's no educational goal. I guess that means that the answer shouldn't be age specific, and probably doesn't have anything to do with pedagogy. The question also asks which step is the *most* important.

Step 2: Use POE to narrow down the answer choices.
Let's look at the answer choices one by one:

> A. Ensure that adequate computer time is available for each student.

Well, I guess that's important, but it seems awfully general. They're probably looking for something else, but let's leave it in until we find something better.

> B.   Ensure that all students are familiar with browser
>   software.

I guess that's important, too, but I don't see why it's more or less important than choice A. Besides, this answer seems to involve some pedagogy (i.e., they have to learn how to use browser software before they can get started), and the question didn't say anything like, "It is most important that the teacher take which of the following steps to prepare students for the assignment?" It just asked what the teacher should do before the students start working on the Internet. Let's cross it out.

> C.   Ensure that software is in place that blocks
>   access to inappropriate sites.

Oh, I see! This has nothing to do with age range, and nothing to do with learning. This is about keeping students shielded from material they shouldn't be seeing. Because student safety is always an assumed goal, in the absence of other decision-making criteria, this is exactly the sort of response they're looking for. Let's keep it.

Be sure to look at the other answer choice, just in case.

> D.   Ensure that students from lower socioeconomic
>   backgrounds are given extra time to familiarize
>   themselves with computer equipment they are
>   less likely to have at home.

Again, this might be important, too, but this would be the right answer if the question had read something like, "It is most important that the teacher take which of the following steps to ensure that all students are able to complete the assignment?" If the question had been phrased that way, then D would probably be the right answer. But it wasn't, so eliminate D.

Step 3: Make a final decision.
Note that in this case, the *absence* of specific information (i.e., age range and goal) was an important clue. That meant that the answer had to be universally applicable in all situations. Student safety, of course, is a paramount concern, so C must be the correct answer.

CLUSTERED ITEMS

On other questions, the TExES will provide you with what they call a stimulus, which is just their way of including extra information that's not given directly in the question. Common examples of stimuli include samples of student work, teacher notes, or descriptions of classroom situations. Sometimes the TExES will ask you more than one question about a given stimulus.

When you encounter a clustered item, take a moment to skim the stimulus. Because you don't yet know what questions will be asked, you don't have to memorize every detail—it'll be right at the top of the page in case you need to look at it again—but you should get a basic idea of what it says before you go to the question. Then, follow the question-answering process as usual, using the stimulus as extra information on which to base your decision.

A typical one-question clustered item might look like this:

Use the information below to answer the question that follows.

A teacher reads the following passage in a fourth-grade student's journal.

> I like bunnys. There cute and soft and cuddly and warm. At nite I dreem about bunnys. I wish I could have one but my Mom and Dad wont let me.

Of the following, which is the most important issue that the teacher needs to address with respect to the journal entry?

A. The student's spelling errors.

B. The student's relationship with her parents.

C. The student's handwriting.

D. The student's understanding of the relationship between how a word sounds and how it is spelled.

Step 1: Identify the scenario.

The stimulus will contain crucial information, so be sure to think about it while you're figuring out the scenario. You probably noticed bad handwriting and many misspelled words while you were reading the stimulus. Combine this with the question, and you're ready to ID the scenario.

- Age range: fourth grade

- Goal: none stated, but asks for the most important issue that's raised by the journal entry

Step 2: Use POE to narrow down the answer choices.

Let's look at the choices:

A. The student's spelling errors.

Maybe. There were lots of spelling errors. Let's keep it and see what the other answer choices say.

B. The student's relationship with her parents.

No. A teacher is required by Texas state law to report suspicion of child abuse, but refusing to allow a child to have a pet clearly doesn't qualify as abuse. Let's cross out choice C.

C. The student's handwriting.

The handwriting is bad, but still legible. Spelling is a more serious problem than that. Let's cross it out.

D. The student's understanding of the relationship between how a word sounds and how it is spelled.

What the heck? What does that have to do with . . . hey, wait. Hmm. Take a look at the spelling errors. They all fall into a pattern, don't they? "Bunnys" should be spelled "bunnies," "There" should be spelled "they're," "nite" should be spelled "night," and so on. The student misspelled the words in a logical way, according to how they sounded. Let's keep this answer choice in.

Step 3: Make a final decision.
So, although choice A seemed like a good answer at first glance, D is actually a better answer, because it goes to the root of the student's problem and addresses the real issue rather than just the symptom. Consequently, it's the most important issue, and the best answer is D.

DECISION SETS

The last type of question format is called a *decision set*. Typically, a decision set will describe a scenario, and then proceed to ask anywhere from three to 12 questions about that scenario, frequently adding information with succeeding questions. The beginning and end of each decision set is clearly marked. A typical example might look like this:

Mr. Swarthout, a high-school economics teacher, is about to begin a three-week unit on product design and marketing. He plans to divide the class into four groups, each of which will design, build, and market a simple product to learn about basic economic concepts such as production costs, profit, and marketing strategies.

3. To ensure that each group picks an appropriate product to develop, which one of the following strategies should he adopt?

   A. Encourage students to brainstorm ideas, discuss their merits and drawbacks, decide on one idea, and submit a proposal for his approval before they proceed to the design and development step.

   B. Make a list of ten approved products, and have each group pick an item from the list.

   C. Have students generate ideas one at a time, and discuss the positives and negatives of each idea before generating the next one.

   D. Provide students with mail-order catalogs to spark their imaginations.

4. Each group must work within a fixed budget that includes the cost of materials and marketing, and the stated goal for each group is to earn the most profit. Which of the following technologies would allow students to most easily compare and contrast different budgets and pricing points?

   A. word-processing software

   B. spreadsheet software

   C. hand-held graphing calculator

   D. access to the Internet

5. The major educational advantage to having students design and build their own products is:

   A. it provides the teacher an opportunity to watch students interact in a group setting.

   B. it puts students on an equal footing with teachers in terms of deciding what the most important educational goals are.

   C. it allows students to address their individual strengths and weaknesses.

   D. it promotes initiative, self-reliance, and a sense of autonomy in students.

6. The day after Mr. Swarthout assigns the project, he receives a telephone call from Mrs. Shannon, the mother of one of his students, Jennifer. Mrs. Shannon questions the value of the assignment, and believes that class time would be better spent lecturing students on the fundamentals of economic theory. In fact, Mrs. Shannon says that the only thing keeping her from filing a formal complaint with the school board is that Jennifer is so excited about the project. Which of the following is the first step that Mr. Swarthout should take in dealing with this situation?

A. Cite Jennifer's excitement about the project as proof of its educational legitimacy.

B. Offer to give Jennifer extra study sheets with traditional economics problems.

C. Thank Mrs. Shannon for her concern, and briefly explain the goals of the project as they relate to the fundamentals of economic theory.

D. Politely end the conversation with Mrs. Shannon and immediately call the head of the Social Studies department.

7. At the end of the sales period, when the project is over, which of the following should Mr. Swarthout require to ensure that students have attained the educational goals he set out?

A. Have each student write a report on the experience, using charts and graphs to illustrate the relationships between formal economic theory and the results of the group project.

B. Formulate a multiple-choice exam similar in style to state competency exams that tests the concepts of formal economic theory.

C. Give top grades to the students that earned the most profit, and lower grades to members of groups that earned less money.

D. Have each group present the results of the project, and ask direct questions of the students as they present their findings that reinforce the links between the results of the project and formal economic theory.

DECISION SET ENDS HERE

Aside from reading the initial situation, there's very little here that differs from single-item questions. Remember the overall goals for the scenario, and treat each question individually.

What was the initial information given?

Mr. Swarthout, a high-school economics teacher, is about to begin a three-week unit on product design and marketing. He plans to divide the class into four groups, each of which will design, build, and market a simple product to learn about basic economic concepts such as production costs, profit, and marketing strategies.

You might be thinking, "Wait! I'm not an economics teacher! I don't know anything about economics! How am I going to answer questions about how to teach basic economic concepts!" If you are thinking this, don't worry. This is still the PPR test. The TExES PPR test can't ask you questions about specific subject matter, and the right answer will never depend on your knowledge of economics, or whatever subject material a given question refers to. So don't worry. Stick to the process:

Step 1: Identify the scenario.

Step 2: Use POE to narrow down the answer choices.

Step 3: Make a final decision.

Now let's take the questions one by one and go through the process:

> 3. To ensure that each group picks an appropriate product to develop, which one of the following strategies should he adopt?

What's the specific goal of this question? To make sure that each group picks an appropriate project. Are we given any criteria for appropriateness? No. So this must be about the teacher having enough information to determine whether a particular product is appropriate.

So, when we ID the scenario, we should include the information from the original set-up, too.

Step 1: Identify the scenario.

- Age range: high school

- Goal: learn basic economic concepts and make sure students have an appropriate product

Step 2: Use POE to narrow down the answer choices.

Let's look at the choices:

> A. Encourage students to brainstorm ideas, discuss their merits and drawbacks, decide on one idea, and submit a proposal for his approval before they proceed to the design and development step.

This sounds good. It makes use of good group decision-making strategies, gives students responsibility, and ensures that the teacher has information upon which to base a sound decision. Let's keep it.

B.   Make a list of ten approved products, and have
each group pick an item from the list.

This does make sure that the students have an appropriate product, but it doesn't sound very exciting for the students, and would substantially limit their creativity. Let's cross it out.

C.   Have students generate ideas one at a time, and
discuss the positives and negatives of each idea
before generating the next one.

This doesn't explicitly give the teacher an opportunity to determine whether a product is inappropriate. In addition, evaluating ideas one at a time is generally a poor strategy for group work. Let's cross this out, too.

D.   Provide students with mail-order catalogs to
spark their imaginations.

Again, Mr. Swarthout isn't given information here to help him make a decision. Let's cross this out, too.

Step 3: Make a final decision.
In this case, answer choice A is the only one remaining.
Question 4 is next:

4.   Each group must work within a fixed budget that
includes the cost of materials and marketing, and the
stated goal for each group is to earn the most profit.
Which of the following technologies would allow
students to most easily compare and contrast different
budgets and pricing points?

Step 1: Identify the scenario.

- Age range: high school

- Goal: learn basic economic concepts and allow students to compare and contrast budgets

Step 2: Use POE to narrow down the answer choices.

A.   word-processing software

Extremely unlikely. Determining budgets and pricing points will involve formulas and calculations that will vary according to the different numbers the students choose. Word-processing software isn't flexible enough. Let's cross it out.

B.   spreadsheet software

Yes. This is exactly the software that would be useful.

> C.   hand-held graphing calculator

This might be useful, too. Let's keep it.

> D.   access to the Internet

Doubtful. Research isn't what's necessary here. Let's cross it off.

Step 3: Make a final decision.

We're down to B and C. The question asks about comparing and contrasting. While you could do the calculations with a hand-held calculator, you can most easily compare different mathematical scenarios with a spreadsheet. The best answer is B.

On to question 5:

> 5.   The major educational advantage to having students
>   design and build their own products is:

Step 1: Identify the scenario.

- Age range: high school

- Goal: to learn basic economic concepts

Notice that this question doesn't mention the overall goal of the project, but simply asks why it's a good idea to put students in charge of their own projects. So we should be looking for a very general answer.

Step 2: Use POE to narrow down the answer choices.

Here are the choices:

> A.   it provides the teacher an opportunity to watch
>   students interact in a group setting.

Maybe. It sounds more like an advantage for the teacher than the student, but let's keep it in for now.

> B.   it puts students on an equal footing with teachers
>   in terms of deciding what the most important
>   educational goals are.

That can't be right. Students shouldn't be on equal footing with teachers about deciding primary educational goals. That's the teacher's job. Cross it out.

> C.   it allows students to address their individual
>   strengths and weaknesses.

Allowing students to address their strengths and weaknesses is a good thing, but I'm not sure how their designing their own products will help with that. Let's get rid of it.

D.   it promotes initiative, self-reliance, and a sense
      of autonomy in students.

That's amazingly general, and remember we were looking for a general answer. Keep this one.

Step 3: Make a final decision.
We're down to A and D, and remember that the question is asking for the major educational advantage. Choice A might be an advantage for a teacher, but D is clearly a worthy educational goal for all students. D is the best answer.

On to question 6:

6.   The day after Mr. Swarthout assigns the project, he
      receives a telephone call from Mrs. Shannon, the
      mother of one of his students, Jennifer. Mrs. Shannon
      questions the value of the assignment, and believes
      that class time would be better spent lecturing students
      on the fundamentals of economic theory. In fact, Mrs.
      Shannon says that the only thing keeping her from
      filing a formal complaint with the school board is that
      Jennifer is so excited about the project. Which of the
      following is the first step that Mr. Swarthout should
      take in dealing with this situation?

Step 1: Identify the scenario.

- Age range: high school

- Goal: learn basic economic concepts

Clearly, we're out of the classroom on this one, and in a situation where we're dealing with parents. Remember the important rule here: treat other adults with respect and professionalism.

Step 2: Use POE to narrow down the answer choices.
Here are the choices again:

A.   Cite Jennifer's excitement about the project as
      proof of its educational legitimacy.

Jennifer might be excited about school being canceled, too, but that doesn't mean it's educationally legitimate. Besides, this sounds like you're arguing with the parent. Cross it off.

B.   Offer to give Jennifer extra study sheets with
      traditional economics problems.

If I were the parent, and Mr. Swarthout suggested that to me, I'd head directly to the school board and tell the members that Mr. Swarthout essentially admitted that the project he was having the students do was useless. In trying to mollify the parent, he's denying the fact that the project has educational value. Cross it off.

> C. Thank Mrs. Shannon for her concern, and briefly
> explain the goals of the project as they relate to
> the fundamentals of economic theory.

Remember that the question asks what the *first* step should be. This is pretty good. Thanking Mrs. Shannon for her concern tells her that Mr. Swarthout is listening to her, and explaining the theory behind the assignment should help her to understand its educational value. This is not to say that Mr. Swarthout shouldn't take other steps, such as offering to set up a meeting to further explain the assignment, but this is a good first step to take.

> D. Politely end the conversation with Mrs. Shannon,
> and immediately call his department head.

This is a cop-out. According to the TExES, good teachers should be able to communicate with parents and caregivers. Running to the department head as a *first* step is passing the buck. Cross it out.

Step 3: Make a final decision.

Here, we crossed out all the choices except C, which is the best answer.

And finally, question 7:

> 7. At the end of the sales period, when the project is over,
> which of the following should Mr. Swarthout require
> to ensure that students have attained the educational
> goals he set out?

Step 1: Identify the scenario.

- Age range: high school

- Goal: learn basic economic concepts

This is a question about assessment methods. In doing a project such as this, students can frequently lose sight of the main goals. How should he test the students?

Step 2: Use POE to narrow down the answer choices.

Here are the choices:

> A. Have each student write a report on the
> experience, using charts and graphs to illustrate
> the relationships between formal economic
> theory and the results of the group project.

Maybe. This forces students to think about what they've done and learned. Let's keep it.

> B. Formulate a multiple-choice exam similar in
> style to state competency exams that tests the
> concepts of formal economic theory.

While it's certainly true that students will be faced with many multiple-choice exams, it's hard to see how such a test would help link the ideas from the project. Let's cross it out.

> C. Give top grades to the students that earned the most profit and lower grades to members of groups that earned less money.

Although this may be how it works in the real world, this does nothing to achieve the educational goals. A group that lost money could learn just as much (or maybe even more) about basic economic concepts as a group that made a lot of money. Cross it off.

> D. Have each group present the results of the project to the rest of the class, and ask direct questions of the students as they present their findings to reinforce the links between the results of the project and formal economic theory.

Maybe. This would force students to think about what they've done and learned. Let's keep this, too.

Step 3: Make a final decision.
This one's tough. Which is better, A or D? The major difference between the two is that the report forces students to do the link-building by themselves, while the class presentation is interactive among the teacher, the presenting students, and the rest of the class. It's quite likely that different groups will have different experiences, and that other groups will learn from hearing about those experiences. To ensure that students meet the educational goals, an in-class presentation is better. The best answer is D.

That's how a decision set works. Notice that although all questions dealt with the same overall scenario, the questions were independent from one another (that is, you didn't have to understand question 5 to answer question 6 correctly) and didn't rely on any specific knowledge of economics.

PACING STRATEGY
Many people feel like they're under a great deal of time pressure on standardized tests. If you're worried about finishing on time, remember these suggestions:

Stick to the Process
The question-answering process outlined in this book is very efficient because it forces you to concentrate on one thing at a time. To identify the scenario, you must read critically and effectively to discern the important information in the question. Using process of elimination to get rid of the obviously incorrect answer choices saves time because you won't spend a lot of time overevaluating incorrect answers. By quickly narrowing the answer choices down to two (or sometimes three), you have enough time left over to carefully make your final, important choice.

Don't Get Bogged Down on One Question
Some questions will be tougher than others, and you may find yourself stuck between two very good answer choices. Keep your decision-making criteria in mind, reexamine the scenario, reread the question, and make your final choice. Then move on.

Don't Leave Anything Blank
Don't leave a question blank and come back to it later. There are about 90 questions on the exam, and it will be difficult for you to keep track of the ones that you've skipped. Furthermore, when you come back to them, you'll have to revisit the details of all the questions that you've skipped, which will take even more time. And there's one final reason not to leave anything blank: if you run out of time, you're throwing away the possibility of one more point—there's no guessing penalty, remember?

If All Else Fails...

If you follow these suggestions, you should find that you have enough time to finish the questions in the two-and-a-half-hour time limit. Time yourself while taking the practice examinations in the back of this book. If you find that you don't have enough time to finish, you have one more option: register for only the PPR examination when you sign up to take the TExES. That way, you'll have up to five hours to complete the test, which will be more than enough time.

PART II

How to Crack the TExES

3

Stages of Development

STAGES OF DEVELOPMENT

We've already discussed the idea that you should identify the age of the students in a given test-question scenario. The reason for this, of course, is that children think and act differently at different ages. Understanding these differences is frequently crucial to picking the right answer. The underlying theory can be broken down into understanding how children develop in three major areas: cognitively, socially, and morally.

This chapter will briefly discuss the dominant theories of these areas of development—those most likely to appear on the TExES. We'll start off with a description of each of these developmental theories, and then we'll group them together according to age range. You should be familiar with the overall concepts as well as some of the jargon—both get tested on the exam.

COGNITIVE DEVELOPMENT

Piaget's Theory

Jean Piaget was a Swiss psychologist whose theory of cognitive development is often alluded to in TExES questions. You should be familiar with the basics of Piaget's theory and some common examples used to illustrate its principles.

Piaget believed that learning happens as people adapt to their environments. He suggested that cognitive development proceeds as follows: when faced with a situation, you first try to use or apply what you already know, and if that doesn't work, you figure out something else based on what's new or different about that situation. The first idea, using your existing framework or *schema*, he called *assimilation*; the second, developing new frameworks, he called *adaptation*. He believed that we are constantly refining our frameworks.

Based on his observations, Piaget theorized that this ongoing process of assimilation and adaptation leads all children to pass through identical stages of cognitive development, but not necessarily at identical times. He identified four stages:

Sensorimotor (birth to 2 years)

Preoperational (2 to 7 years)

Concrete operational (7 to 11 years)

Formal operational (11 to 15 years)

Let's review them in order:

Sensorimotor stage (birth to 2 years)

Because most children pass through this stage by the time they reach the age of formal instruction, it is unlikely that you will see questions dealing with it. You should know, however, that things that babies do and the types of games that parents typically play with babies are all relevant to this stage. For instance, one of the characteristics of the sensorimotor stage is understanding *object permanence*—the concept that things continue to exist even though you can't see them. Some educational psychologists and social anthropologists agree that the game of peek-a-boo is practically universal in human cultures specifically because it reinforces the concept of object permanence. Another hallmark of the sensorimotor stage is the early development of *goal-oriented behavior*. For example, a very young child who is able to roll over at will but not yet able to crawl may consciously roll over multiple times to reach a bottle or favorite toy.

Preoperational stage (2 to 7 years)

At this stage, children are developing language skills quickly. They also begin to use symbols to represent objects. Children in this stage will be able to think through simple problems, but only in one direction (i.e., they won't be able to reverse the steps mentally). They also will have difficulty dealing with more than one aspect of a problem at a time. Children in this stage may have difficulty seeing things from another person's point of view. This idea is called *egocentrism*. Although this sounds like a negative quality, it's best understood as the child's assumption that everyone else sees things the same way the child does. For example, a child may assume that everyone likes orange juice simply because she likes orange juice.

Concrete operational stage (7 to 11 years)

Children in this stage develop the ability to mentally back up operations (reverse the steps in a problem), a concept called *reversibility*. They can *classify* (identify objects according to a specific characteristic, even if the object has many different characteristics) and *seriate* (put things into order according to a given criterion such as height or volume). One important concept is that of *conservation*—the idea that the amount of a substance doesn't change just because it's arranged differently. For example, conservation of mass might be demonstrated by taking a large ball of clay and creating several smaller balls of clay out of it. A child in the concrete operational stage will understand that the total amount of clay hasn't changed; a child in the preoperational stage might think that there is more clay (because there are more balls). At this stage, children can solve concrete, hands-on problems logically.

Formal operational stage (11 to 15 years)

This stage is characterized by the ability to solve abstract problems involving many independent elements. The thought process necessary to frame and solve such problems is called *hypothetico-deductive reasoning*. It is now believed that not all students will reach the formal operational stage. In fact, some theorists estimate that only about 35 percent of the adult population ever achieves this stage.

Vygotsky's Theories

Lev Vygotsky was a Russian educational psychologist in the early twentieth century whose theories you should be familiar with. Here are three of his major ideas that you might be tested on:

- The importance of culture

- The role of language in development

- The zone of proximal development

- Scaffolding

Culture

Vygotsky believed that environmental and cultural factors have an enormous influence on what children learn. While Piaget suggested that children are constantly developing methods of adapting to the world around them, Vygotsky further argued that environment and culture dictate the methods that children will find useful, and what their priorities will be.

Language

To Vygotsky, language use is a critical factor in cognitive development. Young children frequently talk to themselves as they play or solve problems. This is called *private speech*. While Piaget would cite private speech as evidence of egocentrism in the preoperational stage, Vygotsky believed that private speech allows children to use language to help break down a problem and solve it—in effect, the children talk themselves through it. He believed that a fundamental stage in development comes when children begin to carry on this speech internally, without speaking the words aloud.

Zone of Proximal Development

At any given stage, there are problems that a child can solve by herself, and there are other problems that a child couldn't solve even with prodding at each successive step. In between, however, are problems that a child could solve with the guidance of someone who already knows how. That range of problems is what Vygotsky referred to as the *zone of proximal development*. He believed that real learning takes place by solving problems in that zone.

Scaffolding

Scaffolding is another idea fundamental to Vygotsky's notion of social learning. It is about providing children with help from more competent peers and adults. Children are given a lot of support in the early stages of learning and problem solving. Then, as the child is able, he/she takes on more responsibility and the supporter diminishes the support. Supportive techniques include clues, reminders, encouragement, breaking the problem into steps, providing examples, or anything that helps a student develop their learning independence.

Bloom's Taxonomy

- Knowledge

- Comprehension

- Application

- Analysis

- Synthesis

- Evaluation

Students develop thinking skills in the order above, roughly. In the early grades, students are limited to facts and other rote knowledge. As they develop, they are capable of processing information at levels of greater and greater complexity. In general, teachers should try to develop higher-order thinking skills (those at the end of the list). Look at the next page, and let's take a look at the types of questions that would stimulate these types of thinking. Imagine that a teacher was doing a lesson on the colonization of the United States.

Bloom Taxonomy Level	Description	Question Example
Knowledge	Recalling factual information	What were the names of the New England colonies?
Comprehension	Using factual information to answer a specific question	What crops were common to the New England colonies and the Southern colonies? What were the major religious differences between the New England colonies and the Middle colonies?
Application	Taking an abstract concept together with specific facts to answer a question	In which area of the colonies would a Freethinker have been most likely to find like-minded people?
Analysis	Breaking down a question into concepts and ideas in order to answer a question	What characteristics of the New England colonists made them the most likely to rebel against British rule?
Synthesis	Connecting concepts and ideas to create a new product or idea	What steps could the King have taken to appease the New England colonists that might have prevented the American Revolution?
Evaluation	Making considered judgments by breaking down and reconnecting ideas, concepts, and facts and comparing the judgments to standards	In which area of the colonies did the colonists have the best natural resources from an economic standpoint?

So, in planning a U.S. History unit, a good teacher would build a base of facts and concepts and then develop lessons that would encourage students to ask and answer increasingly complicated sorts of questions based on those facts and concepts.

Maslow's Hierarchy of Needs

Abraham Maslow was an educational theorist who believed that children have to have certain needs met before they're ready to learn and grow. He organized these needs into a hierarchy and taught that you couldn't progress to the next level until you'd achieved the previous one. Here's the hierarchy from low to high:

Deficiency Needs

Physiological needs—Food, sleep, clothing, etc.

Safety needs—Freedom from harm or danger

Belongingness and love needs—Acceptance and love from others

Esteem needs—Approval and accomplishment

Growth Needs

Cognitive needs—Knowledge and understanding

Aesthetic needs—Appreciation of beauty and order

Self-actualization needs—Fulfillment of one's potential

Maslow called the first four *deficiency* needs. They are the basic requirements for physical and psychosocial well-being. Desire for these declines once you have them, and you don't think about them unless you lack them. He called the other three *growth* needs. They include the need for knowing, appreciating, and understanding. People try to meet these needs only after their basic needs have been met. He believed that meeting these needs created more desire for them. For example, having adequate shelter and food doesn't make you crave more shelter and food. By contrast, learning and understanding sparks the desire to learn and understand more.

Social Development

Erikson's Eight Stages of Psychosocial Development

You should be familiar with Erikson's Stages of Psychosocial Development. Erik Erikson, a German-born American psychologist, identified eight stages of development, each of which takes the form of a resolution of an identity crisis. Here they are in chronological order:

1. Basic trust vs. basic mistrust (birth to 18 months)

If a child is well cared for during this time, she will become naturally trusting and optimistic. Again, due to the age range involved, you probably will not see questions dealing with this stage.

2. Autonomy vs. shame (18 months to 3 years)

A child learns the mechanical basics of controlling his world—including walking, grasping, and toilet training. The "terrible twos" fall into this stage, with common traits including stubbornness and willful behavior as the child pushes the limits of control. Ideally, a child comes out of this stage proud of his abilities rather than ashamed of them.

3. Initiative vs. guilt (3 to 6 years)

After becoming autonomous, children start wanting to do things. They have ideas and plan and carry out activities. Some activities aren't allowed, and it's important for children to feel that their activities are important and valued by adults. If this feeling isn't there, children believe that what they do is wrong, and guilt develops, which restricts growth.

4. Industry vs. inferiority (6 to 12 years)

In these elementary-school years, children are expected to learn and produce. If children can meet these expectations, they learn to be industrious. If they do not, they risk feeling inferior.

5. Identity vs. role confusion (adolescence)

This is when adolescents answer the question, "Who am I?" It's quite common for teenagers to rebel, some very strongly. Erikson believed that an environment in which adolescents are offered the opportunity and leeway to try out different personalities and roles and decide which ones suit them best is the healthiest environment for resolving this development task.

Because the last three stages, described below, are stages that adults go through, it is unlikely that you will see any questions about them on the exam. They're listed here for completeness's sake only.

6. Intimacy vs. isolation (young adulthood)

Being able to form intimate relationships is the defining task of this stage.

7. Generativity vs. stagnation (middle age)

Adults need to be productive, both procreatively and professionally.

8. Integrity vs. despair (old age)

Finally, adults need to feel complete and comfortable with themselves and the choices they've made in their lives.

PLAY AS A FORM OF SOCIAL DEVELOPMENT

Play is an important way in which children learn to socialize. Because most children will have reached the final stage of cooperative play by age 7, this is a developmental idea that is most likely to show up on the EC–4 exam. However, it's possible that some wrong answer choices on other exams will make reference to these ideas, so it's a good idea to review these no matter which test type you're preparing for.

Parten's Stages of Play Development

Mildred Parten, a child psychologist in the 1930s, was one of the first people to study children at play. Here are her stages of play development, which are linked to different levels of social interaction.

Solitary play
In solitary play, children play by themselves. While children may continue to do this throughout their childhoods, in the context of social interaction, this is usually observed in children younger than 2 years.

Onlooker play
At around 2 years of age, children will watch others play without doing anything themselves or making any effort to join in. This is closely followed in the same time frame by parallel play.

Parallel play
In parallel play, which like onlooker play develops at around 2 years old, children will do the same things or mimic the play of playmates, but will not interact with them.

Associative play
Normally, by age 4 or 5, children engage in associative play, which means that they will interact and share materials, but won't coordinate their efforts.

Cooperative play
Finally, usually by age 5 to 7, children will play together in one activity.

MORAL DEVELOPMENT

Lawrence Kohlberg was a developmental psychologist at Harvard University in the late twentieth century who did extensive research in the field of moral education. You should be familiar with Kohlberg's stage theory of moral reasoning. He split moral development into three levels, each of which contains two stages.

Level 1: Preconventional Moral Reasoning (Elementary School)
This first level is broken down into two stages:

Stage 1: Obedience and Punishment
Young children obey rules simply because they are rules and understand that they risk punishment if they break them. Whether an action is good or bad is understood in terms of its immediate consequences.

Stage 2: Personal Reward
Children internalize the system from Stage 1 and realize that following the rules is generally in their best interests. An action is right or good if it gets you what you want. A simple view of "fair's fair" develops, so that favors are done with the expectation of something in return.

Level 2: Conventional Moral Reasoning (Junior High–High School)

Kohlberg called this level *conventional* because most of society remains at this level. Judgment is based on tradition and the expectations of others. This level is also broken down into two stages:

Stage 3: Good-boy/Good-girl

An action is right or good if it helps, pleases, or is approved by others.

Stage 4: Authority and social-order-maintaining orientation

An action is right or good if it's expected out of a sense of duty or because it supports the morals or laws of the community or country. "It's right because that's the law."

Level three is unlikely to be tested because Kohlberg believed that it's not fully attained until adulthood, if it's ever attained at all. It's included here for completeness:

Level 3: Post-conventional Moral Reasoning

Kohlberg originally broke down this level into two stages (5 and 6). However, in his later years, he decided that stages 5 and 6 were actually the same.

Stage 5: Social contract

An action is right or good if it meets an agreed-upon system of rules and rights (such as the United States Constitution).

Stage 6: Principled conscience

Good and right are relative, not absolute, and require abstract thinking in terms of justice, equality, and human dignity.

WHAT DOES ALL OF THIS MEAN TO ME AS A TEST TAKER?

It is unlikely that a question on the TExES will ask you to identify the stages of Kohlberg's theory of moral reasoning. Instead, you might see a question that looks like this:

1. A sixth-grade teacher is deciding how to establish rules governing acceptable classroom behavior. To best promote an orderly classroom, which of the following strategies should she adopt?

   A. Before the first day of class, mail a list of classroom rules to each child's caregiver.

   B. On the first day of class, post a list of rules for the class and explain each one, including the punishment for failing to obey it.

   C. On the first day of class, start a discussion regarding appropriate and inappropriate behavior, and develop a list of rules with the students' input and agreement.

   D. As the school year progresses, whenever students misbehave, point out their behavior to the class, explain why it's inappropriate, and add that behavior to a list of prohibited activities.

What's the right answer to this question? Follow our question-answering process.

Step 1: Identify the scenario.

- Age range: sixth grade

- Goal: best promote an orderly classroom

Step 2: Use POE to narrow down the answer choices.

> A. Before the first day of class, mail a list of classroom rules to each child's caregiver.

Although answer choice A isn't a bad idea, it does little to promote an orderly classroom because there's no guarantee that caregivers will go over the list with your students in the same way that you would, if at all.

> B. On the first day of class, post a list of rules for the class and explain each one, including the punishment for failing to obey it.

Answer choice B might work. It sets clear guidelines and expectations.

> C. On the first day of class, start a discussion regarding appropriate and inappropriate behavior, and develop a list of rules with the students' input and agreement.

Answer choice C seems difficult to implement, but students would be a part of the learning process. We'll keep it.

> D. As the school year progresses, whenever students misbehave, point out their behavior to the class, explain why it's inappropriate, and add that behavior to a list of prohibited activities.

Answer choice D requires no advance planning and little work for the teacher. Students would be guessing as to whether a given behavior is permissible or not, and it's easy to see chaos ensuing. Eliminate this choice.

Step 3: Make a final decision.

So, we're down to B and C. Remember, you could probably get this one right by thinking about which choice requires more work for the teacher. B is easy to write up ahead of time; C requires a careful classroom discussion with a directed outcome—not an easy feat to manage.

But remember, there's one other clue here: the age range. Sixth graders are morally ready to understand the concept and value of a shared contract, so it would make sense for them to have a say in the discussion. Also, sixth-grade students are more likely to follow rules if they have some say in how the rules are created. The best answer is C.

Look what happens if one word in the question is changed:

2.   A *first*-grade teacher is deciding how to establish rules
     governing acceptable classroom behavior. To best
     promote an orderly classroom, which of the following
     strategies should she adopt?

     A.   Before the first day of class, mail a list of
          classroom rules to each child's caregiver.

     B.   On the first day of class, post a list of rules for
          the class and explain each one, including the
          punishment for failing to obey it.

     C.   On the first day of class, start a discussion
          regarding appropriate and inappropriate
          behavior, and develop a list of rules with the
          students' input and agreement.

     D.   As the school year progresses, whenever
          students misbehave, point out their behavior to
          the class, explain why it's inappropriate, and add
          that behavior to a list of prohibited activities.

All of a sudden, the best answer to this question is B. It has some flaws—a first-grade class wouldn't
be able to remember a long list of rules, discussing punishment for each is somewhat harsh, etc.—but
C can no longer be the right answer because first-grade students typically aren't capable of understanding the reasons behind rules, and A and D are still wrong for the same reasons as explained
above. First graders are content to follow rules simply because they come from an authority figure.

Try this one next:

3.   Miss Rodriguez, a kindergarten teacher, notices that
     during free playtime two of her students are busy
     building sandcastles. Upon closer inspection, she
     sees that although they are working side-by-side, and
     sharing the same bucket and other tools, they are not
     working together in any way. Miss Rodriguez should
     recognize that:

     A.   it is likely that the two students had an argument,
          and she should talk to both students together to
          make sure there are no lingering hostilities.

     B.   the students are passing through a predictable
          stage of social development, and no intervention
          on her part is necessary at this time.

     C.   the students aren't working up to their potential,
          and she should show them that by working
          together they could build a larger, more complex
          sandcastle.

     D.   having to share a bucket is potentially retarding her
          students' progress, and she should make an effort
          to procure another bucket as soon as possible.

Step 1: Identify the scenario.

- Age range: kindergarten

- Goal: none stated, but the teacher is supposed to recognize something

There doesn't seem to be an urgent problem, so whatever the teacher is supposed to recognize probably isn't an emergency.

Step 2: Use POE to narrow down the answer choices.
Let's look at the choices critically:

> A. it is likely that the two students had an argument, and she should talk to both students together to make sure there are no lingering hostilities.

The question says that the students are sharing tools, so it certainly doesn't seem as though they just had an argument. Let's cross this one off.

> B. the students are passing through a predictable stage of social development, and no intervention on her part is necessary at this time.

If you know Parten's stages of play, then you probably recognized the scenario as an example of associative play, and you are fairly confident that this is the right answer. Even if you didn't recognize the scenario, you'd still leave this choice in because you'd already decided the situation wasn't urgent.

> C. the students aren't working up to their potential, and she should show them that by working together they could build a larger, more complex sandcastle.

Maybe, although there's no evidence that the students aren't working up to their potential. Let's leave it in for now, even though we like B better.

> D. having to share a bucket is potentially retarding her students' progress, and she should make an effort to procure another bucket as soon as possible.

Clearly not. Having to share a workbook in which each child is expected to do his or her own work could potentially be a problem; sharing toys during playtime is a positive developmental experience. Cross this one off.

Step 3: Make a final decision.
The more we know about social development, the more we like choice B, but let's look at another reason why C isn't as good.

Again, remember that we were told this was playtime. One of the most important aspects of playtime is that children are given a chance to learn through interaction with other children. If sandcastle building had been an assigned task in which the teacher had specifically divided children into groups of two with the intent that they work together, then this might be the right answer (although there's no evidence the children aren't working up to their potential). In this case, though, we're dealing with playtime, and B is therefore a better answer.

As you can see from the examples, it's more important for you to understand the capabilities and expected stages of development at each age level than to be able to name the stages and who was responsible for developing the theory. So in addition to knowing the structure of each of those theories, you should also be able to apply them to specific teaching situations.

ELLEN'S STAGES OF DEVELOPMENT

To put these ideas together, let's imagine the school-age development of an average student named Ellen. Instead of naming the stages that she grows through, think about how she is likely to respond to a given situation, and imagine interacting with her in ways she's capable of understanding and learning from.

EARLY CHILDHOOD—4TH GRADE

Cognitive Development

Ellen understands things in terms of what she can see or has done herself, so if you're teaching Ellen, you should try to give her examples that relate to her own experiences. Use manipulatives often—she can understand things more if she can literally put her hands on them. As she gets older, choose examples and lessons that help her develop the ability to break problems down into smaller, more easily understood components.

Moral Development

Ellen follows rules at this stage just because they're rules. As long as they're agreed upon ahead of time, and are short and simple, you don't need to give reasons why they are there.

Social Development

Ellen passes from one stage to another during these years. At the beginning, she's interested in a wide variety of things and will want to experiment. Encourage this desire, and answer questions fully and well. As Ellen moves into her later elementary years, she's industrious and measures her self-worth in terms of her ability to keep up with schoolwork and classroom discussions. As a teacher, you should reward effort, even if the results of those efforts are flawed.

4TH GRADE—8TH GRADE

Cognitive Development

Ellen can better analyze things at this stage. Using charts and timelines helps her not only to break things down, but also to build links between separate ideas. Ellen can now use her own experiences to help her reason with simple hypothetical problems that are closely related to her own experiences. You can help her logical and analytical reasoning skills by using puzzles and brainteasers.

Moral Development

Ellen begins to understand that rules are created for a reason and don't exist simply because an authority figure said that they did. As a teacher, you might consider letting students have some say in developing class rules because Ellen and her classmates understand that having rules simultaneously protects their rights and maintains classroom order.

Social Development

Ellen continues to measure her worth by her level of industriousness. Making sure that she has clearly defined assignments of reasonable length and difficulty level helps her meet the goals she has set for herself.

8TH GRADE–12TH GRADE

Cognitive Development

Ellen is developing the ability to think in abstract terms. She can think about multiple scenarios, and can contemplate situations with a number of different factors that interrelate. If you're teaching Ellen at this stage, you can offer her hypothetical situations to think about and describe; you can ask her to debate both sides of an issue, and you can ask her not only to answer a question, but also to design an experiment that would prove the answer correct.

Moral Development

At this stage, Ellen understands that in society overall, everyone is better off if everyone lives by the same rules. She follows them because she understands that it's accepted practice and because she knows that rules are important (partially because she's now capable of imagining the consequences of a life without them).

Social Development

Ellen is trying to answer the question "Who am I?" Peer groups define much of what she considers normal and worthwhile, and Ellen may believe that every nuance of her behavior is being analyzed and commented on by others. It wouldn't be unusual for Ellen to experiment with different personality traits during this time.

Let's take a look at some questions that you might see on the TExES:

A seventh-grade math teacher notices that questions she asks are being answered by only a small number of her students. How should she deal with the quiet students to best promote both their understanding of the material and growth as students?

A. Let them remain silent in class to avoid damaging their self-esteem in case they answer a question incorrectly, but pay close attention to their written work.

B. Divide the class into cooperative learning groups for the rest of the semester, ensuring that at least one vocal student is assigned to each group.

C. Ask specific, directed questions of the quiet students, while being prepared to guide them toward the right answer in an unthreatening manner.

D. Meet with the quiet students privately after class to ensure their understanding.

Step 1: Identify the scenario.

- Age range: seventh grade

- Goal: understanding of mathematical concepts and growth as learners

Step 2: Use POE to narrow down the answer choices.
This one's tough.

> A. Let them remain silent in class to avoid damaging their self-esteem in case they answer a question incorrectly, but pay close attention to their written work.

Let's look at answer choice A. We know self-esteem is a priority, but it seems like a cop-out to do nothing differently in class—how will that promote their growth as learners?

> B. Divide the class into cooperative learning groups for the rest of the semester, ensuring that at least one vocal student is assigned to each group.

How about choice B? Cooperative learning can be an effective strategy in the short term, but not as a default teaching situation. Let's get rid of that one.

> C. Ask specific, directed questions of the quiet students, while being prepared to guide them toward the right answer in an unthreatening manner.

C is okay, but you seem to be running the risk of putting the quiet kids on the spot.

> D. Meet with the quiet students privately after class to ensure their understanding.

D might be all right, too, but as with A, it doesn't seem to promote their growth as learners.

Step 3: Make a final decision.
C is already the best answer because of the clue we've been given that the teacher needs to promote students' growth instead of just ensuring their understanding of the material. But you might also have recognized that C describes a situation in which a teacher is facilitating a student's progress through his or her "zone of proximal development." It's a subtle reference, but it's there, especially the part about guiding the students toward the right answer.

Let's do another:

> In a certain first-grade class, the students display levels of cognitive development ranging from preoperational to concrete operational thought. Which of the following is the best strategy for the teacher to follow to best meet the wide range of student needs?

A. Split the class into smaller instructional groups according to the different levels of cognitive development.

B. Make use of hands-on activities and examples that relate to students' experiences to help foster students' cognitive development as material becomes more complex and abstract.

C. Determine the average level of cognitive development and develop lesson plans to meet that level.

D. Schedule time with each student individually to address specific developmental needs.

Step 1: Identify the scenario.

- Age range: first grade

- Goal: best teach wide range of student needs

Step 2: Use POE to narrow down the answer choices.

A. Split the class into smaller instructional groups according to the different levels of cognitive development.

Answer choice A is a maybe. It doesn't seem practical to do this with only one teacher in the class-room, but we'll see what's next. Keep it for now.

B. Make use of hands-on activities and examples that relate to students' experiences to help foster students' cognitive development as material becomes more complex and abstract.

Answer choice B seems pretty good. Children moving from preoperational to concrete operational will need specific, concrete examples based on their own experiences.

C. Determine the average level of cognitive development and develop lesson plans to meet that level.

Choice C doesn't accommodate the wide range of levels and is too easy for the teacher.

D. Schedule time with each student individually to address specific developmental needs.

Choice D sounds like a good idea, and may be a good supplemental strategy, but fails because it's impractical and involves little planning on the part of the teacher.

Step 3: Make a final decision.

A and D are both impractical, and C and D require too little work for the teacher. The best answer is B.

DRILL

Directions: Each question in this drill is a multiple-choice question with four answer choices. Read each question carefully and choose the ONE best answer.

1. Which of the following actions most clearly demonstrates that a student has grasped the concept of conservation?

   A. Upon pouring water from a large pitcher into four smaller glasses, she claims that there is now more water.

   B. She can take a pile of stuffed animals, order them by size, and then reorganize them by color.

   C. She takes a bucket of sand, uses a scoop to make three small mounds of sand, and then takes the mounds and refills the bucket with them.

   D. She uses a light switch to turn lights on and off.

2. A third-grade boy has been teasing another student. In an effort to stop this behavior, a teacher tries to appeal to the child's moral conscience. Which of the following questions would be most useful?

   A. How would you feel if someone teased you?

   B. Do you know how much trouble you'll get into if you don't stop that?

   C. Don't you think that everyone deserves to be left alone?

   D. Don't you want to be a good boy?

3. Mixed-ability-level small-group learning can be an effective teaching tool because of which of the following?

   A. Teachers can monitor student behavior more effectively.

   B. Students get bored with traditional lecture-based lessons.

   C. Students that understand a concept can help others understand it, too.

   D. Teachers get a break from their daily routine.

4. A teacher's class is filled with students that have an exceptionally wide range of development. To accommodate this range, the teacher should:

   A. allow the students to work on their own exclusively.

   B. group the students according to their level of development.

   C. develop instruction for the lowest level of development in the classroom.

   D. use a variety of teaching techniques for more challenging concepts.

5. Of the following statements, which one most accurately describes the reason it's important for fifth-grade students to be challenged with meaningful yet obtainable educational goals and objectives?

   A. Bored students are more likely to have disciplinary problems.

   B. Failure to accomplish goals at that age can have a damaging impact on a child's self-esteem.

   C. Having a proper understanding of fundamentals will guarantee future academic success.

   D. It is healthier for students to compete against themselves than against others.

6. Which of the following situations should most concern a high school teacher?

   A. A good student suddenly begins dressing differently and dyeing her hair strange colors.

   B. A student consistently claims that the rules he's expected to follow stifle his creative urges.

   C. A previously gregarious student becomes withdrawn and unresponsive.

   D. A student quits the debate team to devote more time to football practice.

7. Upon completing a unit on the settlement of Texas, a teacher breaks her fourth-grade class into small groups and has each group design and create a timeline showing the arrivals of the various peoples. The teacher probably does this to:

   A. give her students a chance to draw and color.

   B. reinforce the knowledge learned in the unit.

   C. give her students an opportunity to learn from one another.

   D. have something to display on the walls of her classroom.

DRILL ANSWER AND EXPLANATIONS

1. Which of the following actions most clearly demonstrates that a student has grasped the concept of conservation?

    A. Upon pouring water from a large pitcher into four smaller glasses, she claims that there is now more water.

    B. She can take a pile of stuffed animals, order them by size, and then reorganize them by color.

    C. She takes a bucket of sand, uses a scoop to make three small mounds of sand, and then takes the mounds and refills the bucket with them.

    D. She uses a light switch to turn lights on and off.

C The question measures Competency 001: The teacher understands human developmental processes and applies this knowledge to plan instruction and ongoing assessment that motivate students and are responsive to their developmental characteristics and needs.

Here's How to Crack It

Step 1: Identify the scenario.

- Age range: none given

- Goal: identify an example of conservation

Step 2: Use POE to narrow down the answer choices.
Conservation is the idea that just because something changes form or shape doesn't mean that there is more or less of it present.

    A. No. This is what a student that hasn't grasped conservation would do.

    B. No. That's an example of seriation.

    C. Maybe. The child seems to understand that he/she has the same amount of sand.

    D. No. That has nothing to do with something changing form or shape.

Step 3: Make a final decision.
It doesn't seem like a perfect answer, but all the others are worse. The best answer is C.

2. A third-grade boy has been teasing another student. In an effort to stop this behavior, a teacher tries to appeal to the child's moral conscience. Which of the following questions would be most useful?

   A. How would you feel if someone teased you?

   B. Do you know how much trouble you'll get into if you don't stop that?

   C. Don't you think that everyone deserves to be left alone?

   D. Don't you want to be a good boy?

A This question measures Competency 001: The teacher understands human developmental processes and applies this knowledge to plan instruction and ongoing assessment that motivate students and are responsive to their developmental characteristics and needs.

Here's How to Crack It

Step 1: Identify the scenario.

- Age range: third grade

- Goal: appeal to a student's moral conscience

Step 2: Use POE to narrow down the answer choices.

A. Maybe. Keep it for now.

B. No. This emphasizes the punitive.

C. No. This moral concept is too advanced for a third grader.

D. No. This moral concept is too advanced for a third grader.

Step 3: Make a final decision.
Choice A is the best answer.

3. Mixed-ability-level small-group learning can be an effective teaching tool because of which of the following?

   A. Teachers can monitor student behavior more effectively.

   B. Students get bored with traditional lecture-based lessons.

   C. Students who understand a concept can help others understand it, too.

   D. Teachers get a break from their daily routine.

C This question measures Competency 004: The teacher understands learning processes and factors that impact students' learning and demonstrates this knowledge by planning effective, engaging instruction and appropriate assessments.

Here's How to Crack It

Step 1: Identify the scenario.

- Age range: none given

- Goal: identify the benefits of small-group learning.

Step 2: Use POE to narrow down the answer choices.

A. Maybe. Teachers spend more time monitoring when small groups are working.

B. No. That may be true, but that's not why small groups are an effective teaching tool.

C. Yes. That's related to Vygotsky's zone of proximal development.

D. No. That makes things easier for the teacher.

Step 3: Make a final decision.
If we read carefully, we find that choice A discusses monitoring student behavior, which makes choice A less likely to be the right answer, which asks about small-group time as an effective teaching tool. The best answer is C.

4. A teacher's class is filled with students that have an exceptionally wide range of development. To accommodate this range, the teacher should:

 A. allow the students to work on their own exclusively.

 B. group the students according to their level of development.

 C. develop instruction for the lowest level of development in the classroom.

 D. use a variety of teaching techniques for more challenging concepts.

D This questions tests Competency 004: The teacher understands learning processes and factors that impact students' learning and demonstrates this knowledge by planning effective, engaging instruction and appropriate assessments.

Here's How to Crack It

Step 1: Identify the scenario.

- Age range: none given

- Goal: accommodate a wide range of development

Step 2: Use POE to narrow down the answer choices.

A. No. The teacher needs to do more than abdicate responsibility.

B. No. Grouping works best when students at different stages are grouped together.

C. No. That will retard the development of the more advanced children.

D. Yes. A variety of techniques will provide the best chance of teaching all students effectively.

Step 3: Make a final decision.
The best answer is D.

> 5. Of the following statements, which one most accurately describes the reason it's important for fifth-grade students to be challenged with meaningful yet obtainable educational goals and objectives?
>
>   A. Bored students are more likely to have disciplinary problems.
>
>   B. Failure to accomplish goals at that age can have a damaging impact on a child's self-esteem.
>
>   C. Having a proper understanding of fundamentals will guarantee future academic success.
>
>   D. It is healthier for students to compete against themselves than against others.

B This question tests Competency 001: The teacher understands human developmental processes and applies this knowledge to plan instruction and ongoing assessment that motivate students and are responsive to their developmental characteristics and needs.

Here's How to Crack It

Step 1: Identify the scenario.

- Age range: fifth grade

- Goal: identify the reason for challenging students

Step 2: Use POE to narrow down the answer choices.

    A. No. That may be true, but it's unlikely that it's the most important reason.

    B. Maybe. Keep it in.

    C. Maybe. Keep it in.

    D. No. The question didn't mention competition.

Step 3: Make a final decision.

Choice B seems very vague, but choice C says that understanding *guarantees* later success. Clearly that's not the case, because nothing can guarantee success, so the best answer is B. Further, choice B matches Erikson's industry stage, which is typical for fifth-grade students.

6.   Which of the following situations should most concern a high school teacher?

    A. A good student suddenly begins dressing differently and dyeing her hair strange colors.

    B. A student consistently claims that the rules he's expected to follow stifle his creative urges.

    C. A previously gregarious student becomes withdrawn and unresponsive.

    D. A student quits the debate team to devote more time to football practice.

C   This question tests Competency 001: The teacher understands human developmental processes and applies this knowledge to plan instruction and ongoing assessment that motivate students and are responsive to their developmental characteristics and needs.

Here's How to Crack It

Step 1: Identify the scenario.

- Age range: high school

- Goal: determine behavior worthy of concern

Step 2: Use POE to narrow down the answer choices.

    A. Maybe. Keep it in.

    B. No. Students are expected to rebel against authority in high school.

    C. Maybe. Keep it in.

    D. No. Making choices and getting deeply involved in extracurricular activities is typical of high school students.

Step 3: Make a final decision.
Between choices A and C, choice C is the greater cause for concern. It's not unusual for a high school student to search for an identity, but withdrawing from social behavior is a clear warning sign. The best answer is C.

> 7. Upon completing a unit on the settlement of Texas, a teacher breaks her fourth-grade class into small groups and has each group design and create a timeline showing the arrivals of the various peoples. The teacher probably does this to:
>
>   A. give her students a chance to draw and color.
>
>   B. reinforce the knowledge learned in the unit.
>
>   C. give her students an opportunity to learn from one another.
>
>   D. have something to display on the walls of her classroom.

B This question tests Competency 004: The teacher understands learning processes and factors that impact students' learning and demonstrates this knowledge by planning effective, engaging instruction and appropriate assessments.

Here's How to Crack It

Step 1: Identify the scenario.

- Age range: none given

- Goal: identify teacher's purpose

Step 2: Use POE to narrow down the answer choices.

    A. No. That's educationally inappropriate at this age.

    B. Maybe. Keep it in.

    C. No. The question says the project happens after the unit is over.

    D. No. That's not an educational purpose.

Step 3: Make a final decision.
Choice B is the only one remaining, but it's also true that fourth graders benefit from the use of timelines and charts that link concepts together.

4

Educational Theory and Practice

EDUCATIONAL THEORY AND PRACTICE

Now that we've reviewed the developmental stages that get tested on the TExES, let's take a look at some different styles of learning and teaching that are likely to show up in test questions.

MULTIPLE INTELLIGENCES

What is intelligence? Who knows? Nonetheless, you should be familiar with Howard Gardner's work because it might show up on the TExES. Howard Gardner is a developmental psychologist at Harvard University who, in the mid-1980s, categorized the following eight types of intelligence:

Logical-Mathematical

This type of intelligence relates to the ability to detect patterns, think logically, and make deductions. Scientists and mathematicians tend to be logical-mathematical thinkers.

Linguistic

People who have linguistic intelligence are particularly sensitive not only to words themselves, but also to the relationship between the meanings of words and the ideas and concepts that words represent. Poets and journalists tend to possess linguistic intelligence.

Musical

Musical intelligence is defined as the ability to recognize and produce rhythm, pitch, and timbre—the three fundamental elements of music. Obviously, composers and musicians possess musical intelligence.

Spatial

People with spatial intelligence have the ability to create and manipulate mental images. They also perceive spatial relationships in the world accurately and can use both the mental and actual perceptions to solve problems. Artists and navigators both use well-developed spatial intelligence.

Bodily-Kinesthetic

Bodily-kinesthetic intelligence is the ability to consciously control and coordinate your body's movements and manipulate objects. Athletes and dancers need a strong bodily-kinesthetic intelligence.

Naturalist

This intelligence relates to being sensitive to natural objects like plants and animals and making fine sensory discriminations. Naturalist, hunters, and botanists excel in this intelligence.

Interpersonal

Interpersonal intelligence is the ability to understand and respond to the emotions and intentions of others. Psychologists and salespeople make good use of interpersonal intelligence.

Intrapersonal

Intrapersonal intelligence is the ability to understand and respond to your own emotions and intentions.

Importantly, Gardner believes that we all possess some degree of these intelligences, and that each of these must be relatively well developed in order for us to function well in society.

Further, although the intelligences are categorized separately, we rarely use them totally independently. It is difficult to think of a profession or activity that doesn't combine some of these intelligences somehow. For instance, a pianist needs not only musical intelligence, but also interpersonal (to be able to relate to an audience) as well as bodily-kinesthetic (to control the actions of his hands on the keyboard).

WHAT DOES THIS MEAN TO ME AS A TEST TAKER?

Remember that most content-based questions on the TExES will ask you to apply this knowledge in a hypothetical classroom situation rather than simply regurgitate it on command. So you might see a question like this:

> Ahmed, a sixth grader, is a good soccer player, but is having a hard time with basic geometry. Which of the following strategies could his teacher use to best help him improve his understanding of math?
>
> A.   Restrict his physical education activities until his math grades improve.
>
> B.   Use extra soccer time as a reward for higher math performance.
>
> C.   Give him extra worksheets to reinforce fundamental concepts.
>
> D.   Plan an outdoor lesson that demonstrates geometric relationships among the players on a soccer field.

Stick to the process:

Here's How to Crack It

Step 1: Identify the scenario.

- Age range: sixth grade

- Goal: improve Ahmed's math understanding

Step 2: Use POE to narrow down the answer choices.

A.   No. This seems punitive and there's no guarantee that he'll improve in math.

B.   Not close enough. This is better because it's rewarding instead of punitive, but again, the teacher isn't directly addressing Ahmed's geometry skills.

C.   Maybe. This seems to talk about learning math, so let's leave it in.

D.   Possibly. This involves both soccer and math. We'll keep it, too.

Step 3: Make a final decision.

Choice C isn't horrible, but it doesn't mention the soccer ability at all. What about answer choice D? It suggests that Ahmed might learn better if the teacher uses Ahmed's apparently strong kinesthetic and spatial intelligence to help improve his mathematical intelligence. In addition, it has the advantage of being a fun approach that might get children excited about math. And, in case you didn't notice, it's the answer choice that involves the most work for the teacher. The best answer is D.

Different Learning Styles

Not all people learn the same way. Different students will process information differently depending on how it's presented. Many theorists split learning styles into the following three categories:

Visual

Visual learners learn by seeing. They prefer graphs and charts to summarize information, rather than text or a spoken summary. They prefer maps and diagrams to step-by-step directions. They're more likely to remember faces than names when they meet someone briefly. Traditional lecture-based lessons can be good for visual listeners as long as the teacher makes good use of visual aids.

Auditory

Aural learners learn by hearing. They're more likely to remember what was said about a painting they've studied than to be able to describe it in great detail. Traditional lecture-based lessons are effective with auditory learners.

Kinesthetic

Kinesthetic learners learn by doing. They remember things best if they try them out and see for themselves. They're more likely to remember what they were doing when they met someone than what they talked about. Traditional lecture-based lessons are not good for kinesthetic learners, but lessons that involve laboratory work or hands-on experimentation tend to be effective.

Of course, students do not fall neatly into one of these three categories. According to the TExES, good teachers should take into account these different learning styles and plan lessons accordingly.

What Does This Mean to Me As a Test Taker?

Again, you won't be asked a question like, "Which of the following is the definition of a kinesthetic learner?" Instead, you might see a question that looks like this:

Mr. Giaudrone, a sixth-grade teacher, is teaching a unit on the criminal justice system. Which of the following activities would be best suited to the kinesthetic learners in his class?

A. Have students write a short report on the justice system that shows the relationships among law enforcement officials, prosecuting attorneys, defense attorneys, defendants, victims, witnesses, and the judge and jury.

B. Show a video in class that dramatizes the justice system and shows the relationships among law enforcement officials, prosecuting attorneys, defense attorneys, defendants, victims, witnesses, and the judge and jury.

C. Stage a mock trial in class in which the students play the roles of law enforcement officials, prosecuting attorneys, defense attorneys, defendants, victims, witnesses, and the judge and jury.

D. Arrange a field trip to a courtroom so students can observe the criminal justice system in action.

Each of these may be effective ways of teaching children about the criminal justice system. For that reason, it's especially important that we stick to the process:

Here's How to Crack It

Step 1: Identify the scenario.

- Age range: sixth grade

- Goal: reach the kinesthetic learners

Step 2: Use POE to narrow down the answer choices.
What's true about kinesthetic learners? They learn by doing. Here are the choices again:

> A.   Have students write a short report on the justice system that shows the relationships among law enforcement officials, prosecuting attorneys, defense attorneys, defendants, victims, witnesses, and the judge and jury.

Maybe. The students are doing something here, even if it's just writing a report. Let's leave it in for now.

> B.   Show a video in class that dramatizes the justice system and shows the relationships among law enforcement officials, prosecuting attorneys, defense attorneys, defendants, victims, witnesses, and the judge and jury.

No. This might be an effective strategy for visual and auditory learners, but not for kinesthetic learners. Cross it out.

> C.   Stage a mock trial in class in which the students play the roles of law enforcement officials, prosecuting attorneys, defense attorneys, defendants, victims, witnesses, and the judge and jury.

Probably. Students here are actively participating, and interacting with each other while they're learning. Keep it.

> D.   Arrange a field trip to a courtroom so students can observe the criminal justice system in action.

No. Although students leave the physical classroom for a field trip, in this case, they're still passively watching the process. From a learning styles perspective, this is no different from watching a video. Cross it out.

Step 3: Make a final decision.
We're down to A and C, but now we can see that A isn't as good. C is the best choice to reach the kinesthetic learners.

Different Teaching Styles

Now that we've looked at the different ways students learn, we need to take a look at what the TExES believes your responsibilities are as far as teaching is concerned. Fundamentally, they're interested in two major areas: instruction and assessment. Or, in other words:

How are you going to teach?

How are you going to tell whether students have learned?

It's probably no surprise to you that the TExES thinks that you should be all things to all students. This means that, according to the test writers, you should vary your teaching style to accommodate different learning styles and intelligences, and tailor your assessment methods to the task at hand. If this sounds logical and sensible, you're right—you just need to make sure that you're picking the answer that the test writers consider logical and sensible.

Let's look at some of the tools they expect you to have:

Communication modes:

Verbal

Nonverbal

Technology-based

Communication strategies:

Simplifying and restating

Responding to nonverbal cues

Summarizing important information

Active listening

What Does This Mean to Me As a Test Taker?

As usual, this is knowledge that will be tested in questions posing hypothetical classroom situations. To apply that knowledge, let's add another criteria to the ones that we've developed: task-appropriateness. Simply put, this is the idea that your teaching and assessment styles should suit the task at hand. Again, common sense is more important than the ability to rattle off the names of four communication strategies.

Let's look at a question:

> Mrs. Soter, a sixth-grade teacher, has students work-
> ing in small groups classifying leaves and categorizing
> them according to different criteria. Each group will
> present a written report stating its findings. Which of
> the following assessment strategies should Mrs. Soter
> use to ensure that all students in a group participated
> equally in creating their report?
>
> A. Have students put their initials next to the
>   specific portions of the report that they wrote.
>
> B. Spend time informally observing each group as
>   students work on the project to determine the
>   level of engagement of each individual student.
>
> C. Have each student submit an additional one-page
>   report explaining the contributions that he or she
>   made to the overall project.
>
> D. Have each group pick a leader, who will have the
>   additional responsibility to ensure the workload
>   is distributed equally among all members of the
>   group.

Follow the process:

Step 1: Identify the scenario.

- Age range: sixth grade

- Goal: equal participation among students in a group project

What's true about group projects? Well, theoretically, with group projects, learning occurs not only from discussing the facts of the situation, but also through interacting with other students. This is a cooperative learning strategy, and it can be very effective if the teacher takes steps to ensure that students are participating equally. We all know from our own experiences that it's easy to sit back and let one motivated person do all the work in a group. What might a teacher do to prevent that from happening?

Step 2: Use POE to narrow down the answer choices.
Let's look at the answer choices.

> A. Have students put their initials next to the
>   specific portions of the report that they wrote.

Maybe, but it's not necessarily true that each student will have written specific portions of the text. If students are truly working as a group, any individual sentence might have been physically written down by one student, but could be the result of work that many students were doing together. Let's leave it in, with some skepticism, and see what the other answer choices look like.

B. Spend time informally observing each group as students work on the project to determine the level of engagement of each individual student.

Maybe. This seems pretty subjective, doesn't it? Observing and evaluating a group dynamic from the outside seems like it would be really hard for the teacher. That's a tough skill. Let's leave it in.

C. Have each student submit an additional one-page report explaining the contributions that he or she made to the overall project.

Again, maybe, but if we thought it was hard for the teacher to determine what each student was contributing, imagine how hard it would be for each student, especially a sixth-grade student, to analyze what he or she brought to the group. Besides, Mrs. Soter would probably want the students to concentrate on the work at hand rather than get distracted by paying specific attention to how they're contributing. Maybe we should leave it in, but we should be very skeptical about this answer choice.

D. Have each group pick a leader, who will have the additional responsibility to ensure the workload is distributed equally among all members of the group.

Probably not. This sounds like Mrs. Soter is abdicating her responsibility and handing it over to a student. Let's cross this off.

Step 3: Make a final decision.

Remember that an assessment is supposed to be task-appropriate. As we mentioned, part of the learning process in group situations occurs through interaction with other students. Of A, B, and C, B is the only answer choice that allows the teacher to observe this interaction first-hand. Also, notice it's the one that requires the most work for the teacher.

To further illustrate the idea of task-appropriateness, let's look at another example:

Miss Bynoe has been teaching a third-grade math class to subtract two-digit numbers. Which of the following assessment strategies should Miss Bynoe use to ensure that students in her class have mastered the skill?

A. Have the students write a one-page report describing, in detail, the process involved in subtracting two-digit numbers.

B. Administer a test with questions ranging in difficulty from easy to hard and require students to show their work on each problem.

C. Assign a worksheet and informally observe students as they solve problems.

D. Have students split into groups of two, quiz each other, and report the results.

Here's How to Crack It

Step 1: Identify the scenario.

- Age range: third grade

- Goal: mastering the skill of subtracting two-digit numbers

Notice that although this question also asks about an assessment method, the task is quite different. Here, we're dealing with a skill, and the only criterion that's important is whether the students have mastered the skill.

Step 2: Use POE to narrow down the answer choices.

Let's look at the answer choices:

> A.   Have the students write a one-page report describing, in detail, the process involved in subtracting two-digit numbers.

No. It's probably true that most third graders who would be able to describe the process fully would also be able to carry it out in practice. But many learners, especially kinesthetic learners, would have difficulty describing the process in words even though they were perfectly capable of accurately subtracting two-digit numbers. Because the only criterion is to ensure that students have mastered the skill, this can't be the right answer. Cross it out.

> B.   Administer a test with questions ranging in difficulty from easy to hard and require students to show their work on each problem.

This looks pretty good. This is a skill-based process, so a test that shows how students solve problems ranging in level of difficulty is probably a good idea. It's appropriate to the task. Leave it in.

> C.   Assign a worksheet and informally observe students as they solve problems.

No. Even though informal observation was the correct answer in the previous example, it's a bad strategy here. Why? Well, to determine a skill level, a teacher will need to see how students approach a variety of problems, not just one. The task is a formal, skill-based process, so it requires a formal assessment method, not an informal one. Cross it out.

> D.   Have students split into groups of two, quiz each other, and report the results.

Again, as we have already discussed, cooperative learning can be an effective teaching strategy, but it's a bad assessment strategy. It also involves less work for the teacher than choice B. Cross it out.

Step 3: Make a final decision.
In this case, B is the only answer left. The other three were bad choices, and B is a task-appropriate strategy.

Let's try another question dealing with assessment methods:

> Mr. Nixon, a seventh-grade math teacher, recently gave what he considered a fair exam on which his class scored an average of 57 out of 100, a failing grade. He concluded that the students had not mastered the subject matter. What should Mr. Nixon's next step be to best meet the students' educational needs?
>
> A.   Write a letter to parents and caregivers describing the results of the examination and suggesting that they become more involved in helping their children with future homework assignments.
>
> B.   Give the students an opportunity to improve their grades by reviewing and correcting the errors they made on the exam.
>
> C.   Revise his lesson plans to include more class time to cover the same material in a new way, and give another test afterward.
>
> D.   Assign extra homework on the material covered on the exam, and encourage students to work harder in the future so that their final grades will be above the passing mark.

Here's How to Crack It

Step 1: Identify the scenario.

- Age range: seventh grade

- Goal: meet students' educational needs.

That is the broadest goal of all, and quite vague. What is Mr. Nixon's fundamental goal? Probably to make sure the students master the material. Clearly, right now, the students haven't yet done so.

Step 2: Use POE to narrow down the answer choices.

> A.   Write a letter to parents and caregivers describing the results of the examination and suggesting that they become more involved in helping their children with future homework assignments.

This is never a correct answer. While communication with parents/caregivers is a huge TExES priority, here the teacher is overstepping the teacher/parent boundary and suggesting that parents do something that many of them might not be prepared to do. In addition, it assigns blame for the students' failure to the students, or, by implication, the parents and caregivers. Cross this one out.

> B.   Give the students an opportunity to improve their
>   grades by reviewing and correcting the errors
>   they made on the exam.

Maybe. Reviewing and correcting errors can be an effective way for children to learn. Let's leave it in.

> C.   Revise his lesson plans to include more class
>   time to reteach the same material that was
>   covered on the exam in a new way, and give
>   another test afterward.

Maybe. Here Mr. Nixon acknowledges that his students didn't learn the material the first time, and he shows that he can use different strategies to teach the same material.

> D.   Encourage students to work harder in the future
>   so that their final grades will be above the
>   passing mark.

No. This choice doesn't address the fact that the students haven't learned the material, and therefore does nothing to reach the goal of mastery. Cross it out.

Step 3: Make a final decision.

We're left with two decent answer choices. Which one is more work for the teacher? C. It's worth mentioning that B might be the best answer if only one or two students had failed the exam, but because the class average was a failing grade, it's clear that Mr. Nixon needs to reteach the material in a better way to the entire class. The best answer is C.

Put all of this together by trying the following drill. Use the clues provided in the question to help guide you to the right answer.

DRILL

Directions: Each question in this practice test is a multiple-choice question with four answer choices. Read each question carefully and choose the ONE best answer.

1. A teacher's goal in classroom behavior management should be to do which of the following?

    A. Motivate students to manage their own behavior.

    B. Stress the importance of conduct grades on report cards.

    C. Allow the students to decide their own punishment for bad behavior.

    D. Provide an environment with clear and concise rules.

2. A history teacher is preparing to start a section about the Vietnam Conflict. To best prepare, the teacher should:

    A. try to find out if the students have a family member who served in Vietnam

    B. have students locate Vietnam on the globe.

    C. prepare a speech about the importance of not repeating past mistakes.

    D. gather information about what the students already know about Vietnam.

3. An elementary school teacher is concerned about the reading level of one of her students. The best way to accurately gauge the student's reading level would be to:

    A. suggest the student be formally tested.

    B. test the student repeatedly.

    C. have the student read to the librarian.

    D. observe the student during reading group time.

4. An English teacher who is worried about his students' reading level has recruited teachers in other areas to work with him to increase students' reading skills. This demonstrates which of the following?

    A. Some teachers are more dedicated than others.

    B. Reading skills are of paramount importance.

    C. Some teachers rely too heavily on others to accomplish their own goals.

    D. Students benefit when teachers collaborate to improve students' education.

Mrs. Keys is an elementary school art teacher. She has been asked to have students create a mural on one of the walls in the school to commemorate the 100-year anniversary of the school.

5. Mrs. Keys has selected a group of students from different grades to work on the project. The students' first step is to come up with ideas for their mural. Then the students must agree on one design. This is an example of which of the following?

   A. parallel thinking, then convergent thinking

   B. parallel thinking, then divergent thinking

   C. brainstorming, then convergent thinking

   D. brainstorming, then divergent thinking

6. After the group has decided on a theme and design for the mural, it could use which of the following to help actualize the design?

   A. spreadsheet software

   B. design software

   C. a projector

   D. the Internet

7. The students have been meeting during study-hall time or free time in their regular classrooms. One of the students' mothers has learned about this project and has called the office to complain about her daughter being taken out of class to work on an art project. To address this concern, the art teacher should:

   A. call or meet with the parent to explain the educational benefit of this project.

   B. remove the student from the project.

   C. speak with the student to address these concerns.

   D. allow someone from administration to speak with the parent.

8. Mrs. Keys has noticed that the creation of the mural has depleted a lot of the supplies she planned to use throughout the year in her art room. To present this information to the administration, she would most likely benefit most from which of the following:

A. a calculator

B. a word document

C. a spreadsheet

D. art catalogs' listed prices

9. At the completion of the mural, which of the following could Mrs. Keys do to demonstrate the educational benefits the students have received while working on the mural?

A. Give a final grade that can be used in place of the classroom grade for the time that was missed.

B. Give an evaluation of the mural and each individual student's contribution to the mural.

C. Have the students present the portion of the mural they worked on and how it relates to the theme.

D. Report on what the students' process was in developing and completing the mural.

DECISION SET ENDS HERE

10. A teacher has just learned that she will have an English language learner join her class. Which of the following locations would be best for this student in the classroom?

    A. in the front row

    B. next to the teacher's desk

    C. next to a buddy who can help him when he doesn't understand

    D. where he will be able to see everything in the classroom

DRILL ANSWERS AND EXPLANATIONS

1. A teacher's goal in classroom behavior management should be to do which of the following?

    A. Motivate students to manage their own behavior.

    B. Stress the importance of conduct grades on report cards.

    C. Allow the students to decide their own punishment for bad behavior.

    D. Provide an environment with clear and concise rules.

A   This item measures Competency 006: The teacher understands strategies for creating an organized and productive learning environment and for managing student behavior. A is the best answer because the student will lead the direction of his/her own education.

Here's How to Crack It

Step 1: Identify the scenario.

- Age range: not given

- Goal: managing classroom behavior

What do we know about managing classroom behavior? Teachers should be fair, consistent, and there are a slew of different theories depending on age range—but wait! The question doesn't mention anything about age range, so the answer can't get too specific. Let's see what we have again.

Step 2: Use POE to narrow down the answer choices.

A. Maybe. Children controlling themselves would be the best-case scenario, right? Let's keep it.

B. Unlikely. That's not a goal, that's a (bad) strategy for motivation. Cross it out.

C. No. Again, that's not a goal, and it goes against what we know about classroom management (even though it allows children control). Cross it out.

D. Maybe. That'll help with classroom management, and it's something a teacher should do.

Step 3: Make a final decision.

Reread the question. It asks for a goal. D isn't really a goal; it's a step. A is the ultimate goal, and is therefore the correct answer.

2. A history teacher is preparing to start a section about the Vietnam Conflict. To best prepare, the teacher should:

A. try to find out if the students have a family member who served in Vietnam

B. have students locate Vietnam on the globe.

C. prepare a speech about the importance of not repeating past mistakes.

D. gather information about what the students already know about Vietnam.

D This item measures Competency 004: The teacher understands learning processes and factors that impact student learning and demonstrates this knowledge by planning effective, engaging instruction and appropriate assessments.

Here's How to Crack It

Step 1: Identify the scenario.

• Age range: none given

• Goal: to best prepare for a history section on the Vietnam Conflict

We must be looking for an answer that could apply to any age range, so this can't be that specific.

Step 2: Use POE to narrow down the answer choices.

A. Unlikely. How would that help the teacher prepare? Cross it out.

B. Perhaps. That might be a good place to start.

C. Unlikely. How would that start the lesson? Cross it out.

D. Perhaps. It's difficult to prepare for a section unless you know what the students' level of knowledge already is.

Step 3: Make a final decision.

Reread the question. The goal is to best prepare. Although B may be a good place to start, it's not going to help the teacher prepare. D is the best answer because the teacher should determine what the students already know in order to plan what they still need to cover.

3. An elementary school teacher is concerned about the reading level of one of her students. The best way to accurately gauge the student's reading level would be to:

   A. suggest the student be formally tested.

   B. test the student repeatedly.

   C. have the student read to the librarian.

   D. observe the student during reading group time.

D This item measures Competency 010: The teacher monitors student performance and achievement; provides students with timely, high-quality feedback; and responds flexibly to promote learning for all students.

Here's How to Crack It

Step 1: Identify the scenario.

- Age range: none given

- Goal: to best gauge the student's reading level

Step 2: Use POE to narrow down the answer choices.

A. Maybe. This seems a little extreme, but it would be one way to go.

B. Unlikely. Repeated testing might give a large number of separate scores, but it would be difficult and time-consuming to implement. Cross it out.

C. No. The librarian is not necessarily trained to measure a student's reading ability. Cross it out.

D. Maybe. Reading group time implies that the student will be reading aloud. The teacher might get a good idea of how the student reads by informally listening.

Step 3: Make a final decision.

It helps here to know that students often feel anxiety about formal reading tests and can consequently perform below their ability level. In other words, formal observation may be less reliable. The best answer is D because informal observation is more likely to reveal the true ability level of the student.

4. An English teacher who is worried about his students' reading level has recruited teachers in other areas to work with him to increase students' reading skills. This demonstrates which of the following?

    A. Some teachers are more dedicated than others.

    B. Reading skills are of paramount importance.

    C. Some teachers rely too heavily on others to accomplish their own goals.

    D. Students benefit when teachers collaborate to improve students' education.

D   This item measures Competency 012: The teacher enhances professional knowledge and skills by effectively interacting with other members of the educational community and participating in various types of professional activities.

Here's How to Crack It

Step 1: Identify the scenario.

- Age range: none given

- Goal: determine what a teacher asking for help constitutes

Step 2: Use POE to narrow down the answer choices.

To begin with, would the SBEC consider a teacher asking for assistance in order to help students a positive or negative thing? Clearly, they'd think it was a good thing.

    A. No. All the teachers described seem dedicated.

    B. Doubtful. The point of the problem seems to be the teachers' collaboration.

    C. No. There's no reason to believe that the teacher is relying *too heavily* on others.

    D. Yes. This is exactly the sort of answer the SBEC likes to see.

Step 3: Make a final decision.

D is the best answer because teachers should support each other regardless of what they teach to improve their students' education.

5. Mrs. Keys has selected a group of students from different grades to work on the project. The students' first step is to come up with ideas for their mural. Then the students must agree on one design. This is an example of which of the following?

   A. parallel thinking, then convergent thinking

   B. parallel thinking, then divergent thinking

   C. brainstorming, then convergent thinking

   D. brainstorming, then divergent thinking

C This item measures Competency 007: The teacher understands and applies principles and strategies for communicating effectively in varied teaching and learning contexts. C is the best answer because the students should first consider many ideas but then in the end, must agree upon one.

Here's How to Crack It

Step 1: Identify the scenario.

- Age range: elementary school

- Goal: identify the decision-making process

Step 2: Use POE to narrow down the answer choices.

If the students must agree on one design at the end, then their thinking must converge, and we can cross out choices B and D. The technique of coming up with ideas is called brainstorming, so we can cross out A.

Step 3: Make a final decision.

The only choice left is C.

6. After the group has decided on a theme and design for the mural, it could use which of the following to help actualize the design?

   A. spreadsheet software

   B. design software

   C. a projector

   D. the Internet

B This item measures Competency 009: The teacher incorporates the effective use of technology to plan, organize, deliver, and evaluate instruction for all students.

Here's How to Crack It

Step 1: Identify the scenario.

- Age range: elementary school

- Goal: choose a good tool to use

Step 2: Use POE to narrow down the answer choices.
We can't be expected to know too much about teaching art, so we'll just have to use common sense.

A. No. A spreadsheet manipulates numerical data.

B. Maybe. There might be software that would be useful.

C. Maybe. You could project the mural onto the wall and then color it in.

D. No. That wouldn't help you "actualize the design."

Step 3: Make a final decision.
Given that we're not expected to know anything about teaching art, which do you think is more likely: that the SBEC is testing your knowledge of a piece of equipment that's been around since your parents were in elementary school, or that the SBEC is testing your knowledge of new technology? The best answer is B.

7. The students have been meeting during study-hall time or free time in their regular classrooms. One of the students' mothers has learned about this project and has called the office to complain about her daughter being taken out of class to work on an art project. To address this concern, the art teacher should:

    A. call or meet with the parent to explain the educational benefit of this project.

    B. remove the student from the project.

    C. speak with the student to address these concerns.

    D. allow someone from administration to speak with the parent.

A This item measures Competency 011: The teacher understands the importance of family involvement in children's education and knows how to interact and communicate effectively with families.

Here's How to Crack It

Step 1: Identify the scenario.

- Age range: elementary school

- Goal: effectively address a parent's concern

Step 2: Use POE to narrow down the answer choices.
Remember the goal is always to address the parent's concern without upsetting the parent.

    A. Yes. This would accomplish both goals.

    B. No. This detracts from the student's education.

    C. No. This doesn't address the parent's concern.

    D. No. Teachers should be able to handle their own problems without involving the administration.

Step 3: Make a final decision.
The best answer is A. By calling or talking to the parent directly, the teacher can assure the parent that there is an educational goal attached to the project and answer any further questions.

8.   Mrs. Keys has noticed that the creation of the mural has depleted a lot of the supplies she planned to use throughout the year in her art room. To present this information to the administration, she would most likely benefit most from which of the following:

    A.   a calculator

    B.   a word document

    C.   a spreadsheet

    D.   art catalogs' listed prices

    C   This item measures Competency 009: The teacher incorporates the effective use of technology to plan, organize, deliver, and evaluate instruction for all students.

Here's How to Crack It

Step 1: Identify the scenario.

- Age range: elementary school

- Goal: identify tool to present budget information

Step 2: Use POE to narrow down the answer choices.

    A. A calculator isn't a mechanism for presentation. Cross it out.

    B. Maybe.

    C. Maybe.

    D. This is important information, but again not something that is good to prepare presentations. Cross it out.

Step 3: Make a final decision.
Although both a word-processing document and a spreadsheet could be used to help deliver a presentation, because this presentation seems specifically directed at supplies and budgetary concerns, the numerical processing capabilities of a spreadsheet would make it the better choice. The best answer is C.

9. At the completion of the mural, which of the following could Mrs. Keys do to demonstrate the educational benefits the students have received while working on the mural?

    A. Give a final grade that can be used in place of the classroom grade for the time that was missed.

    B. Give an evaluation of the mural and each individual student's contribution to the mural.

    C. Have the students present the portion of the mural they worked on and how it relates to the theme.

    D. Report on what the students' process was in developing and completing the mural.

    C   This item measures Competency 010: The teacher monitors student performance and achievement; provides students with timely, high-quality feedback; and responds flexibly to promote learning for all students.

Here's How to Crack It

Step 1: Identify the scenario.

- Age range: elementary school

- Goal: demonstrate educational benefits

Step 2: Use POE to narrow down the answer choices.

    A. No. How does assigning a grade demonstrate an educational benefit?

    B. Maybe. That might show what students learned.

    C. That's even better.

    D. Maybe. That might show what students learned, too.

Step 3: Make a final decision.
Choices B, C, and D are all plausible in this case. However, choices B and D are similar in that the teacher is doing the evaluation and the presentation. Only in choice C is the student expected to build the link between the work he or she did and how it related to the overall theme. Because choice C involves the student, it is more likely to demonstrate the educational benefit, and is therefore the best answer.

10. A teacher has just learned that she will have an English language learner student join her class. Which of the following locations would be best for this student in the classroom?

A. in the front row

B. next to the teacher's desk

C. next to a buddy who can help him when he doesn't understand

D. where he will be able to see everything in the classroom

D This item measures Competency 005: The teacher knows how to establish a classroom climate that fosters learning, equity, and excellence and uses this knowledge to create a physical and emotional environment that is safe and productive.

Here's How to Crack It

Step 1: Identify the scenario.

- Age range: none given

- Goal: place an English language learner in a classroom

Step 2: Use POE to narrow down the answer choices.

Even if you aren't sure exactly how to accommodate an English language learner's needs, you can be sure that, according to the SBEC, the student should feel as included as possible. Let's see what the choices are:

A. Maybe. That might enhance the student's understanding.

B. No. We don't know where the teacher spends most of her time. Cross out B.

C. No. That's not a student's responsibility. Cross out C.

D. Maybe. That would probably make the student feel included.

Step 3: Make a final decision.

The remaining choices are in sharp contrast. *The front row* is a very specific location, where a student might feel put on the spot. *Where he will be able to see everything in the classroom* is quite vague, but it would tend to make the student aware of his surroundings, and perhaps feel more a part of the class than if he were seated in the front row. D is the better answer.

5

Ethical and Legal Standards

ETHICAL AND LEGAL STANDARDS

On the TExES, in addition to finding questions about educational theory and practice, you should also expect to find questions (about nine of them) about legal and ethical standards in Texas. Most of these rules and regulations fall within the boundaries of common sense—you probably already knew that you shouldn't lie about a colleague or have a romantic relationship with a student—but we're including the official code of ethics so you can see for yourself.

Source: www.tcta.org/capital/sbec/codeapproved.htm

REVISED CODE OF ETHICS AND STANDARD PRACTICES FOR TEXAS EDUCATORS (EFFECTIVE SEPT. 1, 2002)

Statement of Purpose

The Texas educator shall comply with standard practices and ethical conduct toward students, professional colleagues, school officials, parents, and members of the community and shall safeguard academic freedom. The Texas educator, in maintaining the dignity of the profession, shall respect and obey the law, demonstrate personal integrity, and exemplify honesty. The Texas educator, in exemplifying ethical relations with colleagues, shall extend just and equitable treatment to all members of the profession. The Texas educator, in accepting a position of public trust, shall measure success by the progress of each student toward realization of his or her potential as an effective citizen. The Texas educator, in fulfilling responsibilities in the community, shall cooperate with parents and others to improve the public schools of the community.

Enforceable Standards

I. Professional Ethical Conduct, Practices, and Performance

Standard 1.1   The educator shall not knowingly engage in deceptive practices regarding official policies of the school district or educational institution.

Standard 1.2   The educator shall not knowingly misappropriate, divert, or use monies, personnel, property, or equipment committed to his or her charge for personal gain or advantage.

Standard 1.3   The educator shall not submit fraudulent requests for reimbursement, expenses, or pay.

Standard 1.4   The educator shall not use institutional or professional privileges for personal or partisan advantage.

Standard 1.5   The educator shall neither accept nor offer gratuities, gifts, or favors that impair professional judgment or to obtain special advantage. This standard shall not restrict the acceptance of gifts or tokens offered and accepted openly from students, parents, or other persons or organizations in recognition or appreciation of service.

Standard 1.6   The educator shall not falsify records, or direct or coerce others to do so.

Standard 1.7   The educator shall comply with state regulations, written local school board policies, and other applicable state and federal laws.

Standard 1.8   The educator shall apply for, accept, offer, or assign a position or a responsibility on the basis of professional qualifications.

II. Ethical Conduct Toward Professional Colleagues

Standard 2.1   The educator shall not reveal confidential health or personnel information concerning colleagues unless disclosure serves lawful professional purposes or is required by law.

Standard 2.2   The educator shall not harm others by knowingly making false statements about a colleague or the school system.

Standard 2.3   The educator shall adhere to written local school board policies and state and federal laws regarding the hiring, evaluation, and dismissal of personnel.

Standard 2.4   The educator shall not interfere with a colleague's exercise of political, professional, or citizenship rights and responsibilities.

Standard 2.5   The educator shall not discriminate against or coerce a colleague on the basis of race, color, religion, national origin, age, sex, disability, or family status.

Standard 2.6   The educator shall not use coercive means or promise of special treatment in order to influence professional decisions or colleagues.

Standard 2.7   The educator shall not retaliate against any individual who has filed a complaint with the SBEC under this chapter.

III. Ethical Conduct Toward Students

Standard 3.1   The educator shall not reveal confidential information concerning students unless disclosure serves lawful professional purposes or is required by law.

Standard 3.2   The educator shall not knowingly treat a student in a manner that adversely affects the student's learning, physical health, mental health, or safety.

Standard 3.3   The educator shall not deliberately or knowingly misrepresent facts regarding a student.

Standard 3.4   The educator shall not exclude a student from participation in a program, deny benefits to a student, or grant an advantage to a student on the basis of race, color, sex, disability, national origin, religion, or family status.

Standard 3.5   The educator shall not engage in physical mistreatment of a student.

Standard 3.6   The educator shall not solicit or engage in sexual conduct or a romantic relationship with a student.

Standard 3.7   The educator shall not furnish alcohol or illegal/unauthorized drugs to any student or knowingly allow any student to consume alcohol or illegal/unauthorized drugs in the presence of the educator.

WHAT DOES THIS MEAN TO ME AS A TEST TAKER?

As we said above, most ethics questions you will see on the TExES can be answered with common sense. Try this one:

> Mr. Hughes, a science teacher, takes the school's DVD player home with him and returns it to the school the next day before classes begin. He has done nothing unethical only if which one of the following is true?
>
> A.   No one else needed the DVD player that night.
>
> B.   No one noticed the DVD player was missing.
>
> C.   He used the DVD player only to preview DVDs that he planned to show to his chemistry class.
>
> D.   He didn't damage the DVD player in any way.

Here's How to Crack It

Step 1: Identify the scenario.

- Age range: unknown

- Goal: unknown

There's no mention of students at all here, and the question is talking about unethical behavior. This must be an ethics question.

Step 2: Use POE to narrow down the answer choices.

> A.   No one else needed the DVD player that night.

Doubtful. Just because no one else needed it doesn't mean that his taking it was ethical. Cross it out.

> B.   No one noticed the DVD player was missing.

It's okay as long as you don't get caught? That doesn't sound ethical at all. Cross it out.

C.   He used the DVD player only to preview DVDs that he planned to show to his chemistry class.

Maybe. He was using the player for school purposes.

D.   He didn't damage the DVD player in any way.

Doubtful. Is it okay to steal a car as long as you don't damage it and give it back later?

Step 3: Make a final decision.

Answer choice C is the only one left. It helps if you remember that Standard 1.2 says: The educator shall not knowingly misappropriate, divert, or use monies, personnel, property, or equipment committed to his or her charge for personal gain or advantage.

So, if Mr. Hughes had used the player to watch his own private DVD collection, that would have been unethical (even if no one else needed it and he didn't damage it).

Try another:

Which of the following is an example of unethical behavior as defined by the Revised Code of Ethics and Standard Practices for Texas Educators?

A.   A female student asks a male teacher a direct question about the teacher's religious beliefs. The teacher refuses to answer the question, believing that his personal beliefs are private.

B.   A superintendent hires a stranger instead of his sister-in-law for a given position. His sister-in-law is clearly better qualified than the stranger, but he knows that he has difficulty getting along with his sister-in-law and he wishes to avoid charges of nepotism.

C.   A female teacher accepts a valuable piece of jewelry as a thank-you gift from a male student just before the student graduates from high school.

D.   A teacher spent $50 on supplies for a project, but lost the sales receipt. The teacher submits the reimbursement request anyway.

Here's How to Crack It

Step 1: Identify the scenario.

- Age range: unknown

- Goal: unknown

There's not much to identify here. One of the situations is unethical. You have to decide which one it is.

Step 2: Use POE to narrow down the answer choices.

> A. A female student asks a male teacher a direct question about the teacher's religious beliefs. The teacher refuses to answer the question, believing that his personal beliefs are private.

Is there any ethical rule that says a teacher must divulge his or her religious beliefs to students when asked? Even if you don't know for sure, it doesn't sound likely, does it? Let's cross it off.

> B. A superintendent hires a stranger instead of his sister-in-law for a given position. His sister-in-law is clearly better qualified than the stranger, but he knows that he has difficulty getting along with his sister-in-law and he wishes to avoid charges of nepotism.

Maybe. It sounds like the superintendent is hiring the less-qualified individual. That's probably not a good idea. Let's keep it.

> C. A female teacher accepts a valuable piece of jewelry as a thank-you gift from a male student just before the student graduates from high school.

Maybe. This seems to raise all sorts of red flags, doesn't it? It's an expensive gift, the student and the teacher are of the opposite sex, and the student is mature. Sounds fishy. Let's keep it for now.

> D. A teacher spent $50 on supplies for a project, but lost the sales receipt. The teacher submits the reimbursement request anyway.

No. A teacher can't submit a fraudulent request, but here the teacher actually spent the money. The teacher may have a problem getting reimbursed without a receipt, but it's not unethical to submit the request.

Step 3: Make a final decision.
We're down to B and C. Although the situation in C may raise a few eyebrows among gossipmongers, the teacher isn't doing anything unethical by accepting the gift. If the gift were given with the expectation of something in return (for example, a higher grade), then it would be unethical.

That leaves B. Although the superintendent's motives may be good, he is ethically obligated to hire on the basis of professional qualifications according to Standard 1.8: The educator shall apply for, accept, offer, or assign a position or a responsibility on the basis of professional qualifications.

In this situation he is not meeting that obligation. The correct answer is B.

LEGAL OBLIGATIONS

While there are many legal obligations that a teacher must fulfill, only a few get tested on the TExES PPR. You should memorize these:

Suspicion of abuse
If a teacher suspects that a student has been abused, the teacher is required to notify the authorities.

Testing for learning disorders

If a teacher suspects that a student has a learning disorder, a teacher must get permission from the student's parent or guardian before testing the student for the disorder.

Students with disabilities

Some topics from the IDEA (Individuals with Disabilities Act) are tested often. You should know these two:

- The IDEA requires that schools provide students with disabilities a satisfactory and equal education to the extent possible.

- An IEP (Individual Education Plan) unites teachers and parents in establishing goals, outlining plans to meet those goals, and determining ways of measuring whether those goals have been met.

Field trip permission

Teachers must have written permission from a parent or guardian before a student may go on a field trip.

Internet protection software

Before allowing students to use the Internet, the teacher must ensure that software blocking access to inappropriate sites is in place.

Guns in school

Teachers must call the police if they have knowledge of or even hear rumors of the presence of firearms on school grounds.

Removing students from class

Teachers are legally allowed to remove a student from class if that student is preventing other students from learning.

WHAT DOES THIS MEAN TO ME AS A TEST TAKER?

In most questions on the PPR, you're asked what a teacher *should* do. You can always tell when a question is about a legal requirement because the question will ask what the teacher *must* do or what the teacher is *required* to do. Try this one:

Mr. Bleckel believes that Suliana, one of his ninth-grade students, suffers from undiagnosed dyslexia. Which of the following must Mr. Bleckel do to confirm his suspicions?

A. Informally test Suliana by monitoring her work closely.

B. Send Suliana to a reading specialist.

C. Get permission from Suliana's parents to arrange for a test.

D. Contact the administration to schedule a dyslexia test.

Here's How to Crack It

Step 1: Identify the scenario.

- Age range: ninth grade

- Goal: determine Mr. Bleckel's action

Step 2: Use POE to narrow down the choices.

The question says *must*, so we're looking for a legal requirement.

- A. No. That's not a legal requirement.

- B. No. That's not a legal requirement.

- C. Yes. That is the legal requirement.

- D. No. That's not a legal requirement.

Step 3: Make a final decision.

Armed with the knowledge of the legal requirements, it was easy to find the right answer. The best answer is C.

TRY IT YOURSELF

Take everything you've learned in this chapter and apply that knowledge to the following drill. Keep in mind that finding the right answers will involve legal and ethical knowledge as well as common sense. Answers and explanations follow the questions.

DRILL

Directions: Each question in this practice test is a multiple-choice question with four answer choices. Read each question carefully and choose the ONE best answer.

1. Which of the following might put a teacher in an unethical position?

    A. Agreeing to baby-sit for a child who is in the teacher's class.

    B. Accepting money for tutoring a student.

    C. Accepting a new watch as a gift before final grades are determined.

    D. Meeting a parent for lunch to discuss a student's progress.

2. A new teacher would be allowed to date a student in which of the following circumstances?

    A. If the student has never been in the teacher's class.

    B. If the student has permission from the parent to date the teacher.

    C. If the principal has knowledge of the situation and has given approval to the teacher.

    D. It would be unethical under any circumstances.

3. Which of the following could a high school coach do to help ensure his star quarterback will have the grades needed to play football?

    A. Insist that the student receive extra help from teachers to raise his grades.

    B. Alter the grade record the student received in the coach's own class.

    C. Temporarily change the grade record of the student as long as it is changed back.

    D. Encourage other teachers to remember how important the student is to the football program when assigning grades.

4. In which of the following situations could a principal share confidential student information?

    A. If the student would likely benefit from the action.

    B. If the student has already transferred to another institution.

    C. After the student graduates from the school.

    D. Under a court order.

5. A teacher took an expensive piece of equipment home where he discovered it was already broken. The teacher:

   A. is liable for the damage.

   B. should report the problem promptly.

   C. should not have taken the equipment home.

   D. could be terminated for taking the equipment.

6. Which of the following would be considered unethical for a teacher?

   A. not reporting suspicious student behavior observed off campus outside of school hours

   B. not reporting the theft of the teacher's prescription drugs by a student

   C. dating the parent of one of the school's students

   D. accepting a gift from a student's family

7. Which of the following should a teacher do if one of his/her students has not been able to bring a written permission slip to attend a field trip?

   A. Provide transportation in another teacher's car instead of putting the student on the bus.

   B. Assume that the parent would have signed the form and allow the student to attend the field trip.

   C. Require the student to stay at the school and miss the field trip.

   D. Reschedule the field trip for another time.

8. Under IDEA (Individuals with Disabilities Act), teachers and schools are required to do which of the following for disabled students?

   A. Provide disabled students with every opportunity available to other students.

   B. Provide an education plan developed by the parents/guardians.

   C. Provide a satisfactory and equal experience to the extent possible.

   D. Provide the best education available.

9. Which of the following is NOT a requirement of the IEP (Individual Education Plan)?

   A. Establish monthly goals for the student during the school year.

   B. Include input from a parent or guardian.

   C. Set parameters to measure the student's success.

   D. Describe the services that will be provided to the student.

10. A fourth-grade teacher suspects that a student who has arrived at school with several bruises on her arms has been physically abused. Texas law requires the teacher to:

    A. talk to the student about how she received the bruises.

    B. report the suspected abuse to the school counselor and principal.

    C. report the suspected abuse to the authorities.

    D. ask the parent/guardian for an explanation of the bruises.

11. The Pledge of Allegiance:

    A. is a requirement for all students under Texas law.

    B. is a requirement for all students under federal law.

    C. is optional for students as students cannot be forced to salute the flag.

    D. is voted on by each school district separately.

12. For which of the following actions could a student be permanently removed from a classroom?

    A. Falling asleep in class.

    B. Continually interrupting the class to argue with the teacher.

    C. Cussing to other students about a test score.

    D. Arguing with another student.

DRILL ANSWERS AND EXPLANATIONS

1. Which of the following might put a teacher in an unethical position?

    A. Agreeing to baby-sit for a child who is in the teacher's class.

    B. Accepting money for tutoring a student.

    C. Accepting a new watch as a gift before final grades are determined.

    D. Meeting a parent for lunch to discuss a student's progress.

C This item measures Competency 013: The teacher understands and adheres to legal and ethical requirements for educators and is knowledgeable of the structure of education in Texas.

Here's How to Crack It

Step 1: Identify the scenario.

- Age range: no age range given

- Goal: no goal stated—relates to ethics

Step 2: Use POE to narrow down the answer choices.

    A. This doesn't seem like an ethical problem in the absence of any other information. Cross it out.

    B. This might be a problem: Is the student being tutored one of the teacher's students? Is tutoring part of the teacher's expected responsibilities? Let's leave it in.

    C. This might be a problem: Maybe the teacher would be unduly influenced by the gift and be tempted to reward the student with a higher grade.

    D. Not a problem: That's something that a good teacher does.

Step 3: Make a final decision.

We're down to B and C. But notice how many questions we had about the rest of the situation described by answer choice B. There are all sorts of things about the specific situation that we don't know, and unless we do, we can't judge whether the situation is unethical. With C, however, we can tell that there's potential for an "appearance of impropriety," which means that even if the teacher wasn't unduly influenced, it might look that way. That's a situation that teachers should avoid, so C is the best answer.

2. A new teacher would be allowed to date a student in which of the following circumstances?

   A. If the student has never been in the teacher's class.

   B. If the student has permission from the parent to date the teacher.

   C. If the principal has knowledge of the situation and has given approval to the teacher.

   D. It would be unethical under any circumstances.

D This item measures Competency 013: The teacher understands and adheres to legal and ethical requirements for educators and is knowledgeable of the structure of education in Texas.

Here's How to Crack It

Step 1: Identify the scenario.

- Age range: no age range given

- Goal: no goal stated—relates to ethics

Step 2: Use POE to narrow down the answer choices.

Even before we hit the answer choices, we can predict where this one's going. NEVER! Go find the answer. It's D.

Step 3: Make a final decision.

No need here. We already did. D is the correct answer as there is absolutely no circumstance under which it would be appropriate for a teacher to date a student.

3. Which of the following could a high school coach do to help ensure his star quarterback will have the grades needed to play football?

   A. Insist that the student receive extra help from teachers to raise his grades.

   B. Alter the grade record the student received in the coach's own class.

   C. Temporarily change the grade record of the student as long as it is changed back.

   D. Encourage other teachers to remember how important the student is to the football program when assigning grades.

A   This item measures Competency 013: The teacher understands and adheres to legal and ethical requirements for educators and is knowledgeable of the structure of education in Texas.

Here's How to Crack It

Step 1: Identify the scenario.

- Age range: high school

- Goal: no goal stated—relates to ethics

Step 2: Use POE to narrow down the answer choices.

A.   Maybe. "Insist" seems a little strong, but there doesn't seem to be anything ethically wrong.

B.   No. You can't alter a grade record. Cross it out.

C.   No. You can't alter a grade record, even temporarily. Cross it out.

D.   Maybe. That doesn't sound terribly unethical. A teacher or coach should not attempt to influence another teacher's grade.

Step 3: Make a final decision.

We're down to A and D. Answer choice A seems okay. Extra help still puts the burden of improving grades on the student, where it belongs. D could be interpreted as coercion, and as usual, a teacher or coach wants to avoid even the appearance of impropriety. Also, D takes the responsibility away from the student and puts it on the teacher. A is the best answer.

4.   In which of the following situations could a principal share confidential student information?

A.   If the student would likely benefit from the action.

B.   If the student has already transferred to another institution.

C.   After the student graduates from the school.

D.   Under a court order.

D   This item measures Competency 013: The teacher understands and adheres to legal and ethical requirements for educators and is knowledgeable of the structure of education in Texas.

Here's How to Crack It

Step 1: Identify the scenario.

- Age range: none given

- Goal: no goal stated—relates to ethics and legalities

Step 2: Use POE to narrow down the answer choices.
Well, the question says the information's confidential, so the teacher should probably be pretty careful. Let's see what we have to choose from:

A. This doesn't seem right. According to whose judgment is the student "likely" to benefit from the action? That criterion seems like it could be abused easily. Cross it out.

B. Maybe. If the student's gone, then what difference would it make? But the information is confidential, after all. Let's keep it in for now.

C. Maybe. If the student's gone, then... Hey, wait! That's the same reasoning we used when we were evaluating B. They can't both be the right answer, so let's be very suspicious of both of them.

D. Okay. That's got some possibility. If a court orders you to release information, you don't have a choice, right? That takes the judgment out of the teacher's hands and into that of the legal system. And this is a question that deals with ethics and legalities. Let's keep it in.

Step 3: Make a final decision.
D seems like the best answer here. B and C are too similar, and you can't argue with a judge. The law is schools are required to keep confidential information confidential unless required by law to disclose this information.

5.   A teacher took an expensive piece of equipment home where he discovered it was already broken. The teacher:

   A.   is liable for the damage.

   B.   should report the problem promptly.

   C.   should not have taken the equipment home.

   D.   could be terminated for taking the equipment.

   B   This item measures Competency 013: The teacher understands and adheres to legal and ethical requirements for educators and is knowledgeable of the structure of education in Texas.

Here's How to Crack It

Step 1: Identify the scenario.

- Age range: none given

- Goal: no goal stated—relates to ethical and legal issues

Step 2: Use POE to narrow down the answer choices.

A. We don't know. Maybe, but if it was already broken then shouldn't the district pay for it? Let's leave it in.

B. It's hard to argue with that. Leave it in.

C. We don't know why the teacher brought the equipment home. Maybe it was for school-related purposes, maybe not.

D. Same thing as C. Maybe.

Step 3: Make a final decision.

We've got three maybes, and an "it's hard to argue with that." Choice A is incorrect as the teacher should not be held liable for damage he/she did not cause. Eliminate C and D because we do not have enough information to know if the teacher should or shouldn't have taken the equipment. The equipment could have been properly removed if the teacher was using it for professional purposes. B is the best answer.

6. Which of the following would be considered unethical for a teacher?

    A. not reporting suspicious student behavior observed off campus outside of school hours

    B. not reporting the theft of the teacher's prescription drugs by a student

    C. dating the parent of one of the school's students

    D. accepting a gift from a student's family

B   This item measures Competency 013: The teacher understands and adheres to legal and ethical requirements for educators and is knowledgeable of the structure of education in Texas.

Here's How to Crack It

Step 1: Identify the scenario.

*   Age range: none given

*   Goal: no goal stated—relates to ethical and legal issues

Step 2: Use POE to narrow down the answer choices.

A. Suspicious student behavior? I don't think so. That sounds a little Big Brother-ish, and it's off campus and not during school hours. Let's leave it in, though, until something better comes along.

B. This is better. Now we can cross out A. Theft of drugs from a teacher sounds pretty serious. Let's leave B in.

C. Teachers can have social lives, too. Could you really prevent teachers from dating the parent of any student in the whole school? Teachers should never date their students, but there are no restrictions on dating parents. Let's cross it out.

D. Maybe, but there's a lot we don't know about the situation. Teachers should be careful to not accept gifts intended to influence students grades, etc., but can accept gifts otherwise.

Step 3: Make a final decision.
If there were more information about D, it could be the right answer (as it was in the earlier problem, when the answer choice explicitly told us that it was before grades were due). In this case, though, B is clearly a more explicit concern, and is therefore the best answer.

7. Which of the following should a teacher do if one of his/her students has not been able to bring a written permission slip to attend a field trip?

A. Provide transportation in another teacher's car instead of putting the student on the bus.

B. Assume that the parent would have signed the form and allow the student to attend the field trip.

C. Require the student to stay at the school and miss the field trip.

D. Reschedule the field trip for another time.

C This item measures Competency 013: The teacher understands and adheres to legal and ethical requirements for educators and is knowledgeable of the structure of education in Texas.

Here's How to Crack It

Step 1: Identify the scenario.

- Age range: none given

- Goal: no goal stated—relates to ethical and legal issues

Step 2: Use POE to narrow down the answer choices.
You have to have a permission slip, right? Let's see what we have to choose from:

A. The student still doesn't have parental permission. Cross it out.

B. The student still doesn't have parental permission. Cross it out.

C. That's kind of harsh, but the teacher doesn't have much choice. Keep it in.

D. The teacher could do that, too, I suppose. Keep it in.

Step 3: Make a final decision.
A written, signed permission slip is required for a student to participate in any field trips. Although the teacher could do either C or D, it seems like a bad idea to reschedule everything because one student forgot to get parental permission. Furthermore, there is no guarantee that the student will get permission for the new date. The best answer is C.

8. Under IDEA (Individuals with Disabilities Act), teachers and schools are required to do which of the following for disabled students?

   A. Provide disabled students with every opportunity available to other students.

   B. Provide an education plan developed by the parents/guardians.

   C. Provide a satisfactory and equal experience to the extent possible.

   D. Provide the best education available.

C   This item measures Competency 013: The teacher understands and adheres to legal and ethical requirements for educators and is knowledgeable of the structure of education in Texas.

Here's How to Crack It

Step 1: Identify the scenario.

- Age range: none given

- Goal: no goal stated—relates to ethical and legal issues

Step 2: Use POE to narrow down the answer choices.

   A. "Every" available opportunity? That's not possible. There are some things that a disability will prevent. Cross it out.

   B. An education plan would also be developed by the teachers. Cross it out.

   C. Maybe. Keep it in.

   D. Maybe. Keep it in.

Step 3: Make a final decision.

We're down to C and D. The question asks what teachers and school are *required* to do, and if you don't know the legal requirements, this one's pretty tough. "The best education available" seems like a worthy goal, but it also seems like it would be tough to fund and enforce. "Satisfactory and equal" sounds much more practical, and in fact, it's the legal requirement. The best answer is C.

9. Which of the following is NOT a requirement of the IEP (Individual Education Plan)?

   A. Establish monthly goals for the student during the school year.

   B. Include input from a parent or guardian.

   C. Set parameters to measure the student's success.

   D. Describe the services that will be provided to the student.

A   This item measures Competency 013: The teacher understands and adheres to legal and ethical requirements for educators and is knowledgeable of the structure of education in Texas.

Here's How to Crack It

Step 1: Identify the scenario.

- Age range: none given

- Goal: no goal stated—relates to ethical and legal issues

Step 2: Use POE to narrow down the answer choices.
What do you know about an IEP? Marshal your facts and hit the answer choices.

A.   Maybe, but is it monthly?

B.   Yes, definitely. Cross this one out.

C.   Yes, definitely. How will you know if the plan's effective if you haven't figured out how you're going to measure it? Cross it out.

D.   Yes, definitely.

Step 3: Make a final decision.
There's only one left, and it was our "maybe." As it turns out, an IEP requires annual—not monthly—goals. The best answer is A.

10.   A fourth-grade teacher suspects that a student who has arrived at school with several bruises on her arms has been physically abused. Texas law requires the teacher to:

A.   talk to the student about how she received the bruises.

B.   report the suspected abuse to the school counselor and principal.

C.   report the suspected abuse to the authorities.

D.   ask the parent/guardian for an explanation of the bruises.

C   This item measures Competency 013: The teacher understands and adheres to legal and ethical requirements for educators and is knowledgeable of the structure of education in Texas.

Here's How to Crack It

Step 1: Identify the scenario.

- Age range: none given

- Goal: no goal stated—relates to ethical and legal issues

Step 2: Use POE to narrow down the answer choices.

What are the legal requirements when a teacher suspects abuse? It must be reported. Let's look at the choices:

A. Is this a requirement? No. Cross it out.

B. Is this a requirement? Maybe. Keep it.

C. Is this a requirement? Maybe. Keep it.

D. Is this a requirement? No, and in the case of actual abuse, it's probably a bad idea. Cross it out.

Step 3: Make a final decision.

We're down to B and C because we know that suspected abuse must be reported. But to whom? If you don't know the correct answer, you might think of it this way: abuse is a criminal act, and should be dealt with by law enforcement officials, not by educators. The best answer is C.

11. The Pledge of Allegiance:

   A. is a requirement for all students under Texas law.

   B. is a requirement for all students under federal law.

   C. is optional for students as students cannot be forced to salute the flag.

   D. is voted on by each school district separately.

C This item measures Competency 013: The teacher understands and adheres to legal and ethical requirements for educators and is knowledgeable of the structure of education in Texas.

Here's How to Crack It

Step 1: Identify the scenario.

- Age range: none given

- Goal: no goal stated—relates to ethical and legal issues

Step 2: Use POE to narrow down the answer choices.

What's the rule here? Do you have to recite the pledge? This one's tough if you don't know the Supreme Court ruling: no child can be compelled to recite the Pledge of Allegiance. Let's look at the answers:

A. No. It's not required.

B. No. It's not required.

C. Yes. That's correct.

D. No. The U.S. Supreme Court made the ruling.

Step 3: Make a final decision.
No need in this case. We narrowed it down to C on the first pass.

12. For which of the following actions could a student be permanently removed from a classroom?

    A. Falling asleep in class.

    B. Continually interrupting the class to argue with the teacher.

    C. Cussing to other students about a test score.

    D. Arguing with another student.

B This item measures Competency 013: The teacher understands and adheres to legal and ethical requirements for educators and is knowledgeable of the structure of education in Texas.

Here's How to Crack It

Step 1: Identify the scenario.

- Age range: none given

- Goal: no goal stated—relates to ethical and legal issues

Step 2: Use POE to narrow down the answer choices.

    A. Doubtful. Why would that warrant removal?

    B. Maybe. Let's leave it in.

    C. Maybe. Let's leave it in.

    D. Doubtful.

Step 3: Make a final decision.
While using inappropriate language may be cause for punishment, the only time a student can be permanently removed from a class is if his or her actions interfere with the other students' ability to learn. Choice B is the best answer.

6

The Domains and Competencies As Defined by the SBEC

THE DOMAINS AND COMPETENCIES AS DEFINED BY THE SBEC

If you've done any preparation on your own, you have probably run into words like *domains* and *competencies*. These terms are used by the SBEC to categorize the content tested on the TExES.

The content is split into four broad areas—called domains—each of which is broken down into several individual competencies. Each individual competency is given about equal weight on the exam, but because some domains contain more competencies than others, the weight of the domains is unequal.

Should you memorize any of this? Probably not. No question will ever ask you to name "Competency 004." You should, however, understand what each of these concepts means, and have some idea of the types of questions that might test whether you understand that competency. The domains and competencies are a good place to start for organizing your studying and identifying any weak areas in your knowledge or training.

Let's start off by listing them all. Then we'll go through them one by one.

Source: www.texes.nesinc.com/prepmanuals/prepman_opener.htm

DOMAIN I

Designing Instruction and Assessment to Promote Student Learning (approximately 31 percent of the test).

Competency 001

The teacher understands human developmental processes and applies this knowledge to plan instruction and ongoing assessment that motivate students and are responsive to their developmental characteristics and needs.

Competency 002

The teacher understands student diversity and knows how to plan learning experiences and design assessments that are responsive to differences among students and that promote all students' learning.

Competency 003

The teacher understands procedures for designing effective and coherent instruction and assessment based on appropriate learning goals and objectives.

Competency 004

The teacher understands learning processes and factors that impact students' learning and demonstrates this knowledge by planning effective, engaging instruction and appropriate assessments.

Domain II

Creating a Positive, Productive Classroom Environment (approximately 15 percent of the test).

Competency 005

The teacher knows how to establish a classroom climate that fosters learning, equity, and excellence and uses this knowledge to create a physical and emotional environment that is safe and productive.

Competency 006

The teacher understands strategies for creating an organized and productive learning environment and for managing student behavior.

Domain III

Implementing Effective, Responsive Instruction and Assessment (approximately 31 percent of the test).

Competency 007

The teacher understands and applies principles and strategies for communicating effectively in varied teaching and learning contexts.

Competency 008

The teacher provides appropriate instruction that actively engages students in the learning process.

Competency 009

The teacher incorporates the effective use of technology to plan, organize, deliver, and evaluate instruction for all students.

Competency 010

The teacher monitors students' performance and achievement; provides students with timely, high-quality feedback; and responds flexibly to promote learning for all students.

Domain IV

Fulfilling Professional Roles and Responsibilities (approximately 23 percent of the test).

Competency 011

The teacher understands the importance of family involvement in children's education and knows how to interact and communicate effectively with families.

Competency 012

The teacher enhances professional knowledge and skills by effectively interacting with other members of the educational community and participating in various types of professional activities.

Competency 013

The teacher understands and adheres to legal and ethical requirements for educators and is knowledgeable of the structure of education in Texas.

What Does This Mean to Me As a Test Taker?

Good question. Let's see what topics might be covered under each competency:

Competency 001

What it says:

The teacher understands human developmental processes and applies this knowledge to plan instruction and ongoing assessment that motivate students and are responsive to their developmental characteristics and needs.

What it means:

This is where all the educational psychology (Chapter 3 of this book) comes in. You should know:

- the typical stages of cognitive, social, physical, and emotional development

- factors that might affect that development (for example, poor nutrition might affect a child's physical or even cognitive development, or a change in family structure might affect a child's social or emotional development)

- how developmental stages affect learning

- how each of the developmental areas (cognitive, social, physical, and emotional) can affect the others

- how you can use that knowledge to help students grow and learn

Competency 002

What it says:

The teacher understands student diversity and knows how to plan learning experiences and design assessments that are responsive to differences among students and that promote all students' learning.

What it means:

All it's saying is that students will be diverse, and you need to recognize that and be ready for it. Specifically, you should know:

- that students will vary according to ethnicity, gender, language background, and socioeconomic status

- that teachers should treat all students with respect

- that teachers are expected to continue to learn about students' differences

- how to create effective lessons to accommodate the needs of all students

Competency 003

What it says:

The teacher understands procedures for designing effective and coherent instruction and assessment based on appropriate learning goals and objectives.

What it means:

Can you implement a curriculum? Can you take stated educational goals and come up with interesting, diverse, age-appropriate, effective lesson plans? You're supposed to take the following things into account:

- curriculum guidelines

- students' needs

- material and resources available to you (including technology)

- different methods of presentation

- logical structure of ideas

Competency 004

What it says:

The teacher understands learning processes and factors that impact students' learning and demonstrates this knowledge by planning effective, engaging instruction and appropriate assessments.

What it means:

Can you put the first three competencies together? This is also the place where the material about different teaching styles and different learning styles gets tested (Chapter 4 of this book).

Competency 005

What it says:

The teacher knows how to establish a classroom climate that fosters learning, equity, and excellence and uses this knowledge to create a physical and emotional environment that is safe and productive.

What it means:

Can you set the right tone in a classroom? You're supposed to do the following things:

- encourage cooperation and respect for others

- convey enthusiasm and understand that your mood affects your students' moods

- know that the physical arrangement of the classroom is important, too

Competency 006

What it says:
The teacher understands strategies for creating an organized and productive learning environment and for managing student behavior.

What it means:
Can you manage a classroom? You're supposed to do all of these:

- use class time effectively

- use technology effectively

- set and enforce behavior standards

- promote good and ethical work habits

- set high academic goals

Competency 007

What it says:
The teacher understands and applies principles and strategies for communicating effectively in varied teaching and learning contexts.

What it means:
Can you communicate with your students? You're supposed to know how to:

- use age-appropriate language

- ask questions and lead discussions

- give explicit directions and instructions

- tailor your communication to the task at hand

Competency 008

What it says:
The teacher provides appropriate instruction that actively engages students in the learning process.

What it means:
Can you make learning fun and interesting? Remember the following:

- vary instructional methods

- help students link new ideas and knowledge to old ideas and knowledge

- vary assessment methods

- vary motivational methods

Competency 009

What it says:

The teacher incorporates the effective use of technology to plan, organize, deliver, and evaluate instruction for all students.

What it means:

Are you up on all the technology stuff? Do you:

- know the basic terminology?

- know how to use important hardware and software?

- understand legal and ethical issues surrounding the use of technology such as copyright protection and Internet plagiarism?

- know how to use technology appropriately in order to teach more effectively?

- understand that your students will have varying levels of understanding of technology?

Competency 010

What it says:

The teacher monitors students' performance and achievement; provides students with timely, high-quality feedback; and responds flexibly to promote learning for all students.

What it means:

Can you assess student work and communicate that assessment to your students? You're supposed to:

- grade assignments and examinations on time

- maintain high expectations

- be flexible and use varied methods

Competency 011

What it says:

The teacher understands the importance of family involvement in children's education and knows how to interact and communicate effectively with families.

What it means:

Can you communicate with parents and caregivers and get them involved? Remember:

- you can call, email, or write depending on the situation

- parents will be just as diverse as your students

- communicate often and appropriately

Competency 012

What it says:

The teacher enhances professional knowledge and skills by effectively interacting with other members of the educational community and participating in various types of professional activities.

What it means:

You don't teach in a vacuum. Can you work well with administrators and other teachers? Will you take advantage of opportunities to learn to be a better teacher? They'll want you to:

- know how to work with other teachers

- know your administrators and the roles they play

- volunteer for activities and committees

- use available resources for professional development

- reflect on the quality of your teaching from time to time

Competency 013

What it says:

The teacher understands and adheres to legal and ethical requirements for educators and is knowledgeable of the structure of education in Texas:

What it means:

- Know your do's and don'ts ethically and legally

- Don't help your students cheat on required state exams

- Don't be afraid to ask for clarification if you're not sure about something.

And that's it.

You might be thinking, "That's a lot of stuff!" And in some ways, it is. But in the previous chapters we've already reviewed the body of actual knowledge that could conceivably be tested on the TExES. The rest of the content (that is, creating a positive mood in the classroom) may seem very subjective. But remember whom the SBEC wants to certify: a hard-working, dedicated, flexible, caring teacher who knows and applies educational theory and knows how to communicate with adults. Keep that ideal in mind, and even the more subjective questions will become easier to answer correctly.

7

What to Do Now

WHAT TO DO NOW

PRACTICE MATERIALS

How do you get to Carnegie Hall? Practice, practice, practice.

At this point, you've read a lot of material, you're an expert on how the TExES is written, the content it tests, and what correct answers look like. Now it's time to practice. You should have already done the drills at the back of each chapter and reviewed the material that you're a little fuzzy on.

In the next chapters, there are three full-length PPR practice exams, one in each category: EC–4, 4–8, and 8–12. If you're preparing to take the EC–12 test, you should take all three. If you're preparing for one of the specific exams, concentrate on the corresponding test, but realize that taking the others may prove useful too, because many questions (such as those dealing with ethics) could apply to any age range, and even those questions that don't may help you solidify your knowledge in your own age area.

In addition, there are other sources of sample questions that you can use to help prepare. Your educational institution may offer a sample PPR test, administered under simulated exam conditions. If this is available to you, we highly recommend that you take advantage of it. Also, the TExES website has many sample questions available, although they're careful to tell you that performance on those questions doesn't necessarily predict performance on the real exam.

As you answer these sample questions, be sure to follow the approach that we've been using all along:

Step 1: Identify the scenario.

- Age range

- Goal

Step 2: Use POE to narrow down the answer choices.

Step 3: Make a final decision.

As you're going through the answer choices, remember to ask yourself not only why a given answer is right, but also why all the others are wrong. Remember, you'll be seeing three times as many wrong answers as right answers, so it's important that you recognize and categorize wrong answers as well as pick the right ones.

WHAT TO DO BEFORE TEST DAY

Establish a time routine

If the test is at 9 A.M., and you normally don't get out of bed until 11 A.M. or so, then you'll want to change your habits about a week before the exam. Force yourself to adopt the new routine so that your body has enough time to adjust to the new schedule.

Scope out the joint

If you can, find the location where you'll be taking the test several days before the actual test. You don't want to have to worry about finding a parking space, finding the building, and finding the room all on the day of the test. Some people find that sitting down inside the room beforehand and imagining taking the exam reduces their anxiety on the actual test day.

Take it easy the night before

Obviously, you shouldn't go out partying until 3 A.M. the night before the exam. Make sure you get enough sleep to be at your peak. By the same token, don't stay up half the night cramming. Take the night off and rent a movie.

WHAT TO DO ON TEST DAY

Physical Preparation

Watch what you eat

If you normally eat a light breakfast, don't suddenly decide to have six pancakes, biscuits and gravy, and a ham steak because you read somewhere that a hearty breakfast is important. If you don't normally drink a lot of coffee, the morning of test day is not a good time to start.

Dress in layers

The testing room will inevitably be too cold or too hot. If you layer up, you'll be able to adjust to a comfortable amount of clothing.

Bring water and a light snack

You'll be there for a couple of hours, at least—better safe than sorry.

Mental Preparation

It's okay to be nervous before the exam. A little nervousness increases adrenaline, which can help you focus your energy and increase your performance. Too much nervousness, however, can be a problem. If you find yourself getting overly stressed during the test, try the following:

- Put your pencil down.

- Lift your head and find the farthest point away from you that you can see. Focus on that point.

- Take two or three deep breaths.

- Tell yourself that no one in the room is better prepared than you are.

- Calmly get back to work.

AFTER THE TEST

When it's over, it's over. The SBEC will mail your result about three weeks after you take the test, so put it out of your mind until then.

Good luck!

PART III

The Princeton Review TExES Practice Tests and Explanations

8

TExES EC–4
Practice Test

Directions: Each question in this practice test is a multiple-choice question with four answer choices. Read each question carefully and choose the ONE best answer.

1. An elementary school computer teacher has been asked to plan an exercise to strengthen the computer skills of a first-grade class. The teacher's first step in the planning process should be to:

    A. check availability of computers for the number of students in the first-grade class.

    B. brainstorm possible projects and activities appropriate for first-grade students.

    C. analyze the first graders' computer skills.

    D. meet with the first-grade teacher to develop a year-long plan for the students.

2. A third-grade teacher notices that Patrick regularly rushes through his seatwork so that he can visit the reading center where he works in a group with his friends. What should the teacher do to help rectify this situation?

    A. Set a minimum time limit that he must spend on his seatwork.

    B. Assign a failing grade for all seatwork not completed correctly.

    C. Reassign Patrick to a different reading group.

    D. Require Patrick to self-evaluate the completeness of his work before going to the reading center.

3. To motivate his fourth-grade music class, Mr. Horn should consider:

    A. requiring students who do not participate in class to attend detention after school.

    B. allowing students the opportunity to try different instruments they might be interested in.

    C. distributing small prizes to students who participate fully.

    D. assigning failing grades to students who do not participate in class.

4. A first-grade teacher would *best* be able to evaluate his/her students' reading progress through:

    A. the students' self assessment.

    B. peer assessment.

    C. frequent, informal observation.

    D. students' performance when reading directly to the teacher.

5. For the first time, Ms. North's second-grade class has a student whose native language is French instead of English. Mrs. Cordoba is the ESL teacher for the school and has volunteered to work with Ms. North to prepare appropriate lessons. Mrs. Cordoba can *best* help Ms. North by:

   A. talking with Ms. North about her lesson plans.

   B. providing French copies of Ms. North's work for the other students.

   C. suggesting that the student be moved to another classroom with another teacher.

   D. dictating lesson plans for the native French-speaking student.

6. A third-grade teacher would be correct in having great concern over which of the following students?

   A. Matthew reacts poorly when teachers or peers offer any criticism of him.

   B. Zachary separates himself from the group and is not interested in spending time with others.

   C. Patrick is very outspoken and spends a lot of time talking in class to the detriment of his schoolwork.

   D. Travis talks constantly about money and tries to elicit monetary bribes from friends for doing favors.

7. A fourth-grade teacher is taking her class on a guided tour of the fine arts museum. The teacher must make special arrangements for a boy in her class who is hearing-impaired and may not be able to understand everything the guide will say. What should the teacher do to accommodate the needs of this student?

   A. Make arrangements for the boy to spend the day at the school in another fourth-grade class.

   B. Make arrangements with the museum to have a tour on tape waiting for the student.

   C. Pair the student with a friend during the tour who can help him follow what the tour guide is saying.

   D. Ask the student's parents to accompany their son on the field trip.

8. A fourth-grade social studies class is reading a passage. To help develop the students' critical reading skills, the teacher could follow the reading with what exercise?

   A. an exercise designed to identify the main parts of the passage such as purpose and conclusion

   B. a multiple-choice quiz about the passage

   C. a class discussion about what the students agree or disagree with in the passage

   D. a class discussion about what evidence the author provided in the passage

9. Miss Redd arranges a field trip to a local supermarket so her fourth-grade students can put their practical math skills to use. The manager of the store has agreed to have the children "shop" for their food, tally their purchases, and provide the students with receipts to take back to the classroom. After the field trip, Miss Redd suggests the students write thank-you notes to the grocery store manager. Her primary instructional purpose for this activity is to allow students at this grade level to:

A. practice writing letters.

B. recognize the value of establishing long-term relationships.

C. develop the bond between the school and the local community.

D. practice socially acceptable behavior.

10. A computer teacher working with a third-grade class assigns small groups of students to work together on a computer project. The teacher assigns these groups so that students of differing abilities will work together. This grouping will:

A. give students who normally don't spend time with each other a chance to get to know one another.

B. give the more advanced students a chance to demonstrate their computer skills.

C. give students the opportunity to learn from each other by teaching less-advanced students or learning from more-advanced students.

D. give the students who have had conflicts in the past time together in a structured environment where they will have to learn to work together.

11. A teacher needs to call the parents of a third-grade boy who was one of a group of children caught throwing rocks on the playground. The teacher should *start* the conversation by:

A. telling the parents their student could be suspended for his actions during recess.

B. telling the parents that no one was hurt but there was an incident on the playground that needs to be addressed.

C. telling the parents that she does not expect perfect behavior from her students.

D. telling the parents that their son was caught throwing rocks but was part of a group and did not start the bad behavior.

12. A teacher who discovers bruising on a student and who cannot establish an innocent explanation for the bruising should first do what?

   A. Schedule a parent/teacher conference immediately.

   B. Report the suspicions of abuse to the school counselor.

   C. Report the suspicions of abuse to the school principal.

   D. Report the suspicions of abuse to the Texas Department of Protective Services.

13. Which type of computer software would be most effective for creating a letter that will be sent home to each parent with individualized information about each child?

   A. database

   B. editing

   C. spreadsheet

   D. word processing

14. A second-grade student who has fallen behind the rest of the class in reading meets with a special tutor during the school day. The tutor works with the student in the classroom. The tutor should arrange to tutor the student during:

   A. class time when students are working in various centers and activities in the room.

   B. ancillary classes such as music or art.

   C. recess.

   D. class time when students are working quietly on projects.

15. A fourth-grade teacher has a student who recently has started performing poorly in class and also seems uninterested in school. What is the *first* step this teacher should take?

   A. talk with the school counselor

   B. talk with the parents

   C. talk with the student's third-grade teacher

   D. talk with the student

16. A new first-grade teacher would do best to employ which of the following practices for motivating her students?

   A. rewarding correct answers with prizes

   B. praising students verbally for correct answers in front of peers

   C. giving students work that is challenging but that they are able to do

   D. publishing an honor roll in a parent newsletter

17. Which of the following questions requires the students to use divergent thinking?

   A. What is the capital of the United States?

   B. How many states start with the letter "A"?

   C. What are you planning to do for summer vacation?

   D. What are the primary colors?

18. At parent night at the beginning of the school year, Ms. Scott invites parents to sign up to come and read to her first-grade class on Friday afternoons. Ms. Scott's motivation for this reading program is to:

A. have time to work on her lesson plan while the parent is reading to the students.

B. allow parents the opportunity to see their child in a classroom setting.

C. include family members in the responsibility for the student's education.

D. allow parents to see what resources the school has versus what is needed.

19. Tristan is a first-grade student who is having trouble finishing his seat-work. His teacher has noted that he can become easily distracted and has problems staying on-task. Which of the following should the teacher do first?

A. Talk to the school counselor about possible testing at the school.

B. Suggest to the parents that Tristan should be tested for attention deficit disorder.

C. Talk to Tristan about techniques he can use to concentrate his efforts.

D. Move Tristan's desk away from the other students.

20. Mrs. Glass is returning to teaching after a ten-year hiatus. She would like to improve her knowledge of technology in the classroom. Which of the following would be the most effective for her?

A. reading articles in professional publications

B. enrolling in a computer course

C. observing how other teachers use technology in their classrooms

D. asking the computer teacher for help incorporating technology into her classroom

21. A parent of a third-grade student is a sheriff's deputy and has offered to talk to the students about safety and strangers. How should the third-grade teacher respond to this offer?

A. Decline the offer because it violates school policy.

B. Decline the offer but agree to send home safety pamphlets with the students.

C. Accept the offer only if all parents agree to the presentation.

D. Accept the offer and notify parents of the upcoming presentation.

22. A second-grade class will soon start studying butterflies. The teacher should do which of the following to prepare the students for the section on butterflies?

   A. Add key words from the butterfly section to their weekly spelling list.

   B. Have the students color a butterfly diagram.

   C. Have a class discussion about what the students want to know about butterflies.

   D. Talk about the different kinds of butterflies and their colorings.

23. A short magazine article could be used in what way to develop critical thinking skills?

   A. Have students consider why the author wrote the article.

   B. Have students find definitions for vocabulary words in the article with which they are unfamiliar.

   C. Have students locate where in the article different examples are given.

   D. Have students find the article's main idea.

24. A teacher witnesses a student teasing another student and causing the other student to cry. How should the teacher intervene in the situation?

   A. Separate the students and send them back to class.

   B. Get the second student to explain how hurt she feels by the first student's words.

   C. Encourage the girl who cried not to show so much emotion.

   D. Talk with the first student about how hurtful words can sometimes be.

25. Mr. Parson has divided his class into small groups and given each of them a differently shaped container and a number of items to put into that container. He challenges each group to arrange the items in their container such that they fit in as many items as possible. Which type of thinking does this activity require?

   A. affective

   B. parallel

   C. convergent

   D. divergent

26. A kindergarten teacher has her students string beads on cording primarily to improve:

A   fine motor skills

B. gross motor skills

C. handwriting

D. behavior

27. Which of the following math exercises requires higher-order thinking?

A. arranging numbers in numerical order from lowest to highest

B. arranging numbers in numerical order from highest to lowest

C. subtracting 2-digit numbers when borrowing is required

D. filling in gaps in a pattern

28. Students in the fourth grade keep a daily journal. Which of the following types of software would be most appropriate for the students to use?

A. database

B. design

C. spreadsheet

D. word processing

29. In order to visit the dinosaur exhibit at the local museum with her students, who have been studying dinosaurs for several weeks, the teacher must first legally:

A. obtain permission from the school board for the field trip.

B. obtain written permission from the parents for the field trip.

C. recruit parents to accompany the students on the field trip.

D. obtain a written release of liability from all field trip volunteers.

30. Mrs. Grant's third-grade class is working together as a group on a year-long project to develop a business. Currently they are developing a budget for setting up their business; they would be helped most by what type of software?

A. database

B. design

C. spreadsheet

D. word processing

31. The librarian at an elementary school has been asked to provide additional resources for testing students who have read books from a list of Newbery Medal winners. The librarian has located resources online and has set up a computer so that the students can come to the library and test themselves. To begin this program, the librarian should first:

A. install child protection software that prohibits the students from visiting inappropriate websites.

B. meet with the teachers to ensure they understand how to use this technology.

C. see what other resources are available online.

D. make sure there are a sufficient number of computer terminals in the library for the students to use.

32. A new first-grade teacher has an English Language Learner in her class. Which of the following would allow an accurate assessment of the student's progress in her classroom?

A. allowing the student more time to complete his homework than other students have to complete their assignments

B. allowing the student more than one opportunity to demonstrate academic progress or use informal observation.

C. allowing the student to help determine his own grade.

D. developing a separate grading scale for English Language Learners.

33. A third-grade teacher plans to have her students study modern art. Her goal is to help her students begin to develop an appreciation of art. To have success in this goal, the teacher should seek out what type of art?

A. art that the students might recognize or have seen before

B. art from different time periods

C. art from local artists

D. art from more than one medium that is of interest to the students

34. A third-grade teacher is starting a new school year off with a new reading center in her classroom. She is hoping this new center will be more effective for the students than the old reading center. To determine this, she should:

A. invite former students to "try out" the center and solicit feedback from them.

B. compare the popularity of the new center versus the old center.

C. test out the new reading center herself from a student's perspective.

D. observe students using the new center and evaluate their work product.

35. First-grade students can be most effectively evaluated with regard to their reading skills by:

A. taking short quizzes about a book when they finish reading it.

B. taking weekly quizzes.

C. frequent teacher observation.

D. reading to their classmates.

36. Mrs. Lynn has high expectations for Sammy, a student in her second-grade class. The most appropriate way for her to communicate those expectations would be to do what?

A. Give Sammy frequent praise and rewards even when he falls short of his goals.

B. Set challenging goals for Sammy and let him know she believes he can accomplish them.

C. Provide Sammy more opportunities to work with other students for which she has high expectations.

D. Remove the emphasis on tasks that would be challenging for Sammy.

37. Which of the following is important to share with parents when seeking out their participation in the classroom?

A. clearly stating goals for the students, teachers, and parents

B. explaining the open-door policy of the classroom

C. making parents more comfortable by providing them with teacher credentials

D. discussing how the home environment affects students

38. The parent of a first-grade student has scheduled a parent/teacher conference because the parent is concerned that the classroom activities are not preparing her student for the second grade. What is the most appropriate response from the teacher?

A. Assure the parent by listing the teacher's credentials and experience.

B. Discuss how some of the activities seem like playtime but are in fact instructional.

C. Solicit the parent's ideas as to how the curriculum could be improved.

D. Suggest the parent meet with a second-grade teacher to better understand what is expected the following year.

39. Which of the following would be the most important use of group self-evaluations after a class works together in small groups on a project?

A. Identify which students in the group worked the hardest.

B. Identify which students in the group did not meet their individual goals.

C. Evaluate the success of working in groups on this particular project.

D. Identify discrepancies between the perceptions of the students and those of the teacher.

40. The parent of a preschool student asks to meet with the teacher as she is concerned that her daughter Myra has regressed after recently transferring to this school from another state. The teacher should assure the parent by:

A. committing to observe Myra more often to help determine the problem.

B. encouraging the parent to explain to Myra that this is unacceptable.

C. explaining this is typical behavior after a traumatic event such as a move.

D. asking the parent to examine the expectations she is placing on her own child.

41. A preschool class has an established schedule for center time, recess time, lunch time, and free-choice time. What is the likely purpose for this schedule?

A. To have students begin to develop an awareness of time.

B. To allow teachers to have a structured schedule and rotate easily between different groups.

C. To establish continuity for the students in hopes of increasing participation in the different activities.

D. To encourage parents to structure schedules for after-school activities.

42. Two third-grade boys repeatedly have physical conflicts with each other. Their teacher's primary goal should be to do what?

A. Determine if either of the students exhibits a pattern of aggressive behavior.

B. Teach the students how to work through their problems without becoming physical.

C. Separate the boys from each other in as many activities as possible.

D. Involve school administrators in the situation as additional resources.

43. A kindergarten teacher has noticed that suddenly Carla is unmotivated and withdrawn. The teacher has talked to Carla but her situation has not improved. The teacher has asked to meet with Carla's parents. Which of the following would most likely help Carla the most?

   A. asking the parents to consider testing Carla for various problems

   B. asking for the parents' interpretation of Carla's behavior

   C. sharing with the parents concerns about the negative impact of Carla's home environment on her education

   D. not contacting Carla's parents

44. A second-grade teacher will meet with the parents of a student who performed poorly on a recent examination. What is the best way for the teacher to begin this meeting?

   A. List a few of the student's strengths that were revealed on this examination.

   B. Explain why this examination is important.

   C. Determine if there were factors from the home environment that impacted the result.

   D. Assure the parents that their student is not the only poor performer.

45. A preschool program has a set of morning teachers and a set of afternoon teachers. The success of this program probably depends most heavily on which of the following factors?

   A. a clear division of labor between the morning and afternoon teachers

   B. a full-time administrative staff

   C. matching teaching styles between the morning and afternoon teachers

   D. daily communication about issues that have come up and that affect the children

46. Cameron, a third-grade student, is at the center of a bitter custody battle between his parents. The result is that Cameron regularly spends some days at his mother's house, some days at his father's house, some days at a grandmother's house, and some days at an after-school daycare center. Knowing this, his teacher should be sure to:

   A. have Cameron visit the school counselor.

   B. involve the mother, father, and grandmother in parent conferences.

   C. provide a predictable schedule during school time.

   D. monitor Cameron's behavior.

47. A fourth-grade student asks his teacher for help in understanding a book he is reading. The teacher asks what the student does and doesn't understand in an attempt to:

A. determine how much of the book the student has read so far.

B. determine what specifically the student needs help understanding.

C. require the student to verbalize the problem.

D. help the student realize his weaknesses himself.

48. Mrs. Collins has been teaching for ten years and is a well-liked and highly respected teacher, yet she continues to subscribe to professional teaching journals. The most important benefit she receives from doing this is:

A. supporting publications she feels are important in her field.

B. staying apprised of the activities in the various professional organizations.

C. remaining current on trends in education and technology.

D. building a resource center for other teachers to use.

49. Ms. Spivey is concerned that a student who has just transferred into her class from another school may have a learning disorder. The student's file indicates nothing about a learning disorder or any previous testing. What step should the teacher take?

A. Refer the student to the special education staff.

B. Suggest the parents have the student tested.

C. Arrange for support from the special education staff.

D. Try to meet the student's needs through the regular education curriculum.

50. A teacher shows his class a picture of a cat sleeping. Which of the following questions should he ask his kindergarten students about the cat to encourage higher-order thinking?

A. What do you think the cat is dreaming about?

B. What is a sound a cat might make?

C. Can you describe the cat in this picture?

D. What color is the cat in the picture?

51. A second-grade teacher is preparing to start studying the solar system. Which of the following should be her first step in the process of preparing to study the solar system?

A. Select resources that will be used by the students.

B. Develop individual and small group activities.

C. Quiz the students informally to assess their current knowledge of the solar system.

D. Find out if a field trip to the planetarium will be possible.

52. A new student will soon be joining Mr. Simon's class. To help make the student feel welcome, Mr. Simon might consider which of the following?

A. Ask the new student to tell a bit about herself to the class.

B. Give the new student more time than other students are given to complete assignments until she becomes acclimated.

C. Ask the other students to smile at or talk to the new student.

D. Ask the students to treat her like any other student.

53. In which of the following instances would it be permissible for a teacher to take a video camera from the audio/visual department home with her?

A. only when the use of the camera is for school purposes

B. only if the equipment is not needed by others at the school

C. only if the use has been approved by the administration

D. only if the teacher signs an agreement to pay for losing or damaging the camera if that should happen

54. An example of convergent thinking in the classroom might be:

A. the teacher reading a book out loud to the class.

B. having the students brainstorm a problem and come up with a proposed solution.

C. having the students memorize the names of the planets.

D. having the students brainstorm possible names for the new class hamster.

55. A kindergarten teacher will soon start a unit about reptiles. She plans to take her students to the reptile center at the local zoo to encourage the students':

A. curiosity.

B. imagination.

C. dependency.

D. good behavior.

56. Which type of thinking would the following question promote? "How many different ways could you go to get to school in the morning?"

A. convergent

B. divergent

C. memory recall

D. routine

57. A fourth-grade teacher has assigned his students a report on a famous person. Some of the students have expressed interest in researching their subject on the Internet. The teacher agrees but insists the students list the websites they use in researching and writing their report. What is the primary purpose behind his request?

A. The teacher will be able to verify the students' information.

B. The teacher will know where the student's' information originated.

C. The students will learn how to cite sources in their work.

D. The students know the teacher will have access to the same information they used.

Use the information below to answer the two questions that follow.

Mr. Brook's fourth grade class spends an hour in the computer lab each Tuesday and Thursday afternoon. Mr. Brook accompanies his students even though they are instructed by Mrs. Diaz, the computer teacher.

58. Because many of Mr. Brook's students do not have access to computers outside of school, the majority of his students are not very comfortable using a computer. Knowing this, what should Mrs. Diaz focus on primarily?

A. teaching the students keyboard skills

B. teaching the students how to use the mouse

C. showing the students how computers are used in business

D. allowing the students to explore uses of the computer on their own

59. What is an important benefit to the students in Mr. Brook accompanying his students to the computer lab?

A. The two teachers can easily coordinate projects with class topics.

B. Mr. Brook is able to monitor his students' progress.

C. Mr. Brook is able to ensure the students behave in the computer lab.

D. Mr. Brook is aware of what software resources are available.

◆ ◆ ◆ ◆ ◆ ◆ ◆

60. A second-grade teacher is concerned about one of her students who is withdrawn and seems to lack self-confidence. The teacher should consider which of the following to help the student feel more comfortable participating in the classroom?

A. Require weekly presentations by the students in which they share information about themselves with the other students.

B. Assign the student a leadership role in the classroom.

C. Move the student's desk next to a student with a similar problem.

D. Praise the student in front of the class for an excellent drawing, paper, or similar project.

A third-grade teacher and a college art professor have decided to have their respective classes collaborate on an art project. Students from the college art class will create a book about their younger partners and what they want to be when they grow up. The art students will be partnered with the third graders as pen pals. They will write a series of letters to each other allowing the art students the opportunity to get to know the third graders. The older students will then create a story about what their pen pal partners want to be when they grow up. During a field trip to the college near the end of the project, their college partners will present the third graders with the final project—the book.

61. What might the third-grade teacher do to prepare his class for working with college students?

A. Explain what the art classroom at the college will look like.

B. Explain the objective of the art project.

C. Have a class discussion about what college students are like.

D. Have a class discussion about artists.

62. For the field trip to the college, the primary concern for the third-grade teacher should be:

A. to ensure that parents know what time the students will leave from and return to the school.

B. to make sure that the third-grade students are not exposed to anything inappropriate.

C. to make sure that the third-grade students know where they will be going.

D. to make sure that the third-grade students follow directions when they are in the college art room.

63. To consider this project a success, the third-grade teacher should:

A. observe what the third-grade students have learned during the joint project.

B. discuss expectations of the collaborative art project with the college professor.

C. follow the same grading structure that the college professor will be using for the project.

D. set objectives before the project begins against which the final product can be measured.

64. During a science class, a group of third-grade students read about an experiment that has failed. After having the students read about the experiment, the teacher could follow with which of the following to help the students develop critical thinking skills?

A. a brainstorming session about ideas for new experiments

B. ask the class to identify the premise of the experiment

C. discuss ways the experiment could have succeeded

D. give the students a quick quiz on the facts of the experiment

65. George is a bright student in Mrs. Sutton's fourth-grade class, however he often does not complete his work in the same amount of time others do because he is continually distracted and talking to the students around him. Which of the following ideas might help George?

A. Require George to sit away from the other students until his work is done.

B. Require George to permanently move his desk away from the other students.

C. Remind George that his grades are the consequence of this action.

D. Allow George to use the timer on his watch to better manage his time.

66. Students in Mr. Raymond's third-grade class will soon be writing a report on a president. The students are dreading the report. In an effort to increase enthusiasm about the report, Mr. Raymond could consider:

A. allowing students to choose the presidential subject of their report instead of assigning presidents to them.

B. threatening to increase the number of pages required in the report.

C. threatening to deduct points for lack of enthusiasm.

D. postponing the report until later in the school year.

Mrs. Landon's fourth-grade class will start a new unit about health soon. Included in this unit are themes on exercise, healthy eating, and a positive attitude.

67. Each student in Mrs. Landon's class will be required to make a project demonstrating the importance of healthy eating. Each student will be allowed to set the parameters for their own project provided:

A. they are approved by Mrs. Landon before the student completes the project.

B. the parent or guardian monitors the student to make sure parameters are met.

C. the project's parameters fall within the basic guidelines given by Mrs. Landon when the project was assigned.

D. they are approved by a parent or guardian before the student begins the project.

68. Mrs. Landon has made an arrangement with the physical education teacher to take the students to a public park next to the school property. The park has an exercise trail with activities and the students will complete the trail instead of attending their regular physical education class. Mrs. Landon must legally do what?

A. Obtain written permission from parents to allow the children to leave school property and complete the trail.

B. Contact the transportation department to arrange for a bus to drive the students to the park even though the park is next to the school.

C. Have an adult at each exercise station available to help students.

D. Provide drinks at the end of the exercise trail.

69. Mrs. Landon is approached by the mother of one of the girls in the class. The mother has volunteered to teach a yoga session as part of the unit dealing with having a positive attitude. Mrs. Landon agrees to arrange a yoga session. At the beginning of the session, a couple of the boys announce they don't want to try yoga because it is for girls. Which of the following is the most appropriate response for Mrs. Landon?

A. Refer to professional trade magazines that might address the issue.

B. Tell the boys they will receive a failing grade for this exercise if they do not try it.

C. Stop for a moment and consider if any gender stereotypes exist.

D. Talk to other boys in the class to see if they feel the same way.

DECISION SET ENDS HERE

70. Mr. Todd taught in another state for 12 years. He recently moved to Texas and feels he needs to learn more about the TEKS so that he can better prepare her students. Mr. Todd attends a seminar, which another teacher had recommended, given by a professional teachers' organization. This shows that Mr. Todd:

   A. understands how different Texas is from his previous home state.

   B. is preparing his students appropriately.

   C. has carefully planned his curriculum around the TEKS.

   D. has tapped into resources around him.

71. A teacher should be *most* concerned about which of the following students?

   A. a first-grade girl who cries when her name is put on the board for talking

   B. a first-grade boy who pushes a girl who has been teasing him

   C. a third-grade boy who brags about things that cannot be true

   D. a second-grade girl whose grades have plummeted

72. A kindergarten teacher has decided to try to recruit sixth-grade students to read to her class during library time. When choosing books for the sixth graders to read, she should:

   A. search for books the sixth-grade students would enjoy reading themselves.

   B. search for books related to topics covered in class.

   C. search for books the kindergarten students will likely have interest in.

   D. search for books without difficult vocabulary.

73. A first-grade teacher just instituted new policies about classroom behavior. The students will have to work together as a group with everyone behaving well in order to earn rewards for the whole class. The teacher will evaluate the change in behavior in six weeks. What is the best way for the teacher to evaluate the policies?

   A. Compare weekly conduct grades before and after instituting the new policy.

   B. Informally observe and note if the students are modifying their behavior in hopes of earning the reward for the class.

   C. Create a separate system for monitoring the new policy.

   D. Have a class discussion at the end of the six weeks to hear from the students if they think that the new policy is effective.

74. Fourth-grade students will attend various activities during their Drug-Free week at a local elementary school. Students will hear from a nurse, watch a video, watch a weight-lifting presentation, and take a field trip. Each activity will feature the same drug-free message. The crucial advantage of this plan is that:

A. it allows students to hear the same message multiple times and in multiple ways.

B. it allows students to enjoy diverse activities during the week.

C. it allows teachers to attend these activities as well.

D. teachers will not be required to plan the activities individually.

75. What should teachers encourage parents to do with regard to standardized assessment scores?

A. Trust that the teacher will evaluate the scores and pass along relevant information.

B. Work with the teacher to evaluate the scores of their student.

C. Advise teachers of problems that may have occurred during assessment.

D. Keep standardized assessment scores secret from the student.

76. A first-grade teacher has planned a field trip to an aquarium. The teacher and students will be accompanied by several mothers who will serve as group leaders. To ensure the success of the field trip, the teacher should make sure to:

A. share the goals of the field trip with the group leaders/mothers.

B. ask the mothers to sign waivers for the field trip.

C. inform the aquarium that several mothers will serve as group leaders.

D. balance the small groups with equal numbers of boys and girls.

77. A third-grade teacher wants to talk about an abstract concept in class. The best way for the students to understand this concept would be to:

A. discuss the concept in class several times in a week.

B. invite an expert to visit the class and talk to the students about the concept.

C. liken the concept to something familiar to the students.

D. create worksheets for students to take home and discuss with parents.

78. Recently, assessment scores were sent home to parents. One parent who is concerned about her daughter's low scores has asked for a conference with the teacher. The teacher should begin the conference by:

A. providing an objective analysis of the student's scores and areas of improvement.

B. assuring the parent that the scores are a poor indication of the student's abilities.

C. explaining where the student's scores fall compared to other students in the class.

D. reviewing the positive and negative aspects of the student's assessment scores.

79. The parent of a third-grade girl meets with her daughter's teacher and expresses concern over her handwriting skills. The mother is concerned because her daughter had beautiful printing but is having difficulty with cursive writing. The parent is concerned with the ability of the teacher to instruct her daughter in this area. How *best* could the teacher respond?

A. Provide examples of other students' handwriting so the parent can see that her daughter's handwriting is not as bad as first thought.

B. Assure the parent that the fourth-grade teachers the student will have the next year do not expect perfect cursive handwriting from the students at the beginning of the year.

C. Ask the parent to trust in her teaching methods.

D. Explain that it is common for students to perform poorly when they first learn something new and that her daughter will start to show improvement soon.

80. A student working on a math problem raises his hand for help. The teacher comes over to help and asks the student to tell him what the problem is and what work he has done so far. The teacher has asked these questions so that the student might be able to:

A. prove to the teacher that he is actually working.

B. understand the importance of what it is he needs help with.

C. spend more time thinking about the problem himself while the teacher helps the other students who are asking questions.

D. solve the problem himself while reviewing it with the teacher.

81. Mrs. Baker is preparing to turn her class over to Mrs. Fence while she is on maternity leave. The administration has asked Mrs. Fence to start working in Mrs. Baker's classroom on the 10th even though Mrs. Baker will not leave until the 24th. What is the administration's primary reason for the early start date?

A. The administration wants to allow sufficient time for all necessary communication to happen between the two teachers before Mrs. Baker leaves.

B. The administration is concerned that Mrs. Baker might leave earlier.

C. The administration would like Mrs. Fence to evaluate Mrs. Baker's teaching style.

D. The administration would like Mrs. Baker to evaluate Mrs. Fence's teaching style.

82. A second-year teacher has decided to start regularly attending professional seminars in his area. The primary benefit he will receive is that:

A. he will meet other professionals who may be good resources for him.

B. he will be able to learn things he may have previously missed.

C. he will stay current on trends in his area.

D. he will be able to socialize with other teachers.

83. During the administration of the TAKS, the teacher is able to answer which of the following questions from a student taking the TAKS?

A. What is the meaning of this word?

B. Can I start the next section now instead of waiting?

C. Did I get this question right?

D. What is the name of this figure?

84. A pre-kindergarten teacher is meeting a new student for the first time. The student is clinging to his mother and crying uncontrollably. The best reaction from the teacher would be to:

A. make constant eye contact with the student while talking to the parent about leaving the student.

B. wait for the student to calm down before approaching him.

C. send the parent away and lead the child into the classroom crying.

D. kneel down and talk to the student directly in a soft, reassuring tone.

Use the information below to answer the two questions that follow.

The fourth-grade math teacher, Ms. Santos, overhears a group of students talking about how many trading cards each student has. She plans to start a new project in class and decides to use the students and their trading cards as inspiration.

85. During math class, Ms. Santos announces the new project. The class will be divided into small groups. Each group will survey at least 50 students and graph the results. Each group can design their own question for the survey. Ms. Santos has:

    A. provided a framework for the project that will allow students to proceed on their own.

    B. designed the project to facilitate group interaction.

    C. provided students with the tools needed to complete the project.

    D. recognized the contribution of the group overheard.

86. The most important advantage of having students design their own questions and survey the students is to:

    A. allow the group to maximize the strengths of the different students.

    B. increase communication skills.

    C. allow students to structure their own learning.

    D. improve the students' graphing capabilities.

◆ ◆ ◆ ◆ ◆ ◆ ◆

Use the information below to answer the two questions that follow.

A group of kindergarten children visited a local restaurant during a field trip to learn what happens behind the scenes when you eat at a restaurant.

87. Within a short time following the field trip, it is *most* important that the students:

    A. talk to their parents about the field trip.

    B. persuade their parents to frequent that restaurant.

    C. draw pictures to thank the restaurant manager and staff.

    D. recognize the unique opportunity.

88. Shortly after the students' drawings were mailed to the restaurant as a thank-you, the students received a letter from the restaurant manager thanking them for the beautiful pictures and letting them know he had displayed them in the restaurant. The teacher should share this letter with the students in order to:

    A. help the students understand the value of people's time.

    B. justify to the students the purpose of their artwork.

    C. encourage the students to visit the restaurant to eat.

    D. encourage the students to remember to thank people.

◆ ◆ ◆ ◆ ◆ ◆ ◆

89. A preschool teacher sees two students playing at the water table. One child is pouring a liquid back and forth between two containers. The second child begins to mimic this behavior. This is an example of what kind of play?

A. associative

B. cooperative

C. parallel

D. solitary

90. A teacher is shocked when a female student in her class announced during a discussion of airplanes that women can't be pilots. How should the teacher respond?

A. Invite a female pilot to speak to the class.

B. Invite both a female and male pilot to speak to the class.

C. Invite females and males to speak to the class from many professions.

D. Have students write a report about a famous woman who worked in a traditionally male job.

91. A new first-grade teacher is trying to decide how to arrange her classroom. What is the most important aspect for her to take into consideration?

A. future discipline issues

B. the furniture available to her

C. the approach she plans to teach with in her classroom

D. how the other first-grade teachers arrange their classrooms

92. A third-grade teacher has decided to call a class meeting for the students to deal with the problems associated with cliques that are developing in the class. Talking as a group is important because:

A. the students will understand the expectations of their teachers.

B. the students will communicate better in the future.

C. the students will not discuss the problem individually.

D. the students will be able to recognize the consequences of their actions.

93. Two children who are playing in the same area but are not playing together are exhibiting what type of play?

A. associative

B. cooperative

C. parallel

D. solitary

94. A teacher asks the students to come up with as many ways that they can think of to recycle. This is an example of what type of thinking?

A. convergent

B. divergent

C. affective

D. associative

95. Which of the following situations demonstrates solitary play?

A. a child playing trucks with one other child

B. a girl who is brushing her doll's hair and who will not share the brush

C. a child copying what her friend does

D. two boys building a sand castle together

9

TExES EC–4 Practice Test: Answers and Explanations

TExES PPR EC–4 PRACTICE TEST ANSWER KEY

1. C	26. A	51. C	76. A
2. D	27. D	52. C	77. C
3. B	28. D	53. A	78. D
4. C	29. B	54. B	79. D
5. A	30. C	55. A	80. D
6. B	31. A	56. B	81. A
7. B	32. B	57. C	82. C
8. D	33. D	58. D	83. B
9. D	34. D	59. A	84. D
10. C	35. C	60. D	85. A
11. B	36. B	61. C	86. C
12. D	37. A	62. B	87. C
13. D	38. B	63. D	88. D
14. A	39. D	64. C	89. C
15. D	40. C	65. D	90. C
16. C	41. C	66. A	91. C
17. C	42. B	67. C	92. D
18. C	43. B	68. A	93. A
19. C	44. A	69. C	94. B
20. D	45. D	70. D	95. B
21. D	46. C	71. D	
22. C	47. B	72. C	
23. A	48. C	73. B	
24. B	49. D	74. A	
25. C	50. A	75. B	

1. An elementary school computer teacher has been asked to plan an exercise to strengthen the computer skills of a first-grade class. The teacher's first step in the planning process should be to:

    A. check availability of computers for the number of students in the first-grade class.

    B. brainstorm possible projects and activities appropriate for first-grade students.

    C. analyze the first graders' computer skills.

    D. meet with the first-grade teacher to develop a year-long plan for the students.

C This question tests Competency 003: The teacher understands procedures for designing effective and coherent instruction and assessment based on appropriate learning goals and objectives.

Here's How to Crack It

Step 1: Identify the scenario.

- Age range: first grade

- Goal: plan a computer exercise to strengthen skills

Note that the question asks what the teacher's *first* step should be.

Step 2: Use POE to narrow down the answer choices.

A. Unlikely. That may need to be done, but it's a first step as far as the implementation is concerned, not the planning. Cross it out.

B. Maybe. Keep it in.

C. Maybe. Keep it in.

D. No. This is beyond the stated goal of the question, which is only about one exercise. Cross it out.

Step 3: Make a final decision.

Although brainstorming may help eventually, the question asks what the first step should be. Because the goal is strengthening skills, the teacher needs to find out what the current student skill level is. The best answer is C.

2. A third-grade teacher notices that Patrick regularly rushes through his seatwork so that he can visit the reading center where he works in a group with his friends. What should the teacher do to help rectify this situation?

A. Set a minimum time limit that he must spend on his seatwork.

B. Assign a failing grade for all seatwork not completed correctly.

C. Reassign Patrick to a different reading group.

D. Require Patrick to self-evaluate the completeness of his work before going to the reading center.

D This question tests Competency 006: The teacher understands strategies for creating an organized and productive learning environment and for managing student behavior.

Here's How to Crack It

Step 1: Identify the scenario.

- Age range: third grade

- Goal: get Patrick to spend more focused time on his seatwork

Step 2: Use POE to narrow down the answer choices.

A. Unlikely. There's no guarantee that the same amount of time would be appropriate in all situations. Cross it out.

B. Unlikely. This is overly punitive, and uses negative reinforcement.

C. Unlikely. This again seems punitive, and doesn't address the underlying issue.

D. Maybe. This has the added advantage of forcing Patrick to take responsibility for the situation.

Step 3: Make a final decision.

There's no decision to be made. Choice D is the only answer left.

3. To motivate his fourth-grade music class, Mr. Horn should consider:

    A. requiring students who do not participate in class to attend detention after school.

    B. allowing students the opportunity to try different instruments they might be interested in.

    C. distributing small prizes to students who participate fully.

    D. assigning failing grades to students who do not participate in class.

B This question tests Competency 008: The teacher provides appropriate instruction that actively engages students in the learning process.

Here's How to Crack It

Step 1: Identify the scenario.

- Age range: fourth grade

- Goal: motivate a music class

Step 2: Use POE to narrow down the answer choices.

    A. Unlikely. This is punitive. Positive reinforcement would be better. Cross it out.

    B. Maybe. Motivation will be higher if it's internal.

    C. Maybe. This is positive reinforcement.

    D. No. This is also punitive.

Step 3: Make a final decision.
Internal motivation is the best of all. The best answer is B.

4. A first-grade teacher would *best* be able to evaluate his/her students' reading progress through:

    A. the students' self assessment.

    B. peer assessment.

    C. frequent, informal observation.

    D. students' performance when reading directly to the teacher.

C This question tests Competency 010: The teacher monitors student performance and achievement; provides students with timely, high-quality feedback; and responds flexibly to promote learning for all students.

Here's How to Crack It

Step 1: Identify the scenario.

- Age range: first grade

- Goal: *best* evaluate students' reading progress

Step 2: Use POE to narrow down the answer choices.

A. No. First graders can't assess themselves.

B. No. First graders can't assess each other.

C. Maybe.

D. Maybe.

Step 3: Make a final decision.

Not only is C better because it allows for more than one observation, but it's also better because young children especially can freeze up and underperform when they are directly in front of a teacher. The best answer is C.

5. For the first time, Ms. North's second-grade class has a student whose native language is French instead of English. Mrs. Cordoba is the ESL teacher for the school and has volunteered to work with Ms. North to prepare appropriate lessons. Mrs. Cordoba can *best* help Ms. North by:

A. talking with Ms. North about her lesson plans.

B. providing French copies of Ms. North's work for the other students.

C. suggesting that the student be moved to another classroom with another teacher.

D. dictating lesson plans for the native French-speaking student.

A This question tests Competency 012: The teacher enhances professional knowledge and skills by effectively interacting with other members of the educational community and participating in various types of professional activities.

Here's How to Crack It

Step 1: Identify the scenario.

- Age range: second grade

- Goal: provide help to regular teacher

Step 2: Use POE to narrow down the answer choices.

A. Maybe. Let's leave it in.

B. No. Why would the other students need French copies?

C. No. We have no reason to believe this is necessary or helpful.

D. Maybe. Perhaps translation is part of Mrs. Cordoba's responsibilities.

Step 3: Make a final decision.

We're down to A and D. It's important to remember that ESL teachers have plans of their own and aren't simply translators. To best help, the two teachers should communicate their plans to each other to make sure the plans are compatible. Choice A is the best answer.

6. A third-grade teacher would be correct in having great concern over which of the following students?

   A. Matthew reacts poorly when teachers or peers offer any criticism of him.

   B. Zachary separates himself from the group and is not interested in spending time with others.

   C. Patrick is very outspoken and spends a lot of time talking in class to the detriment of his schoolwork.

   D. Travis talks constantly about money and tries to elicit monetary bribes from friends for doing favors.

B   This question tests Competency 001: The teacher understands human developmental processes and applies this knowledge to plan instruction and ongoing assessment that motivate students and are responsive to their developmental characteristics and needs.

Here's How to Crack It

Step 1: Identify the scenario.

- Age range: third grade

- Goal: identify cause for concern

Step 2: Use POE to narrow down the answer choices.

A. Maybe.

B. Maybe.

C. No. That's normal behavior for many third graders.

D. No. That's also normal behavior for many third graders.

Step 3: Make a final decision.

We're down to A and B. Notice the question asks about "great concern." In answer choice A, Matthew reacts "poorly." Do you know anyone who reacts well? That may be something that Matthew will need to work on, but it's probably not a cause for great concern. How about B? It's very unusual for a third grader to be that antisocial. The best answer is B.

7. A fourth-grade teacher is taking her class on a guided tour of the fine arts museum. The teacher must make special arrangements for a boy in her class who is hearing-impaired and may not be able to understand everything the guide will say. What should the teacher do to accommodate the needs of this student?

   A. Make arrangements for the boy to spend the day at the school in another fourth-grade class.

   B. Make arrangements with the museum to have a tour on tape waiting for the student.

   C. Pair the student with a friend during the tour who can help him follow what the tour guide is saying.

   D. Ask the student's parents to accompany their son on the field trip.

B This question tests Competency 002: The teacher understands student diversity and knows how to plan learning experiences and design assessments that are responsive to differences among students and that promote all students' learning.

Here's How to Crack It

Step 1: Identify the scenario.

- Age range: fourth grade

- Goal: accommodate the needs of a hearing-impaired student

Step 2: Use POE to narrow down the answer choices.

A. No. A hearing-impaired student should participate fully in a field trip.

B. Maybe. Will a tape be better than the guide?

C. Maybe. Perhaps the friend will be able to better communicate with the student.

D. No. The teacher needs to find a way to accommodate the student's needs.

Step 3: Make a final decision.

We're down to B and C. B seems odd because there's no guarantee that the student will be able to hear the tape—we're not told the extent of his impairment. C seems like a bad choice because it seems as though the teacher is giving important responsibility to a young (fourth-grade) student. So neither answer is very good. Remember, though, that the choice that is *more work for the teacher* is more likely to be right. Because arranging for special accommodations from the museum is more work than asking a student to help, B is the best answer.

8. A fourth-grade social studies class is reading a passage. To help develop the students' critical reading skills, the teacher could follow the reading with what exercise?

A. an exercise designed to identify the main parts of the passage such as purpose and conclusion

B. a multiple-choice quiz about the passage

C. a class discussion about what the students agree or disagree with in the passage

D. a class discussion about what evidence the author provided in the passage

D   This question tests Competency 007: The teacher understands and applies principles and strategies for communicating effectively in varied teaching and learning contexts.

Here's How to Crack It

Step 1: Identify the scenario.

- Age range: fourth grade

- Goal: help develop students' critical reading skills

Step 2: Use POE to narrow down the answer choices.

A. No. That's lower-order thinking.

B. No. That's likely to test lower-order thinking, too.

C. Maybe.

D. Maybe.

Step 3: Make a final decision.

We're down to C and D. Remember, the goal is to develop critical reading skills. D is a better answer than C because the discussion will relate the higher-order thinking skills directly to the reading itself.

9. Miss Redd arranges a field trip to a local supermarket so her fourth-grade students can put their practical math skills to use. The manager of the store has agreed to have the children "shop" for their food, tally their purchases, and provide the students with receipts to take back to the classroom. After the field trip, Miss Redd suggests the students write thank-you notes to the grocery store manager. Her primary instructional purpose for this activity is to allow students at this grade level to:

A. practice writing letters.

B. recognize the value of establishing long-term relationships.

C. develop the bond between the school and the local community.

D. practice socially acceptable behavior.

D   This question tests Competency 001: The teacher understands human developmental processes and applies this knowledge to plan instruction and ongoing assessment that motivate students and are responsive to their developmental characteristics and needs.

Here's How to Crack It

Step 1: Identify the scenario.

- Age range: fourth grade

- Goal: identify instructional purpose of writing thank-you letters

Step 2: Use POE to narrow down the answer choices.

Why should people write thank-you notes? Because it's polite. Let's see what we've got:

A. Unlikely, but let's keep it until we see what it else is there.

B. No. The relationship with the manager will not be long-term.

C. No. That's a teacher's responsibility, but not the students'.

D. Yes.

Step 3: Make a final decision.

Choice D matches our initial concept of politeness, and is therefore the correct answer.

10. A computer teacher working with a third-grade class assigns small groups of students to work together on a computer project. The teacher assigns these groups so that students of differing abilities will work together. This grouping will:

A. give students who normally don't spend time with each other a chance to get to know one another.

B. give the more advanced students a chance to demonstrate their computer skills.

C. give students the opportunity to learn from each other by teaching less-advanced students or learning from more-advanced students.

D. give the students who have had conflicts in the past time together in a structured environment where they will have to learn to work together.

C   This question tests Competency 005: The teacher knows how to establish a classroom climate that fosters learning, equity, and excellence and uses this knowledge to create a physical and emotional environment that is safe and productive.

Here's How to Crack It

Step 1: Identify the scenario.

- Age range: third grade

- Goal: none stated, but the goal seems to be what the problem is asking—the problem seems to be describing a collaborative or cooperative learning scenario

Step 2: Use POE to narrow down the answer choices.

A. That doesn't seem to be an educational goal. Cross it out.

B. Why would showing off be an educational goal? Cross it out.

C. Yes. That's the educational goal of a collaborative learning strategy.

D. Maybe, but the question doesn't provide us with enough information to determine whether that's the situation.

Step 3: Make a final decision.

There's not much of a decision to be made. C is clearly the best answer.

11. A teacher needs to call the parents of a third-grade boy who was one of a group of children caught throwing rocks on the playground. The teacher stopped the children before anyone was hurt. The teacher should *start* the conversation with the parents by:

A. telling the parents their student could be suspended for his actions during recess.

B. telling the parents that no one was hurt but there was an incident on the playground that needs to be addressed.

C. telling the parents that she does not expect perfect behavior from her students.

D. telling the parents that their son was caught throwing rocks but was part of a group and did not start the bad behavior.

B   This question tests Competency 011: The teacher understands the importance of family involvement in children's education and knows how to interact and communicate effectively with families.

Here's How to Crack It

Step 1: Identify the scenario.

- Age range: third grade

- Goal: determine how to start a conversation with parents

Step 2: Use POE to narrow down the answer choices.

When a question concerns parents, the answer choice should emphasize communication and respect. Let's see what we've got:

A. No. This seems confrontational. Cross it out.

B. Maybe. This is factual without being confrontational.

C. No. This is not necessarily true, and irrelevant to the matter at hand.

D. No. We don't know who was responsible for starting the rock throwing.

Step 3: Make a final decision.

The best answer is B.

12. A teacher who discovers bruising on a student and who cannot establish an innocent explanation for the bruising should first do what?

    A. Schedule a parent/teacher conference immediately.

    B. Report the suspicions of abuse to the school counselor.

    C. Report the suspicions of abuse to the school principal.

    D. Report the suspicions of abuse to the Texas Department of Protective Services.

D   This question tests Competency 013: The teacher understands and adheres to legal and ethical requirements for educators and is knowledgeable of the structure of education in Texas.

Here's How to Crack It

Step 1: Identify the scenario.

- Age range: none given

- Goal: none stated

This seems to be a question dealing with legal requirements.

Step 2: Use POE to narrow down the answer choices.

    A. No. Suspicion of abuse must be reported.

    B. Maybe.

    C. No. That wouldn't be the principal's job.

    D. Maybe, but it might seem like an overreaction.

Step 3: Make a final decision.

We're down to B and D. It may seem like an overreaction, but a teacher is required to report the suspicion of abuse to the Texas Department of Protective Services. The best answer is D.

13.   Which type of computer software would be most effective for creating a letter that will be sent home to each parent with individualized information about each child?

    A. database

    B. editing

    C. spreadsheet

    D. word processing

D   This question tests Competency 009: The teacher incorporates the effective use of technology to plan, organize, deliver, and evaluate instruction for all students.

Here's How to Crack It

Step 1: Identify the scenario.

- Age range: none given

- Goal: determine which software is most appropriate for individualized information

Step 2: Use POE to narrow down the answer choices.

    A. No. A database may store a great deal of individualized information, but it's not ideal for communicating with parents.

    B. What's editing software? Who knows? But we'd better leave it in for now.

    C. No. Spreadsheet software is good for collecting and analyzing information for large numbers of students, not individual ones.

    D. Maybe. If you're writing parents, you'll need a word processor.

Step 3: Make a final decision.
We may not know what editing software is, but we know that word-processing software would meet our goal. The best answer is D.

14. A second-grade student who has fallen behind the rest of the class in reading meets with a special tutor during the school day. The tutor works with the student in the classroom. The tutor should arrange to tutor the student during:

   A. class time when students are working in various centers and activities in the room.

   B. ancillary classes such as music or art.

   C. recess.

   D. class time when students are working quietly on projects.

A This question tests Competency 002: The teacher understands student diversity and knows how to plan learning experiences and design assessments that are responsive to differences among students and that promote all students' learning.

Here's How to Crack It

Step 1: Identify the scenario.

   • Age range: second grade

   • Goal: scheduling a tutoring session

Step 2: Use POE to narrow down the answer choices.

   A. Maybe. This seems a little vague, though.

   B. No. A tutoring session shouldn't take away time from other activities.

   C. No. That seems like it's punishing the student.

   D. Maybe. This seems a little vague, too.

Step 3: Make a final decision.
We're down to A and D. D suggests that other students are working quietly on projects. If that's the case, then the student working with the teacher may be disrupting the others, and may be drawing unwanted attention to him- or herself. Both A and D are vague, but D has drawbacks, and A doesn't. A is the best answer.

15. A fourth-grade teacher has a student who recently has started performing poorly in class and also seems un-interested in school. What is the *first* step this teacher should take?

    A.   talk with the school counselor

    B.   talk with the parents

    C.   talk with the student's third-grade teacher

    D.   talk with the student

D   This questions tests Competency 010: The teacher monitors student performance and achievement; provides students with timely, high-quality feedback; and responds flexibly to promote learning for all students.

Here's How to Crack It

Step 1: Identify the scenario.

- Age range: fourth grade

- Goal: address student situation

Notice that the question asks about the *first* step the teacher should take.

Step 2: Use POE to narrow down the answer choices.

    A.   Maybe, but what would the teacher tell the counselor at this point?

    B.   Doubtful. What would the teacher say? The teacher doesn't have any real information.

    C.   Doubtful. If the student has just recently become withdrawn, then talking to the previous teacher probably won't be that useful.

    D.   Probably. The best place to start is at the source. The teacher can talk to the student to get more information, and then decide what to do next.

Step 3: Make a final decision.

There's not much of a decision to make here. The *first* thing the teacher should do is talk to the student (choice D).

16. A new first-grade teacher would do best to employ which of the following practices for motivating her students?

    A.   rewarding correct answers with prizes

    B.   praising students verbally for correct answers in front of peers

    C.   giving students work that is challenging but that they are able to do

    D.   publishing an honor roll in a parent newsletter

C   This question tests Competency 005: The teacher knows how to establish a classroom climate that fosters learning, equity, and excellence and uses this knowledge to create a physical and emotional environment that is safe and productive.

Here's How to Crack It

Step 1: Identify the scenario.

- Age range: first grade

- Goal: best motivate students

Step 2: Use POE to narrow down the answer choices.

- A.   No. This would set a bad precedent. Will all correct answers deserve prizes? Cross it out.

- B.   Perhaps. Keep it in.

- C.   Perhaps. This is related to motivation. Keep it in.

- D.   No. That may please the parents, but it won't motivate the students.

Step 3: Make a final decision.
This is where it helps to remember the difference between intrinsic and extrinsic motivation. The SBEC prefers intrinsic motivation to extrinsic motivation. The best answer is C.

17.   Which of the following questions requires the students to use divergent thinking?

- A.   What is the capital of the United States?

- B.   How many states start with the letter "A"?

- C.   What are you planning to do for summer vacation?

- D.   What are the primary colors?

C   This question tests Competency 007: The teacher understands and applies principles and strategies for communicating effectively in varied teaching and learning contexts.

Here's How to Crack It

Step 1: Identify the scenario.

- Age range: none given

- Goal: identify the example of divergent thinking

Step 2: Use POE to narrow down the answer choices.
There's not much going on here. Do you know what divergent thinking is?

    A.   That has a concrete answer.

    B.   That has a more complex, but still concrete answer.

    C.   That could involve a number of possibilities. There is no one correct answer.

    D.   That has a concrete answer.

Step 3: Make a final decision.
Even if you're not sure of the definition of divergent thinking, one of these choices is clearly different from all the rest. The best answer is C. Answer choices A, B, and D are not examples of divergent thinking because there is a finite, predictable, correct answer for each of these questions.

18. At parent night at the beginning of the school year, Ms. Scott invites parents to sign up to come and read to her first-grade class on Friday afternoons. Ms. Scott's motivation for this reading program is to:

    A.   have time to work on her lesson plan while the parent is reading to the students.

    B.   allow parents the opportunity to see their child in a classroom setting.

    C.   include family members in the responsibility for the student's education.

    D.   allow parents to see what resources the school has versus what is needed.

   C   This question tests Competency 011: The teacher understands the importance of family involvement in children's education and knows how to interact and communicate effectively with families.

Here's How to Crack It

Step 1: Identify the scenario.

- Age range: first grade

- Goal: identify why it's important to involve parents

Step 2: Use POE to narrow down the answer choices.

    A.   No. This is a cop-out for the teacher.

    B.   Maybe. That could be a reason.

    C.   Maybe. That could also be a reason.

    D.   No. That's not an educational goal.

Step 3: Make a final decision.

Which one sounds like the more likely educational reason? It's nice to have parents get to see their children in class, but is that likely to contribute to their education? No. So, choice B is out and C is the answer.

19. Tristan is a first-grade student who is having trouble finishing his seatwork. His teacher has noted that he can become easily distracted and has problems staying on-task. Which of the following should the teacher do first?

    A. Talk to the school counselor about possible testing at the school.

    B. Suggest to the parents that Tristan should be tested for attention deficit disorder.

    C. Talk to Tristan about techniques he can use to concentrate his efforts.

    D. Move Tristan's desk away from the other students.

C This questions tests Competency 013: The teacher understands and adheres to legal and ethical requirements for educators and is knowledgeable of the structure of education in Texas.

Here's How to Crack It

Step 1: Identify the scenario.

- Age range: first grade

- Goal: identify first step in dealing with Tristan

Step 2: Use POE to narrow down the answer choices.

    A. By law, parents must be informed before students can be tested for a learning disability. Cross out A.

    B. Maybe.

    C. Maybe.

    D. No. There's no evidence that proximity to other students is a factor.

Step 3: Make a final decision.

Notice that the question asks what the teacher's first step should be. The teacher should try to teach Tristan to overcome his difficulties before broaching the subject of a possible learning disorder with the parents. The best answer is C.

20. Mrs. Glass is returning to teaching after a ten-year hiatus. She would like to improve her knowledge of technology in the classroom. Which of the following would be the most effective for her?

   A. reading articles in professional publications

   B. enrolling in a computer course

   C. observing how other teachers use technology in their classrooms

   D. asking the computer teacher for help incorporating technology into her classroom

D This question tests Competency 012: The teacher enhances professional knowledge and skills by effectively interacting with other members of the educational community and participating in various types of professional activities.

Here's How to Crack It

Step 1: Identify the scenario.

- Age range: none given

- Goal: improve knowledge of technology in the classroom

Step 2: Use POE to narrow down the answer choices.

   A. Maybe. That might help.

   B. No. That doesn't necessarily apply to teaching.

   C. Maybe. That might help.

   D. Maybe. That might help, too.

Step 3: Make a final decision.

This is tough. We only eliminated one answer choice in Step 2. Let's look at the remaining choices in more detail. Compared to C and D, A isn't as good. Reading journals may be a helpful supplemental thing to do, but interaction with other teachers is a better step. Cross out A. C is okay, but would put an undue burden on both teachers and the students. D looks pretty good. The computer teacher is a specialist, after all, and would be a great source of information. It's the best of the bunch. The best answer is D.

21. A parent of a third-grade student is a sheriff's deputy and has offered to talk to the students about safety and strangers. How should the third-grade teacher respond to this offer?

   A. Decline the offer because it violates school policy.

   B. Decline the offer but agree to send home safety pamphlets with the students.

   C. Accept the offer only if all parents agree to the presentation.

   D. Accept the offer and notify parents of the upcoming presentation.

D   This question tests Competency 003: The teacher understands procedures for designing effective and coherent instruction and assessment based on appropriate learning goals and objectives.

Here's How to Crack It

Step 1: Identify the scenario.

- Age range: third grade

- Goal: respond to offer of parental visit

Step 2: Use POE to narrow down the answer choices.

   A. In general, we know that parental visitation is a good thing, so we can get rid of answer choice A.

   B. As noted in A, we know that parental visitation is a good thing, so we can get rid of answer choice B.

   C. There's no legal requirement that parents must agree to each classroom visitor that a teacher arranges for, so we can get rid of C.

   D. There's no requirement that teachers must inform parents of upcoming classroom visits either, but it's the only answer left, and it's not unreasonable to notify parents. The best answer is D.

Step 3: Make a final decision.
There's no decision to be made here. We narrowed it down to D.

22. A second-grade class will soon start studying butter-flies. The teacher should do which of the following to prepare the students for the section on butterflies?

    A.   Add key words from the butterfly section to their weekly spelling list.

    B.   Have the students color a butterfly diagram.

    C.   Have a class discussion about what the students want to know about butterflies.

    D.   Talk about the different kinds of butterflies and their colorings.

C This question tests Competency 004: The teacher understands learning processes and factors that impact student learning and demonstrates this knowledge by planning effective, engaging instruction and appropriate assessments.

Here's How to Crack It

Step 1: Identify the scenario.

- Age range: second grade

- Goal: prepare students for a section on butterflies

Step 2: Use POE to narrow down the answer choices.
Here we're trying to prepare the students, so we're probably looking for an answer choice that suggests that relating new information to previously learned information is a good thing, or that building motivation is a good thing, or something along those lines.

    A.   Maybe. That would familiarize students with some of the vocabulary and could build links. Keep it.

    B.   No. That sounds like a step in the lesson itself rather than preparation. Cross it out.

    C.   Maybe. That sounds like it has something to do with motivation.

    D.   No. That's a first step, not a preparation. Cross it out.

Step 3: Make a final decision.
We're down to A and C. Of the two remaining choices, C is better. Simply adding words to a spelling list isn't much of a link-building idea, and the discussion outlined in C would be a strong motivator for the lesson. C is the best answer. It actively engages the students in their own education, by involving them in the planning process.

23. A short magazine article could be used in what way to develop critical thinking skills?

    A. Have students consider why the author wrote the article.

    B. Have students find definitions for vocabulary words in the article with which they are unfamiliar.

    C. Have students locate where in the article different examples are given.

    D. Have students find the article's main idea.

A This question tests Competency 007: The teacher understands and applies principles and strategies for communicating effectively in varied teaching and learning contexts.

Here's How to Crack It

Step 1: Identify the scenario.

- Age range: none given

- Goal: develop critical thinking skills

Step 2: Use POE to narrow down the answer choices.
Critical thinking skills are higher-order thinking skills with complex answers. Let's hit the answer choices:

    A. Maybe. "Why" is a higher-order question.

    B. No. Learning vocabulary is a lower-order skill.

    C. No. Finding information in an article is a lower-order skill.

    D. Maybe. The main idea requires summarizing.

Step 3: Make a final decision.
We're down to A and D. A is the better answer because it promotes more critical thinking skills than does D. Pick A.

24. A teacher witnesses a student teasing another student and causing the other student to cry. How should the teacher intervene in the situation?

    A.   Separate the students and send them back to class.

    B.   Get the second student to explain how hurt she feels by the first student's words.

    C.   Encourage the girl who cried not to show so much emotion.

    D.   Talk with the first student about how hurtful words can sometimes be.

B   This question tests Competency 006: The teacher understands strategies for creating an organized and productive learning environment and for managing student behavior.

Here's How to Crack It

Step 1: Identify the scenario.

- Age range: none given

- Goal: intervene in a teasing situation

Step 2: Use POE to narrow down the answer choices.

Clearly, the SBEC believes that a teacher should take some strong action here. Let's see what we've got:

    A.   No. That's not a strong action. Cross it out.

    B.   Maybe.

    C.   No. That sounds like the teacher is blaming the victim.

    D.   Maybe.

Step 3: Make a final decision.

We're down to B and D. The SBEC believes that intervention works best if both students are involved. The best answer is B.

25. Mr. Parson has divided his class into small groups and given each of them a differently shaped container and a number of items to put into that container. He challenges each group to arrange the items in their container such that they fit in as many items as possible. Which type of thinking does this activity require?

A.   affective

B.   parallel

C.   convergent

D.   divergent

C   This question tests Competency 008: The teacher provides appropriate instruction that actively engages students in the learning process.

Here's How to Crack It

Step 1: Identify the scenario.

- Age range: none given

- Goal: identify the thinking

Step 2: Use POE to narrow down the answer choices.

A.   I've never heard of "affective" thinking. Leave it in.

B.   No. That's a category of play.

C.   Maybe. That's when you have a large number of choices and you narrow them down to one.

D.   No. That's when you have an open-ended question with many possible answers.

Step 3: Make a final decision.

We still don't know what "affective" thinking is, but C is a good word to describe the kind of thinking going on. The best answer is C.

26. A kindergarten teacher has her students string beads on cording primarily to improve:

A   fine motor skills

B.   gross motor skills

C.   handwriting

D.   behavior

A   This question tests Competency 001: The teacher understands human developmental processes and applies this knowledge to plan instruction and ongoing assessment that motivate students and are responsive to their developmental characteristics and needs.

Here's How to Crack It

Step 1: Identify the scenario.

- Age range: kindergarten

- Goal: identify the goal

Step 2: Use POE to narrow down the answer choices.

A. Maybe.

B. No. Gross motor skills involve larger muscle groups.

C. No. Handwriting?

D. No. It might keep the kids busy, but how would it improve behavior?

Step 3: Make a final decision.
We've got it narrowed down to A. It's the best answer.

27. Which of the following math exercises requires higher-order thinking?

    A. arranging numbers in numerical order from lowest to highest

    B. arranging numbers in numerical order from highest to lowest

    C. subtracting 2-digit numbers when borrowing is required

    D. filling in gaps in a pattern

D This question tests Competency 004: The teacher understands learning processes and factors that impact student learning and demonstrates this knowledge by planning effective, engaging instruction and appropriate assessments.

Here's How to Crack It

Step 1: Identify the scenario.

- Age range: none given

- Goal: identify the higher-order thinking

Step 2: Use POE to narrow down the answer choices.

A. A and B must both be wrong because they're essentially the same task.

B. A and B must both be wrong because they're essentially the same task.

C. C is a complex task, so keep it.

D. D is also a complex task, so it stays.

Step 3: Make a final decision.
D is a better example of higher-order thinking because C describes a task that, although complex, is still rule-based and mechanical. D is the best answer.

28. Students in the fourth grade keep a daily journal. Which of the following types of software would be most appropriate for the students to use?

   A. database

   B. design

   C. spreadsheet

   D. word processing

D   This question tests Competency 009: The teacher incorporates the effective use of technology to plan, organize, deliver, and evaluate instruction for all students.

Here's How to Crack It

Step 1: Identify the scenario.

- Age range: fourth grade

- Goal: determine the best software

Step 2: Use POE to narrow down the answer choices.

   A. This is used for storing and sorting large amount of data.

   B. This is used for art and design tasks.

   C. This is used for computing.

   D. This is used for writing and looks like a good answer. It's a journal, so they should be writing.

Step 3: Make a final decision.
We got rid of all the others. The best answer is D.

29. In order to visit the dinosaur exhibit at the local museum with her students, who have been studying dinosaurs for several weeks, the teacher must first legally:

   A. obtain permission from the school board for the field trip.

   B. obtain written permission from the parents for the field trip.

   C. recruit parents to accompany the students on the field trip.

   D. obtain a written release of liability from all field trip volunteers.

B This question tests Competency 013: The teacher understands and adheres to legal and ethical requirements for educators and is knowledgeable of the structure of education in Texas.

Here's How to Crack It

Step 1: Identify the scenario.

- Age range: none given

- Goal: determine what the teacher must do

Step 2: Use POE to narrow down the answer choices.

The question uses the word *must*, so this must be a question about legal requirements.

A. No. School board permission is not legally required.

B. Yes. Written permission from a parent or guardian is required.

C. No. The teacher may, in fact, do this, but it is not legally required.

D. No. Written permission, not release of liability, is legally required.

Step 3: Make a final decision.

We crossed out all the others. The best answer must be B.

30. Mrs. Grant's third-grade class is working together as a group on a year-long project to develop a business. Currently they are developing a budget for setting up their business; they would be helped most by what type of software?

    A. database

    B. design

    C. spreadsheet

    D. word processing

C This question tests Competency 009: The teacher incorporates the effective use of technology to plan, organize, deliver, and evaluate instruction for all students.

Here's How to Crack It

Step 1: Identify the scenario.

- Age range: third grade

- Goal: pick software for a budget

Step 2: Use POE to narrow down the answer choices.
It's for a budget, so the answer must involve numbers.

> A. Maybe. Databases are used for storing and manipulating information.
>
> B. No. This is used for art or design tasks.
>
> C. Maybe. This is a good tool for manipulating numbers.
>
> D. Doubtful. This is a good writing tool.

Step 3: Make a final decision.
Databases can be used to store numerical information, but we're not interested in storing as much as manipulating, and for that a spreadsheet is better. The best answer is C.

31. The librarian at an elementary school has been asked to provide additional resources for testing students who have read books from a list of Newbery Medal winners. The librarian has located resources online and has set up a computer so that the students can come to the library and test themselves. To begin this program, the librarian should first:

    A. install child protection software that prohibits the students from visiting inappropriate websites.

    B. meet with the teachers to ensure they understand how to use this technology.

    C. see what other resources are available online.

    D. make sure there are a sufficient number of computer terminals in the library for the students to use.

A   This question tests Competency 009: The teacher incorporates the effective use of technology to plan, organize, deliver, and evaluate instruction for all students.

Here's How to Crack It

Step 1: Identify the scenario.

- Age range: not specified

- Goal: to start a library program

Step 2: Use POE to narrow down the answer choices.

There's not a lot of information here, but it's obviously a technology question.

A.   Safety first. This sounds good, so hold onto it for now.

B.   No. There's no evidence that teachers need to know how to use this.

C.   No. That seems backward. She wants to start the program, and she's already located resources online.

D.   No. She's ready to start the program now. She can add more terminals later.

Step 3: Make a final decision.

There's only one answer choice left. The best answer is A.

32.   A new first-grade teacher has an English Language Learner in her class. Which of the following would allow an accurate assessment of the student's progress in her classroom?

A.   allowing the student more time to complete his homework than other students have to complete their assignments

B.   allowing the student more than one opportunity to demonstrate academic progress or use informal observation.

C.   allowing the student to help determine his own grade.

D.   developing a separate grading scale for English Language Learners.

B   This question tests Competency 002: The teacher understands student diversity and knows how to plan learning experiences and design assessments that are responsive to differences among students and that promote all students' learning.

Here's How to Crack It

Step 1: Identify the scenario.

- Age range: first grade

- Goal: accurately assess an English Language Learner's progress

Step 2: Use POE to narrow down the answer choices.

The student is in first grade, so there should be a variety of assessment mechanisms. While the teacher shouldn't change requirements or standards for an English Language Learner, there should be some recognition that progress should be measured in comparison with the student's starting level.

Let's see what we have:

A. No. That changes a standard.

B. That's a reasonable idea. Hold onto this one.

C. No. First grade is too young for that.

D. Definitely not. This is the worst answer of all.

Step 3: Make a final decision.
There's only one choice left. The best answer is B.

33. A third-grade teacher plans to have her students study modern art. Her goal is to help her students begin to develop an appreciation of art. To have success in this goal, the teacher should seek out what type of art?

   A. art that the students might recognize or have seen before

   B. art from different time periods

   C. art from local artists

   D. art from more than one medium that is of interest to the students

D This question tests Competency 003: The teacher understands procedures for designing effective and coherent instruction and assessment based on appropriate learning goals and objectives.

Here's How to Crack It

Step 1: Identify the scenario.

- Age range: third grade

- Goal: begin to develop an appreciation of art

Step 2: Use POE to narrow down the answer choices.
Obviously, the teacher will need to spark students' interest. A creative teacher would come up with interesting ideas. Let's see what the choices say:

A. This might be a good place to start. The teacher could use that common experience to begin to introduce new concepts and styles. Keep it.

B. This doesn't provide enough information, and it isn't as good a choice as A. Cross it out.

C. Like A, this might be a good place to start. If it's local, students might be more interested. Keep it.

D. This suggests a variety of media and specifies interest—a good way to spark student interest. Keep it.

Step 3: Make a final decision.

Choices A and C are good single ideas, but D gives us the general all-encompassing idea we're looking for and is therefore the best answer.

34. A third-grade teacher is starting a new school year off with a new reading center in her classroom. She is hoping this new center will be more effective for the students than the old reading center. To determine this, she should:

    A. invite former students to "try out" the center and solicit feedback from them.

    B. compare the popularity of the new center versus the old center.

    C. test out the new reading center herself from a student's perspective.

    D. observe students using the new center and evaluate their work product.

D   This question tests Competency 010: The teacher monitors student performance and achievement; provides students with timely, high-quality feedback; and responds flexibly to promote learning for all students.

Here's How to Crack It

Step 1: Identify the scenario.

- Age range: third grade

- Goal: measure effectiveness of new reading center

Step 2: Use POE to narrow down the answer choices.

How can you measure effectiveness? Students will have to use the reading center first. Let's take a look at the answers:

    A. This is possible, but it might be tough to implement. Keep it for now.

    B. This choice is unlikely because popularity doesn't guarantee effectiveness, but keep it for now.

    C. No. Students need to use it.

    D. This answer looks pretty good.

Step 3: Make a final decision.

Remember that the goal was to measure the effectiveness. Choice D suggests that the teacher evaluate students' performance after they use the reading center, which will determine whether the center was effective. The best answer is D.

35. First-grade students can be most effectively evaluated with regard to their reading skills by:

    A. taking short quizzes about a book when they finish reading it.

    B. taking weekly quizzes.

    C. frequent teacher observation.

    D. reading to their classmates.

C This question tests Competency 010: The teacher monitors student performance and achievement; provides students with timely, high-quality feedback; and responds flexibly to promote learning for all students.

Here's How to Crack It

Step 1: Identify the scenario.

- Age range: first grade

- Goal: effectively evaluate reading skills

Step 2: Use POE to narrow down the answer choices.

There will likely be a wide variation in ability level at this age range. A one-size-fits-all answer will be incorrect.

    A. This is a one-size-fits-all answer.

    B. So is this one.

    C. This is a good choice.

    D. Maybe.

Step 3: Make a final decision.

Choice D might be one way to evaluate students, but probably would work most effectively in the context of frequent teacher observation in other contexts, too. Because choice C allows for many different possibilities, it's the best answer.

36. Mrs. Lynn has high expectations for Sammy, a student in her second-grade class. The most appropriate way for her to communicate those expectations would be to do what?

A. Give Sammy frequent praise and rewards even when he falls short of his goals.

B. Set challenging goals for Sammy and let him know she believes he can accomplish them.

C. Provide Sammy more opportunities to work with other students for which she has high expectations.

D. Remove the emphasis on tasks that would be challenging for Sammy.

B This question tests Competency 005: The teacher knows how to establish a classroom climate that fosters learning, equity, and excellence and uses this knowledge to create a physical and emotional environment that is safe and productive.

Here's How to Crack It

Step 1: Identify the scenario.

- Age range: second grade

- Goal: appropriately communicate high expectations

Step 2: Use POE to narrow down the answer choices.

A. No. This suggests to Sammy that it's okay not to do well. Cross it out.

B. Good. This provides a challenge and positive reinforcement.

C. Also good. This offers a challenge and the kids can reinforce each other.

D. No. This removes the incentive for Sammy to meet the challenge.

Step 3: Make a final decision.
Reread the question. The goal is for Mrs. Lynn to communicate the goal. While answer choice C provides Sammy the challenge, choice B does a better job of making sure the teacher is communicating the goal. B is the best answer.

37. Which of the following is important to share with parents when seeking out their participation in the classroom?

    A. clearly stating goals for the students, teachers, and parents

    B. explaining the open-door policy of the classroom

    C. making parents more comfortable by providing them with teacher credentials

    D. discussing how the home environment affects students

A   This question tests Competency 011: The teacher understands the importance of family involvement in children's education and knows how to interact and communicate effectively with families.

Here's How to Crack It

Step 1: Identify the scenario.

- Age range: none specified

- Goal: what to discuss when attempting to encourage parental involvement in the classroom

Step 2: Use POE to narrow down the answer choices.

What would parents like to know? Probably that their contributions would be important to the class and their children. Let's see what we've got:

A. Maybe. That could show parents how their involvement would help. Keep it.

B. Maybe. This might make parents feel more welcome.

C. No. This could make parents more uneasy if they have less formal education or a complete lack of educational training themselves. Cross it out.

D. No. This might have been the right answer if the question had asked about parental involvement at home, but the question is about parental involvement in the classroom. Cross it out.

Step 3: Make a final decision.

While answer choice B might make parents feel more welcome, answer choice A shows parents what their contributions would mean in the overall context of their children's education, and is therefore a better answer. The best answer is A.

39. Which of the following would be the most important use of group self-evaluations after a class works together in small groups on a project?

    A.   Identify which students in the group worked the hardest.

    B.   Identify which students in the group did not meet their individual goals.

    C.   Evaluate the success of working in groups on this particular project.

    D.   Identify discrepancies between the perceptions of the students and those of the teacher.

D This question tests Competency 001: The teacher understands human developmental processes and applies this knowledge to plan instruction and ongoing assessment that motivate students and are responsive to their developmental characteristics and needs.

Here's How to Crack It

Step 1: Identify the scenario.

- Age range: none given

- Goal: identify most important use of self-evaluations

Step 2: Use POE to narrow down the answer choices.

Why would the teacher want the students to evaluate themselves? Perhaps as a mechanism for reflection, or perhaps to give students a chance to explain their particular contributions. Let's see what we've got:

    A.   No. Self-evaluation wouldn't help with that.

    B.   Maybe. Leave it in.

    C.   No. We don't know how "success" is measured, and it's unlikely that a teacher would rely solely on students' self-evaluations to measure it in any case.

    D.   Maybe. Assessing group work is difficult, and this would alert the teacher to something he or she might have overlooked through informal observation.

Step 3: Make a final decision.

The question asks about the most important use, and it seems that more information relevant to overall assessment is probably more beneficial than knowing whether a student met an individual goal. The best answer is D.

40. The parent of a preschool student asks to meet with the teacher as she is concerned that her daughter Myra has regressed after recently transferring to this school from another state. The teacher should assure the parent by:

A. committing to observe Myra more often to help determine the problem.

B. encouraging the parent to explain to Myra that this is unacceptable.

C. explaining this is typical behavior after a traumatic event such as a move.

D. asking the parent to examine the expectations she is placing on her own child.

C   This question tests Competency 004: The teacher understands learning processes and factors that impact student learning and demonstrates this knowledge by planning effective, engaging instruction and appropriate assessments.

Here's How to Crack It

Step 1: Identify the scenario.

- Age range: preschool

- Goal: assure a parent regarding a student's regression

Step 2: Use POE to narrow down the answer choices.

When dealing with parents, the rules are to address the concern without irritating the parents. It will also help the parents to know that Myra's regression is not unexpected: disruption of routine is difficult for small children. Let's see what we've got:

A. No. This might be something that the teacher should do, but it's hardly assuring. Cross it out.

B. No. This will make the problem worse.

C. Yes. This is an appropriate response.

D. No. This is not assuring.

Step 3: Make a final decision.

There's only one left. The best answer is D. C

41. A preschool class has an established schedule for center time, recess time, lunch time, and free-choice time. What is the likely purpose for this schedule?

A. To have students begin to develop an awareness of time.

B. To allow teachers to have a structured schedule and rotate easily between different groups.

C. To establish continuity for the students in hopes of increasing participation in the different activities.

D. To encourage parents to structure schedules for after-school activities.

C This question tests Competency 006: The teacher understands strategies for creating an organized and productive learning environment and for managing student behavior.

Here's How to Crack It

Step 1: Identify the scenario.

- Age range: preschool

- Goal: identify the purpose behind a schedule

Step 2: Use POE to narrow down the answer choices.
Why do you tightly schedule preschool? Small children need routine. Let's see what we've got:

A. Maybe. Learning about time is an important skill.

B. No. This suggests that you're making life easier for the teacher. Get rid of it.

C. Maybe. Establishing continuity is important.

D. No. This is not a purpose for a school schedule.

Step 3: Make a final decision.
Although learning about time is important, preschool-aged children typically aren't ready for it. The best answer is C.

42. Two third-grade boys repeatedly have physical conflicts with each other. Their teacher's primary goal should be to do what?

A. Determine if either of the students exhibits a pattern of aggressive behavior.

B. Teach the students how to work through their problems without becoming physical.

C. Separate the boys from each other in as many activities as possible.

D. Involve school administrators in the situation as additional resources.

B. This question tests Competency 006: The teacher understands strategies for creating an organized and productive learning environment and for managing student behavior. Here's How to Crack It

Step 1: Identify the scenario.

- Age range: third grade

- Goal: identify the teacher's primary goal in dealing with two fighting boys

Step 2: Use POE to narrow down the answer choices.

Clearly, the teacher's primary goal should be to get the boys to stop fighting. Let's see what we've got:

A. Will this get them to stop fighting? No. Cross it out.

B. Will this get them to stop fighting? Maybe. Keep it.

C. Will this get them to stop fighting? Maybe. Keep it.

D. Will this get them to stop fighting? No. Besides, according to the SBEC, a teacher should solve his or her own problems without involving the administration unless it's required.

Step 3: Make a final decision.

Although answer choice C might get the boys to stop fighting, it's hardly an educational goal. B should be the teacher's primary goal — how she ends up reaching that goal is up to her and outside the scope of this question. B is the best answer because it is the only one that gives the students control over their behavior and the tools to prevent further problems.

43. A kindergarten teacher has noticed that suddenly Carla is unmotivated and withdrawn. The teacher has talked to Carla but her situation has not improved. The teacher has asked to meet with Carla's parents. Which of the following would most likely help Carla the most?

    A. asking the parents to consider testing Carla for various problems

    B. asking for the parents' interpretation of Carla's behavior

    C. sharing with the parents concerns about the negative impact of Carla's home environment on her education

    D. not contacting Carla's parents

B This question tests Competency 010: The teacher monitors student performance and achievement; provides students with timely, high-quality feedback; and responds flexibly to promote learning for all students.

Here's How to Crack It

Step 1: Identify the scenario.

- Age range: kindergarten

- Goal: help Carla while talking to her parents

Step 2: Use POE to narrow down the answer choices.
The teacher wants to inform the parents about the situation without alarming them. Let's see what we've got:

    A. No. This might alarm the parents.

    B. Yes. Soliciting the parents' insight promotes involvement in the child's education and sets the stage for a solution- rather than a problem-based discussion.

    C. No. This blames the parents, and would likely offend them.

    D. No. Unless there's evidence of abuse, it's appropriate for the teacher to contact the parents.

Step 3: Make a final decision.
There's only one answer left. B is the best answer.

44. A second-grade teacher will meet with the parents of a student who performed poorly on a recent examination. What is the best way for the teacher to begin this meeting?

A. List a few of the student's strengths that were revealed on this examination.

B. Explain why this examination is important.

C. Determine if there were factors from the home environment that impacted the result.

D. Assure the parents that their student is not the only poor performer.

A This question tests Competency 011: The teacher understands the importance of family involvement in children's education and knows how to interact and communicate effectively with families.

Here's How to Crack It

Step 1: Identify the scenario.

- Age range: second grade

- Goal: how to start to talk to parents about a student's poor performance on an exam

Step 2: Use POE to narrow down the answer choices.
The teacher should communicate concern without alarming or upsetting the parents. Let's see what we've got:

A. Yes. This is a good ice-breaker.

B. No. That strengthens the impact of the fact that the student didn't do well. That might alarm the parents.

C. No. That blames the parents, which will upset them.

D. No. That suggests the teacher is to blame, which could easily upset the parents.

Step 3: Make a final decision.
There's only one left. The best answer is A.

45. A preschool program has a set of morning teachers and a set of afternoon teachers. The success of this program probably depends most heavily on which of the following factors?

A. a clear division of labor between the morning and afternoon teachers

B. a full-time administrative staff

C. matching teaching styles between the morning and afternoon teachers

D. daily communication about issues that have come up and that affect the children

D This question tests Competency 012: The teacher enhances professional knowledge and skills by effectively interacting with other members of the educational community and participating in various types of professional activities.

Here's How to Crack It

Step 1: Identify the scenario.

- Age range: preschool

- Goal: determine why a program is successful

Step 2: Use POE to narrow down the answer choices.

It would be difficult to coordinate the two sets of faculty, so the right answer must have something to do with making sure the faculty are on the same page. Let's see what we've got:

A. Maybe. This helps keep the teachers' roles well-defined and would reduce confusion.

B. No. This might help, but isn't what we're looking for.

C. Maybe. Matching teaching styles might provide a smooth transition between morning and afternoon sessions, which in turn might help the program.

D. Maybe. Daily communication would undoubtedly help to ensure that faculty is on the same page.

Step 3: Make a final decision.

This is tougher. We're asked for the most important factor for the success of the program. Let's assume that success is measured according to the students. That means answer choice A is wrong because that seems more geared to the faculty than the students. Between choices C and D, D is better because it is centered on the students, and because communication is always vital to the success of any program. The best answer is D.

46. Cameron, a third-grade student, is at the center of a bitter custody battle between his parents. The result is that Cameron regularly spends some days at his mother's house, some days at his father's house, some days at a grandmother's house, and some days at an after-school daycare center. Knowing this, his teacher should be sure to:

   A. have Cameron visit the school counselor.

   B. involve the mother, father, and grandmother in parent conferences.

   C. provide a predictable schedule during school time.

   D. monitor Cameron's behavior.

C This question tests Competency 002: The teacher understands student diversity and knows how to plan learning experiences and design assessments that are responsive to differences among students and that promote all students' learning.

Here's How to Crack It

Step 1: Identify the scenario.

- Age range: third grade

- Goal: support Cameron

Step 2: Use POE to narrow down the answer choices.

   A. No. We don't have any evidence that counseling is required.

   B. Maybe. Involving all of Cameron's caretakers in conferences might be helpful, but it also might be somewhat chaotic. But, keep this one for now.

   C. Maybe. Cameron needs structure.

   D. No. This should be happening already.

Step 3: Make a final decision.

In the absence of any other information, the best thing the teacher can do is make Cameron's school environment as stable as possible. The best answer is C.

47. A fourth-grade student asks his teacher for help in understanding a book he is reading. The teacher asks what the student does and doesn't understand in an attempt to:

    A.   determine how much of the book the student has read so far.

    B.   determine what specifically the student needs help understanding.

    C.   require the student to verbalize the problem.

    D.   help the student realize his weaknesses himself.

B This question tests Competency 008: The teacher provides appropriate instruction that actively engages students in the learning process.

Here's How to Crack It

Step 1: Identify the scenario.

- Age range: fourth grade

- Goal: help student understand a book he is reading

Step 2: Use POE to narrow down the answer choices.

    A.   Probably not. The teacher is trying to help the student understand, not quiz him about how much he has or has not read.

    B.   Yes. It would help the teacher to know what it is exactly that the student does not understand.

    C.   Maybe. The teacher might think it would help the student understand if he can put it into words.

    D.   No. This is something that would not be helpful and could be detrimental to the student.

Step 3: Make a final decision.
We're down to B and C. Eliminate C because the student may not be able to verbalize what it is he does not understand because he doesn't understand it! B is the best answer.

48. Mrs. Collins has been teaching for ten years and is a well-liked and highly respected teacher, yet she continues to subscribe to professional teaching journals. The most important benefit she receives from doing this is:

   A. supporting publications she feels are important in her field.

   B. staying apprised of the activities in the various professional organizations.

   C. remaining current on trends in education and technology.

   D. building a resource center for other teachers to use.

C This question tests Competency 012: The teacher enhances professional knowledge and skills by effectively interacting with other members of the educational community and participating in various types of professional activities.

Here's How to Crack It

Step 1: Identify the scenario.

- Age range: none given

- Goal: determine why teachers should subscribe to journals

Step 2: Use POE to narrow down the answer choices.

According to the SBEC, good teachers should continue to learn about teaching. Let's see what we have:

   A. No. That won't make her a better teacher.

   B. Maybe. Professional activities are one way to continue to learn.

   C. Yes. This is better than answer choice B.

   D. No. That won't make her a better teacher.

Step 3: Make a final decision.

Although answer choice B was a possibility, C is a better answer because remaining current is the ultimate goal.

49. Ms. Spivey is concerned that a student who has just transferred into her class from another school may have a learning disorder. The student's file indicates nothing about a learning disorder or any previous testing. What step should the teacher take?

    A.   Refer the student to the special education staff.

    B.   Suggest the parents have the student tested.

    C.   Arrange for support from the special education staff.

    D.   Try to meet the student's needs through the regular education curriculum.

D   This question tests Competency 013: The teacher understands and adheres to legal and ethical requirements for educators and is knowledgeable of the structure of education in Texas.

Here's How to Crack It

Step 1: Identify the scenario.

- Age range: none specified

- Goal: determine what the teacher should do with a student with a potential learning disability

Step 2: Use POE to narrow down the answer choices.

There are legal issues involved here. Remember that a teacher can't have a student tested for learning disabilities without parental permission. Let's see what we've got:

    A.   No. This would require parental permission.

    B.   Maybe. This could, however, unnecessarily worry or incite the parents.

    C.   No. This would require parental permission.

    D.   Maybe. It is usually a good idea, at least initially, to try to work with the student in the regular classroom environment.

Step 3: Make a final decision.

This is a tough call. The best clue in the question is that the student has only just transferred into the class. Perhaps it's best to wait for further evidence before approaching the parents. The best answer is D.

50. A teacher shows his class a picture of a cat sleeping. Which of the following questions should he ask his kindergarten students about the cat to encourage higher-order thinking?

    A. What do you think the cat is dreaming about?

    B. What is a sound a cat might make?

    C. Can you describe the cat in this picture?

    D. What color is the cat in the picture?

A This question tests Competency 007: The teacher understands and applies principles and strategies for communicating effectively in varied teaching and learning contexts.

Here's How to Crack It

Step 1: Identify the scenario.

- Age range: kindergarten

- Goal: encourage higher-order thinking

Step 2: Use POE to narrow down the answer choices.
Higher-order thinking moves beyond repetition of facts and involves analysis beyond plain comprehension. Let's see what we have:

    A. Maybe. That would require some imagination.

    B. No. That's a factual question.

    C. No. That's also a factual question.

    D. No. That's even worse than C.

Step 3: Make a final decision.
There's only one answer left. A is the best answer choice because it is the only answer choice that asks an open-ended question for which there are many different possible answers.

51. A second-grade teacher is preparing to start studying the solar system. Which of the following should be her first step in the process of preparing to study the solar system?

    A. Select resources that will be used by the students.

    B. Develop individual and small group activities.

    C. Quiz the students informally to assess their current knowledge of the solar system.

    D. Find out if a field trip to the planetarium will be possible.

C This question tests Competency 003: The teacher understands procedures for designing effective and coherent instruction and assessment based on appropriate learning goals and objectives.

Here's How to Crack It

Step 1: Identify the scenario.

- Age range: second grade

- Goal: first step in preparing to teach students about the solar system

Step 2: Use POE to narrow down the answer choices.
Let's see what we have:

    A. Maybe. But that doesn't sound like a first step. First she has to decide exactly what she will teach.

    B. No. That's definitely not a first step.

    C. Yes. It would be helpful to know what the students know in order to tailor the lesson plans to their level of knowledge.

    D. No. That's something to do later.

Step 3: Make a final decision.
C is the best answer.

52. A new student will soon be joining Mr. Simon's class. To help make the student feel welcome, Mr. Simon might consider which of the following?

A. Ask the new student to tell a bit about herself to the class.

B. Give the new student more time than other students are given to complete assignments until she becomes acclimated.

C. Ask the other students to smile at or talk to the new student.

D. Ask the students to treat her like any other student.

C This question tests Competency 007: The teacher understands and applies principles and strategies for communicating effectively in varied teaching and learning contexts.

Here's How to Crack It

Step 1: Identify the scenario.

- Age range: none specified

- Goal: make a new student feel welcome

Step 2: Use POE to narrow down the answer choices.
Let's see what we have:

A. No. Shy students wouldn't like this, and it's other students' reactions that will make a student feel welcome.

B. No. How would reducing expectations make a student feel welcome?

C. Maybe. Those would be welcoming gestures.

D. No. That wouldn't make a new student feel welcome.

Step 3: Make a final decision.
There's only one answer left. The best answer is C because a nonverbal friendly gesture or talking to someone new should make the new student feel welcome. On the other hand, singling the student out in answer choice A and B might cause additional problems for the student. Eliminate D as treating someone no differently than anyone else is not a welcoming gesture.

53. In which of the following instances would it be permissible for a teacher to take a video camera from the audio/visual department home with her?

    A. only when the use of the camera is for school purposes

    B. only if the equipment is not needed by others at the school

    C. only if the use has been approved by the administration

    D. only if the teacher signs an agreement to pay for losing or damaging the camera if that should happen

A This question tests Competency 013: The teacher understands and adheres to legal and ethical requirements for educators and is knowledgeable of the structure of education in Texas.

Here's How to Crack It

Step 1: Identify the scenario.

- Age range: none given

- Goal: determine permissibility of taking school property home

Step 2: Use POE to narrow down the answer choices.
This shouldn't be too bad. You can't take school property home unless it's for school-related reasons. Let's look at the choices:

    A. Yup. That seems pretty good.

    B. No. This is not an ethical or legal requirement for using school equipment.

    C. No. This is not an ethical or legal requirement for using school equipment.

    D. No. This is not an ethical or legal requirement for using school equipment.

Step 3: Make a final decision.
There's only one left, and it matches our prediction. The best answer is A.

54. An example of convergent thinking in the classroom might be:

A. the teacher reading a book out loud to the class.

B. having the students brainstorm a problem and come up with a proposed solution.

C. having the students memorize the names of the planets.

D. having the students brainstorm possible names for the new class hamster.

B This question tests Competency 008: The teacher provides appropriate instruction that actively engages students in the learning process.

Here's How to Crack It

Step 1: Identify the scenario.

- Age range: none given

- Goal: identify an example of convergent thinking

Step 2: Use POE to narrow down the answer choices.
Convergent thinking involves deciding on the best answer from a field of possible answers—sort of like the TExES exam. Let's look at our options:

A. No. That doesn't necessarily involve thinking on the part of the students at all.

B. Yes. That's exactly the definition.

C. No. That's not convergent thinking.

D. No, not without deciding which one's best.

Step 3: Make a final decision.
There's only one choice left. The best answer is B.

55. A kindergarten teacher will soon start a unit about reptiles. She plans to take her students to the reptile center at the local zoo to encourage the students':

A. curiosity.

B. imagination.

C. dependency.

D. good behavior.

A This question tests Competency 004: The teacher understands learning processes and factors that impact student learning and demonstrates this knowledge by planning effective, engaging instruction and appropriate assessments.

Here's How to Crack It

Step 1: Identify the scenario.

- Age range: kindergarten

- Goal: determine why the teacher is planning a field trip to the zoo

Step 2: Use POE to narrow down the answer choices.

She hasn't started the lesson yet, so this must have something to do with preparing the children for the unit. It might have something to do with determining how much they already know. Let's see what we've got:

A. Maybe. The trip could make them ask questions they would then want answered.

B. Maybe. The trip could stimulate imagination and interest in the subject.

C. No. This is a bad idea in general.

D. No. This has nothing to do with the reptile unit.

Step 3: Make a final decision.

Choices A and B are both possible, but because the teacher's goal is to prepare them for the lesson, it's more likely that she planned the trip to spark her students' curiosity. The best answer is A.

56. Which type of thinking would the following question promote? "How many different ways could you go to get to school in the morning?"

A. convergent

B. divergent

C. memory recall

D. routine

B   This question tests Competency 007: The teacher understands and applies principles and strategies for communicating effectively in varied teaching and learning contexts.

Here's How to Crack It

Step 1: Identify the scenario.

- Age range: none given

- Goal: identify the type of thinking required to answer a question

Step 2: Use POE to narrow down the answer choices.
We ought to be able to predict this one. The question isn't geared toward one solution, so we're probably looking for divergent thinking. Let's see:

A. No. That type of thinking is for problems requiring one solution.

B. Yes. We're looking for thinking that could generate many different responses.

C. No. This is just memorization and recall.

D. No. This is not a kind of thinking that is tested on the TExES.

Step 3: Make a final decision.
There's only one answer left. The best answer is B.

57. A fourth-grade teacher has assigned his students a report on a famous person. Some of the students have expressed interest in researching their subject on the Internet. The teacher agrees but insists the students list the websites they use in researching and writing their report. What is the primary purpose behind his request?

   A. The teacher will be able to verify the students' information.

   B. The teacher will know where the students' information originated.

   C. The students will learn how to cite sources in their work.

   D. The students know the teacher will have access to the same information they used.

   C   This question tests Competency 009: The teacher incorporates the effective use of technology to plan, organize, deliver, and evaluate instruction for all students.

Here's How to Crack It

Step 1: Identify the scenario.

- Age range: fourth grade

- Goal: determine why a teacher requires website references

Step 2: Use POE to narrow down the answer choices.
According to the SBEC, a good teacher should know that the Internet can be used as source material. Why would a teacher require that a source be cited? Probably because it's good practice. Let's see what we have to choose from:

A. No. That's not a primary purpose.

B. Maybe. The teacher might want to know this, but does this choice emphasize learning?

C. Yes. This answer choice emphasizes learning.

D. No. This isn't a reason for requiring citation.

Step 3: Make a final decision.
The question asks about the primary purpose. While it might be important for a teacher to know the source of students' information, the teacher's primary purpose is to teach students the importance of accurately citing sources. The best answer is C.

58. Because many of Mr. Brook's students do not have access to computers outside of school, the majority of his students are not very comfortable using a computer. Knowing this, what should Mrs. Diaz focus on primarily?

    A.   teaching the students keyboard skills

    B.   teaching the students how to use the mouse

    C.   showing the students how computers are used in business

    D.   allowing the students to explore uses of the computer on their own

D This question tests Competency 009: The teacher incorporates the effective use of technology to plan, organize, deliver, and evaluate instruction for all students.

Here's How to Crack It

Step 1: Identify the scenario.

- Age range: fourth grade

- Goal: identify the computer specialist's primary focus

Step 2: Use POE to narrow down the answer choices.
Let's see what we've got:

    A.   Maybe. This might help students use the computers.

    B.   Maybe. This might help students use the computers.

    C.   No. That's too advanced for fourth grade.

    D.   Maybe. This involves students in their learning experience—usually a good thing to do and a sign of a good answer choice.

Step 3: Make a final decision.
Mrs. Diaz's main goal is to increase familiarity and confidence. While she might try answer choices A and B on an individual basis, students will learn more by experimenting. The best answer is D.

59.   What is an important benefit to the students in Mr. Brook's accompanying his students to the computer lab?

    A.   The two teachers can easily coordinate projects with class topics.

    B.   Mr. Brook is able to monitor his students' progress.

    C.   Mr. Brook is able to ensure the students behave in the computer lab.

    D.   Mr. Brook is aware of what software resources are available.

A   This question tests Competency 009: The teacher incorporates the effective use of technology to plan, organize, deliver, and evaluate instruction for all students.

Here's How to Crack It

Step 1: Identify the scenario.

- Age range: fourth grade

- Goal: benefit of Mr. Brook's accompanying his class to computer lab

Step 2: Use POE to narrow down the answer choices.
Let's see what we have:

    A.   Yes. That sounds like it would be a very beneficial reason.

    B.   No. That's not Mr. Brook's responsibility.

    C.   No. Not Mr. Brook's responsibility.

    D.   Maybe. But that is not necessarily a benefit to the students.

Step 3: Make a final decision.
There's only one answer left. The best answer is A.

60. A second-grade teacher is concerned about one of her students who is withdrawn and seems to lack self-confidence. The teacher should consider which of the following to help the student feel more comfortable participating in the classroom?

   A. Require weekly presentations by the students in which they share information about themselves with the other students.

   B. Assign the student a leadership role in the classroom.

   C. Move the student's desk next to a student with a similar problem.

   D. Praise the student in front of the class for an excellent drawing, paper, or similar project.

D This question tests Competency 005: The teacher knows how to establish a classroom climate that fosters learning, equity, and excellence and uses this knowledge to create a physical and emotional environment that is safe and productive.

Here's How to Crack It

Step 1: Identify the scenario.

- Age range: second grade

- Goal: increase a shy student's participation rate

Step 2: Use POE to narrow down the answer choices.
We should be looking for a nonthreatening way to increase the child's participation. Let's see what we have:

   A. No. That would be threatening.

   B. No. That would also be threatening.

   C. No. That could make the problem worse.

   D. Yes. That would be a good thing to try.

Step 3: Make a final decision.
There's only one answer choice remaining. The best answer is D.

61. What might the third-grade teacher do to prepare his class for working with college students?

A. Explain what the art classroom at the college will look like.

B. Explain the objective of the art project.

C. Have a class discussion about what college students are like.

D. Have a class discussion about artists.

C This question tests Competency 004: The teacher understands learning processes and factors that impact student learning and demonstrates this knowledge by planning effective, engaging instruction and appropriate assessments.

Here's How to Crack It

Step 1: Identify the scenario.

- Age range: third grade

- Goal: prepare the class for working with college students

Step 2: Use POE to narrow down the answer choices.

A. No. The students won't see the room until the end of the project. How would that help them work with college students as pen pals?

B. Maybe. Knowing the purpose of the project might help students prepare for the project. Keep this answer for now.

C. Maybe. That might help them prepare.

D. No. The goal is to prepare them to work with college students.

Step 3: Make a final decision.
Remember that the goal is to prepare the third graders to work with college students. Answer choice C is better than answer choice B for that reason. The best answer is C.

62. For the field trip to the college, the primary concern for the third-grade teacher should be:

A. to ensure that parents know what time the students will leave from and return to the school.

B. to make sure that the third-grade students are not exposed to anything inappropriate.

C. to make sure that the third-grade students know where they will be going.

D. to make sure that the third-grade students follow directions when they are in the college art room.

B This question tests Competency 005: The teacher understands how to establish a classroom climate that fosters learning, equity, and excellence and uses this knowledge to create a physical and emotional environment that is safe and productive.

Here's How to Crack It

Step 1: Identify the scenario.

- Age range: third grade

- Goal: identify primary concern before field trip

Step 2: Use POE to narrow down the answer choices.
In the absence of any other information, we can assume that this has something to do with students' safety.

A. Maybe, but this doesn't sound like a primary concern. Let's see what else we have.

B. Quite possibly. Keep it for now.

C. No. It's the teacher's responsibility to know where they're going.

D. Maybe. This might have something to do with safety.

Step 3: Make a final decision.
We can cross out choice A now, because choices B and D are both better choices. Of the two, which is more likely to be a correct answer on the TExES? Probably choice B. If students were exposed to anything inappropriate, there could be a huge parental outcry. The best answer is B.

63. To consider this project a success, the third-grade teacher should:

    A. observe what the third-grade students have learned during the joint project.

    B. discuss expectations of the collaborative art project with the college professor.

    C. follow the same grading structure that the college professor will be using for the project.

    D. set objectives before the project begins against which the final product can be measured.

D This question tests Competency 003: The teacher understands procedures for designing effective and coherent instruction and assessment based on appropriate learning goals and objectives.

Here's How to Crack It

Step 1: Identify the scenario.

- Age range: third grade

- Goal: measure the project's success

Step 2: Use POE to narrow down the answer choices.

How do you measure the success of any project? By comparing the result to the goals. Let's see what we've got:

    A.   Maybe. Observing student progress might help to measure a project's success.

    B.   No. The goals need to be set for the third graders.

    C.   No. That's totally inappropriate.

    D.   Yes. Goals need to be set ahead of time in order to measure success later on.

Step 3: Make a final decision.

Although answer choice A looked good at first, D is the best answer.

64.   During a science class, a group of third-grade students read about an experiment that has failed. After having the students read about the experiment, the teacher could follow with which of the following to help the students develop critical thinking skills?

    A.   a brainstorming session about ideas for new experiments

    B.   ask the class to identify the premise of the experiment

    C.   discuss ways the experiment could have succeeded

    D.   give the students a quick quiz on the facts of the experiment

    C   This question tests Competency 003: The teacher understands procedures for designing effective and coherent instruction and assessment based on appropriate learning goals and objectives.

Here's How to Crack It

Step 1: Identify the scenario.

- Age range: third grade

- Goal: develop critical thinking skills

Step 2: Use POE to narrow down the answer choices.

Critical thinking involves combining rules, facts, and reasoning skills. Let's see what we've got:

    A.   No. Brainstorming doesn't involve reasoning.

    B.   No. That's a single-response question.

    C.   Yes. That would involve critical thinking.

    D.   No. That would only test those facts.

Step 3: Make a final decision.
There's only one choice left. The best answer is C.

65. George is a bright student in Mrs. Sutton's fourth-grade class, however he often does not complete his work in the same amount of time others do because he is continually distracted and talking to the students around him. Which of the following ideas might help George?

   A. Require George to sit away from the other students until his work is done.

   B. Require George to permanently move his desk away from the other students.

   C. Remind George that his grades are the consequence of this action.

   D. Allow George to use the timer on his watch to better manage his time.

D This question tests Competency 006: The teacher understands strategies for creating an organized and productive learning environment and for managing student behavior.

Here's How to Crack It

Step 1: Identify the scenario.

- Age range: fourth grade

- Goal: help George better manage his time

Step 2: Use POE to narrow down the answer choices.
He's in fourth grade, so he's old enough to accept some responsibility for his own progress. Let's see what we've got:

   A. No. This doesn't teach George anything.

   B. No. This is worse than A.

   C. Maybe, but the teacher isn't doing anything but threatening.

   D. Maybe. This is a step in the right direction and gives George some degree of control.

Step 3: Make a final decision.
None of the answers is perfect, but answer choice C is worse than answer choice D. D is the best answer.

66. Students in Mr. Raymond's third-grade class will soon be writing a report on a president. The students are dreading the report. In an effort to increase enthusiasm about the report, Mr. Raymond could consider:

A. allowing students to choose the presidential subject of their report instead of assigning presidents to them.

B. threatening to increase the number of pages required in the report.

C. threatening to deduct points for lack of enthusiasm.

D. postponing the report until later in the school year.

A   This question tests Competency 008: The teacher provides appropriate instruction that actively engages students in the learning process.

Here's How to Crack It

Step 1: Identify the scenario.

- Age range: third grade

- Goal: increase enthusiasm for a project

Step 2: Use POE to narrow down the answer choices.
Enthusiasm stems from student interest. We should be looking for something that increases students' interest.

A. Maybe. Giving students choices might increase interest.

B. No. That will decrease interest.

C. No. That will decrease interest further.

D. No. That will teach students that they can control the curriculum by complaining.

Step 3: Make a final decision.
There's only one choice left. The best answer is A.

67. Each student in Mrs. Landon's class will be required to make a project demonstrating the importance of healthy eating. Each student will be allowed to set the parameters for their own project provided:

A. they are approved by Mrs. Landon before the student completes the project.

B. the parent or guardian monitors the student to make sure parameters are met.

C. the project's parameters fall within the basic guidelines given by Mrs. Landon when the project was assigned.

D. they are approved by a parent or guardian before the student begins the project.

C This question tests Competency 003: The teacher understands procedures for designing effective and coherent instruction and assessment based on appropriate learning goals and objectives.

Here's How to Crack It

Step 1: Identify the scenario.

- Age range: fourth grade

- Goal: determine under which provision students should be allowed to set their own parameters for a project

Step 2: Use POE to narrow down the answer choices.
Clearly, there should be some sort of teacher approval. Let's see:

A. Maybe. This discusses teacher approval.

B. No. It's not the parents' responsibility.

C. Maybe. A project should be in line with the teacher's guidelines.

D. No. This relies on parental, rather than teacher, approval.

Step 3: Make a final decision.
We're down to A or C. The project should be approved before the student starts, not just sometime before it's completed, so eliminate A. The best answer is C because the project's parameters should definitely fall within the teacher's guidelines.

68. Mrs. Landon has made an arrangement with the physical education teacher to take the students to a public park next to the school property. The park has an exercise trail with activities and the students will complete the trail instead of attending their regular physical education class. Mrs. Landon must legally do what?

A. Obtain written permission from parents to allow the children to leave school property and complete the trail.

B. Contact the transportation department to arrange for a bus to drive the students to the park even though the park is next to the school.

C. Have an adult at each exercise station available to help students.

D. Provide drinks at the end of the exercise trail.

A This question tests Competency 013: The teacher understands and adheres to legal and ethical requirements for educators and is knowledgeable of the structure of education in Texas.

Here's How to Crack It

Step 1: Identify the scenario.

- Age range: fourth grade

- Goal: identify the legal requirement

Step 2: Use POE to narrow down the answer choices.
This is about a legal requirement. Let's be careful:

A. Yes. That's a legal requirement.

B. No. That's not a requirement.

C. No. That's not a requirement.

D. No. That's not a requirement.

Step 3: Make a final decision.
There's only one answer left. The best answer is A.

69. Mrs. Landon is approached by the mother of one of the girls in the class. The mother has volunteered to teach a yoga session as part of the unit dealing with having a positive attitude. Mrs. Landon agrees to arrange a yoga session. At the beginning of the session, a couple of the boys announce they don't want to try yoga because it is for girls. Which of the following is the most appropriate response for Mrs. Landon?

A. Refer to professional trade magazines that might address the issue.

B. Tell the boys they will receive a failing grade for this exercise if they do not try it.

C. Stop for a moment and consider if any gender stereotypes exist.

D. Talk to other boys in the class to see if they feel the same way.

C   This question tests Competency 002: The teacher understands student diversity and knows how to plan learning experiences and design assessments that are responsive to differences among students and that promote all students' learning.

Here's How to Crack It

Step 1: Identify the scenario.

- Age range: fourth grade

- Goal: respond appropriately to the situation

Step 2: Use POE to narrow down the answer choices.

Clearly, the situation has a gender-role component. Let's see what the answers look like:

A. No. The situation requires an immediate response.

B. No. Threats aren't an effective teaching mechanism.

C. Maybe, but this doesn't seem like much of a response.

D. Maybe, but this doesn't seem like the teacher is adequately addressing the situation. What if the other boys agreed?

Step 3: Make a final decision.

Neither answer C nor D seems good, but choice C at least allows the teacher a moment to consider her options and think about the problem. Choice D commits her to a path that could backfire. C is the best answer.

70. Mr. Todd taught in another state for 12 years. He recently moved to Texas and feels he needs to learn more about the TEKS so that he can better prepare his students. Mr. Todd attends a seminar, which another teacher had recommended, given by a professional teachers' organization. This shows that Mr. Todd:

A. understands how different Texas is from his previous home state.

B. is preparing his students appropriately.

C. has carefully planned his curriculum around the TEKS.

D. has tapped into resources around him.

D This question tests Competency 012: The teacher enhances professional knowledge and skills by effectively interacting with other members of the educational community and participating in various types of professional activities.

Here's How to Crack It

Step 1: Identify the scenario.

- Age range: none given

- Goal: determine what is shown by Mr. Todd's attending the recommended seminar

Step 2: Use POE to narrow down the answer choices.
We're looking for something that suggests Mr. Todd is a conscientious teacher.

A. Maybe, but he already understands that Texas is different.

B. No. Other things would be required to show that.

C. No. Other things would be required to show that.

D. Yes. It proves that he is taking advantage of resources around her.

Step 3: Make a final decision.
Choice A looked like a possibility, but D is a better answer. The best answer is D.

71. A teacher should be *most* concerned about which of the following students?

    A.   a first-grade girl who cries when her name is put on the board for talking

    B.   a first-grade boy who pushes a girl who has been teasing him

    C.   a third-grade boy who brags about things that cannot be true

    D.   a second-grade girl whose grades have plummeted

D   This question tests Competency 001: The teacher understands human developmental processes and applies this knowledge to plan instruction and ongoing assessment that motivate students and are responsive to their developmental characteristics and needs.

Here's How to Crack It

Step 1: Identify the scenario.

- Age range: none given

- Goal: identify the student with the biggest problem

Step 2: Use POE to narrow down the answer choices.
We can't predict much here—we're just looking for the worst problem

    A.   No. That seems like an age-appropriate reaction.

    B.   Maybe. That's behavior that shouldn't be tolerated.

    C.   No. That seems like age-appropriate behavior.

    D.   Yes. That's a major cause for concern at any age.

Step 3: Make a final decision.
Choice B is second-best, but D is the *best* answer.

72. A kindergarten teacher has decided to try to recruit sixth-grade students to read to her class during library time. When choosing books for the sixth graders to read, she should:

    A.   search for books the sixth-grade students would enjoy reading themselves.

    B.   search for books related to topics covered in class.

    C.   search for books the kindergarten students will likely have interest in.

    D.   search for books without difficult vocabulary.

C This question tests Competency 003: The teacher understands procedures for designing effective and coherent instruction and assessment based on appropriate learning goals and objectives.

Here's How to Crack It

Step 1: Identify the scenario.

- Age range: kindergarten

- Goal: pick good books for a sixth-grader to read to a kindergarten class

Step 2: Use POE to narrow down the answer choices.

A. No. These would likely be age-inappropriate for kindergarteners.

B. Maybe. This might be a good idea, but would it always work best? Hold onto this answer for now.

C. Probably. They're kindergarteners. We want to get them excited about reading.

D. No. There should be challenging vocabulary.

Step 3: Make a final decision.

Although it might be nice to have books relate to topics in class, it's more important for books read at library time to hold students' interest, especially if the reader is going to be a student herself. The best answer is C.

73. A first-grade teacher just instituted new policies about classroom behavior. The students will have to work together as a group with everyone behaving well in order to earn rewards for the whole class. The teacher will evaluate the change in behavior in six weeks. What is the best way for the teacher to evaluate the policies?

   A. Compare weekly conduct grades before and after instituting the new policy.

   B. Informally observe and note if the students are modifying their behavior in hopes of earning the reward for the class.

   C: Create a separate system for monitoring the new policy.

   D. Have a class discussion at the end of the six weeks to hear from the students if they think that the new policy is effective.

B This question tests Competency 010: The teacher monitors student performance and achievement; provides students with timely, high-quality feedback; and responds flexibly to promote learning for all students.

Here's How to Crack It

Step 1: Identify the scenario.

- Age range: first grade

- Goal: determine whether new policies have been effective

Step 2: Use POE to narrow down the answer choices.

A. Maybe. Think. We're looking for an answer that addresses behavior and the motivation behind it.

B. Maybe. This choice accommodates the desire to evaluate motivation as well as behavior.

C. Vague. Why would creating a separate system help with evaluation? And, what system are we suggesting, anyway?

D. No. First graders are too young to have that kind of input.

Step 3: Make a final decision.

This is a tough call. Choice C gives us no information about the kind of system, so it doesn't seem like a great idea. Choice A might work, but conduct grades wouldn't necessarily reflect the motivation behind the students' grades. Choice B would let the teacher see the plan in action, and gauge its effectiveness relatively well. The best answer is B.

74. Fourth-grade students will attend various activities during their Drug-Free week at a local elementary school. Students will hear from a nurse, watch a video, watch a weight-lifting presentation, and take a field trip. Each activity will feature the same drug-free message. The crucial advantage of this plan is that:

A. it allows students to hear the same message multiple times and in multiple ways.

B. it allows students to enjoy diverse activities during the week.

C. it allows teachers to attend these activities as well.

D. teachers will not be required to plan the activities individually.

A This question tests Competency 008: The teacher provides appropriate instruction that actively engages students in the learning process.

Here's How to Crack It

Step 1: Identify the scenario.

- Age range: fourth grade

- Goal: identify why a multifaceted message is important in an anti-drug campaign

Step 2: Use POE to narrow down the answer choices.

A multifaceted anti-drug message is important because not all children will respond to the same message. Let's see what we've got:

   A. Yes. That's the advantage.

   B. No. That may be true, but that's not the advantage.

   C. No. That may also be true, but that's not the advantage.

   D. No. Answers that make things easier for the teacher are usually wrong.

Step 3: Make a final decision.

There's only one answer left. The best choice is A.

75. What should teachers encourage parents to do with regard to standardized assessment scores?

   A. Trust that the teacher will evaluate the scores and pass along relevant information.

   B. Work with the teacher to evaluate the scores of their student.

   C. Advise teachers of problems that may have occurred during assessment.

   D. Keep standardized assessment scores secret from the student.

B   This question tests Competency 010: The teacher monitors student performance and achievement; provides students with timely, high-quality feedback; and responds flexibly to promote learning for all students.

Here's How to Crack It

Step 1: Identify the scenario.

- Age range: none given

- Goal: what to suggest to parents about test score results

Step 2: Use POE to narrow down the answer choices.

As always, the goal with parents is to include them without offending them. Let's look at our choices:

A. No. Parents should be equal partners in their children's education.

B. Yes. This suggests working together.

C. Maybe. That's something parents should do.

D. No. Students should be involved in their educational decision making, too, and we're not given an age range or other circumstances that would suggest otherwise.

Step 3: Make a final decision.

Choices C and B are both good, but choice C is encompassed within the scope of choice B, which is the ultimate goal. B is the best answer.

76. A first-grade teacher has planned a field trip to an aquarium. The teacher and students will be accompanied by several mothers who will serve as group leaders. To ensure the success of the field trip, the teacher should make sure to:

A. share the goals of the field trip with the group leaders/mothers.

B. ask the mothers to sign waivers for the field trip.

C. inform the aquarium that several mothers will serve as group leaders.

D. balance the small groups with equal numbers of boys and girls.

A   This question tests Competency 011: The teacher understands the importance of family involvement in children's education and knows how to interact and communicate effectively with families.

Here's How to Crack It

Step 1: Identify the scenario.

- Age range: first grade

- Goal: a successful field trip with parent supervisors

Step 2: Use POE to narrow down the answer choices.

A. Maybe. Sharing the goals with the leaders would put everyone on the same page.

B. No. The question makes no mention of a legal requirement.

C. No. Why would that make a difference to the success of the trip?

D. No. That has no bearing on the success of the trip.

Step 3: Make a final decision.
The best answer is A. Sharing goals would help to promote the identified goals of the trip.

> 77. A third-grade teacher wants to talk about an abstract concept in class. The best way for the students to understand this concept would be to:
>
> A. discuss the concept in class several times in a week.
>
> B. invite an expert to visit the class and talk to the students about the concept.
>
> C. liken the concept to something familiar to the students.
>
> D. create worksheets for students to take home and discuss with parents.

C   This question tests Competency 007: The teacher understands and applies principles and strategies for communicating effectively in varied teaching and learning contexts.

Here's How to Crack It

Step 1: Identify the scenario.

- Age range: third grade

- Goal: have students understand an abstract concept

Step 2: Use POE to narrow down the answer choices.
Most educational theorists discuss the idea of building new knowledge onto existing knowledge. Further, because the new concept is abstract, the students should be introduced to it in a way that relates it to their concrete experiences. Let's see what we've got:

A. No. That doesn't discuss what we're looking for.

B. No. That just changes the messenger.

C. Yes. That's close.

D. No. It's the teacher's job.

Step 3: Make a final decision.
There's only one answer that came close to our prediction. C is the best answer.

78. Recently, assessment scores were sent home to parents. One parent who is concerned about her daughter's low scores has asked for a conference with the teacher. The teacher should begin the conference by:

    A   providing an objective analysis of the student's scores and areas of improvement.

    B.   assuring the parent that the scores are a poor indication of the student's abilities.

    C.   explaining where the student's scores fall compared to other students in the class.

    D.   reviewing the positive and negative aspects of the student's assessment scores.

D   This question tests Competency 011: The teacher understands the importance of family involvement in children's education and knows how to interact and communicate effectively with families.

Here's How to Crack It

Step 1: Identify the scenario.

- Age range: none given

- Goal: determine how to begin a parent conference

Step 2: Use POE to narrow down the answer choices.

As always, teachers should address the concern without upsetting the parents. Let's take a look at our choices:

    A.   Maybe. An objective analysis seems like a good idea.

    B.   No. This would upset the parent, who would immediately want to know why the tests were being given if they are poor indicators.

    C.   Maybe. Letting the parent know where his/her child falls on the continuum doesn't seem like a bad idea.

    D.   Maybe. This seems like a good balance.

Step 3: Make a final decision.

Answer choices A, C, and D all address the concern, but, by focusing on the positives as well as the negatives, D does the best job of ensuring that the parent doesn't get upset. D is the best answer. In addition, the question asks how the conference should begin. It's always best to begin with not only negative but also positive feedback.

79. The parent of a third-grade girl meets with her daughter's teacher and expresses concern over her handwriting skills. The mother is concerned because her daughter had beautiful printing but is having difficulty with cursive writing. The parent is concerned with the ability of the teacher to instruct her daughter in this area. How best could the teacher respond?

A. Provide examples of other students' handwriting so the parent can see that her daughter's handwriting is not as bad as first thought.

B. Assure the parent that the fourth-grade teachers the student will have the next year do not expect perfect cursive handwriting from the students at the beginning of the year.

C. Ask the parent to trust in her teaching methods.

D. Explain that it is common for students to perform poorly when they first learn something new and that her daughter will start to show improvement soon.

D This question tests Competency 011: The teacher understands the importance of family involvement in children's education and knows how to interact and communicate effectively with families.

Here's How to Crack It

Step 1: Identify the scenario.

- Age range: third grade

- Goal: respond to parental concern

Step 2: Use POE to narrow down the answer choices.
Address the concern; don't upset the parent. Let's see:

A. No. That might address the concern, but the teacher shouldn't show other students' work to the parent.

B. No. The parent is concerned that the teacher isn't teaching well. It would likely upset the mother to tell her that her child's upcoming teacher has low standards.

C. Maybe, but that doesn't really address the underlying concern.

D. Yes. This explains the problem and treats the parent with respect.

Step 3: Make a final decision.
D is the best answer.

80. A student working on a math problem raises his hand for help. The teacher comes over to help and asks the student to tell him what the problem is and what work he has done so far. The teacher has asked these questions so that the student might be able to:

A. prove to the teacher that he is actually working.

B. understand the importance of what it is he needs help with.

C. spend more time thinking about the problem himself while the teacher helps the other students who are asking questions.

D. solve the problem himself while reviewing it with the teacher.

D This question tests Competency 008: The teacher provides appropriate instruction that actively engages students in the learning process.

Here's How to Crack It

Step 1: Identify the scenario.

- Age range: none given

- Goal: identify why the teacher asked specific questions

Step 2: Use POE to narrow down the answer choices.

A. Does that sound like the right answer to a TExES question? That's what a mean, critical teacher might do. Cross it out.

B. Maybe. It depends what "importance" means.

C. No. This choice starts out well, but ends up sounding like it's trying to make the teacher's job easier. Cross it out.

D. Maybe. Engaging the student in his own process might help him to find solutions independently.

Step 3: Make a final decision.

Both choices B and D could be correct, but choice D is the one that suggests that there is active teaching going on. Further, we don't know what "importance" means in this context. Therefore, D is the best answer.

81. Mrs. Baker is preparing to turn her class over to Mrs. Fence while she is on maternity leave. The administration has asked Mrs. Fence to start working in Mrs. Baker's classroom on the 10th even though Mrs. Baker will not leave until the 24th. What is the administration's primary reason for the early start date?

A. The administration wants to allow sufficient time for all necessary communication to happen between the two teachers before Mrs. Baker leaves.

B. The administration is concerned that Mrs. Baker might leave earlier.

C. The administration would like Mrs. Fence to evaluate Mrs. Baker's teaching style.

D. The administration would like Mrs. Baker to evaluate Mrs. Fence's teaching style.

A This question tests Competency 012: The teacher enhances professional knowledge and skills by effectively interacting with other members of the educational community and participating in various types of professional activities.

Here's How to Crack It

Step 1: Identify the scenario.

- Age range: not given

- Goal: determine why an administration would ask a substitute to arrive early

Step 2: Use POE to narrow down the answer choices.
This must have something to do with ensuring a smooth transition for the students. Let's see what the choices are:

A. Maybe. The two-week overlap would allow time for the teachers to communicate and work toward a smooth transition.

B. No. This may be true, but it wouldn't be the primary reason.

C. No. Again, we're looking for something that suggests a smooth transition.

D. No. This is not about teacher evaluation, it's about classroom transition.

Step 3: Make a final decision.
There's only one choice left. The best answer is A.

82. A second-year teacher has decided to start regularly attending professional seminars in his area. The primary benefit he will receive is that:

    A.   he will meet other professionals who may be good resources for him.

    B.   he will be able to learn things he may have previously missed.

    C.   he will stay current on trends in his area.

    D.   he will be able to socialize with other teachers.

C   This question tests Competency 012: The teacher enhances professional knowledge and skills by effectively interacting with other members of the educational community and participating in various types of professional activities.

Here's How to Crack It

Step 1: Identify the scenario.

- Age range: none given

- Goal: determine the primary benefit of attending professional seminars

Step 2: Use POE to narrow down the answer choices.
As we've seen, the primary benefit of professional development is keeping up-to-date. Let's see what we've got:

    A.   Maybe. The teacher would likely meet other professionals.

    B.   Maybe. The seminars would likely provide new information and learning opportunities.

    C.   Yes. That's a match. Staying current is the primary benefit of attending professional seminars.

    D.   Maybe, but that's hardly a primary educational benefit.

Step 3: Make a final decision.
We predicted this one ahead of time. The best answer is C.

83. During the administration of the TAKS, the teacher is able to answer which of the following questions from a student taking the TAKS?

    A.   What is the meaning of this word?

    B.   Can I start the next section now instead of waiting?

    C.   Did I get this question right?

    D.   What is the name of this figure?

B   This question tests Competency 013: The teacher understands and adheres to legal and ethical requirements for educators and is knowledgeable of the structure of education in Texas.

Here's How to Crack It

Step 1: Identify the scenario.

- Age range: none given

- Goal: decide which question is appropriate to answer in administering the TAKS

Step 2: Use POE to narrow down the answer choices.
Ethically, the teacher can only answer administration-related questions.

    A. No. That's content-based.

    B. Yes. That relates only to the administration of the exam.

    C. No. That's really unethical.

    D. No. That's content-based.

Step 3: Make a final decision.
There's only one choice left. The best answer is B.

84.   A pre-kindergarten teacher is meeting a new student for the first time. The student is clinging to his mother and crying uncontrollably. The best reaction from the teacher would be to:

    A. make constant eye contact with the student while talking to the parent about leaving the student.

    B. wait for the student to calm down before approaching him.

    C. send the parent away and lead the child into the classroom crying.

    D. kneel down and talk to the student directly in a soft, reassuring tone.

D   This question tests Competency 007: The teacher understands and applies principles and strategies for communicating effectively in varied teaching and learning contexts.

Here's How to Crack It

Step 1: Identify the scenario.

- Age range: preschool

- Goal: make a new student comfortable

Step 2: Use POE to narrow down the answer choices.

    A. No. This could scare the student even more.

    B. Maybe. The teacher could wait for the student to calm down on his own, but this wouldn't necessarily promote the beginnings of a teacher-student relationship. Hang on to this one for now, though.

    C. No. This could scare the student even more.

    D. Maybe. This sounds pretty good.

Step 3: Make a final decision.
The teacher could do either choice B or D. But because the teacher wants to start developing a relationship with the student, D is a better answer. The best answer is D.

85. During math class, Ms. Santos announces the new project. The class will be divided into small groups. Each group will survey at least 50 students and graph the results. Each group can design their own question for the survey. Ms. Santos has:

    A. provided a framework for the project that will allow students to proceed on their own.

    B. designed the project to facilitate group interaction.

    C. provided students with the tools needed to complete the project.

    D. recognized the contribution of the group overheard.

    A   This question tests Competency 004: The teacher understands learning processes and factors that impact student learning and demonstrates this knowledge by planning effective, engaging instruction and appropriate assessments.

Here's How to Crack It

Step 1: Identify the scenario.

- Age range: fourth grade

- Goal: identify what Ms. Santos has accomplished

Step 2: Use POE to narrow down the answer choices.
It seems as though she has given her students the assignment and is allowing them a fair amount of freedom in implementing it.

    A. Yes, she did that.

    B. No, there's not much room for interaction among groups.

    C. No. That seems to be up to the students.

    D. No. There's no evidence that she did that.

Step 3: Make a final decision.
There's only one choice left. A is the best answer.

    86. The most important advantage of having students design their own questions and survey the students is to:

        A. allow the group to maximize the strengths of the different students.

        B. increase communication skills.

        C. allow students to structure their own learning.

        D. improve the students' graphing capabilities.

    C   This question tests Competency 004: The teacher understands learning processes and factors that impact student learning and demonstrates this knowledge by planning effective, engaging instruction and appropriate assessments.

Here's How to Crack It

Step 1: Identify the scenario.

- Age range: fourth grade

- Goal: identify the advantage of having students design their own questions

Step 2: Use POE to narrow down the answer choices.
Students will be more motivated if they get to design things themselves. Let's see:

    A. No. That might be a benefit of working in groups, but not of self-design.

    B. No. That's not the primary advantage of having students design their own projects.

    C. Maybe. This sounds like it promotes student involvement in the learning process, which is an educational goal.

    D. No. That might be the primary goal of the project overall, but the question asks about the most important advantage of having the students design their own project.

Step 3: Make a final decision.
The best answer is C.

> 87. Within a short time following the field trip, it is *most* important that the students:
>
> A.   talk to their parents about the field trip.
>
> B.   persuade their parents to frequent that restaurant.
>
> C.   draw pictures to thank the restaurant manager and staff.
>
> D.   recognize the unique opportunity.

C   This question tests Competency 001: The teacher understands human developmental processes and applies this knowledge to plan instruction and ongoing assessment that motivate students and are responsive to their developmental characteristics and needs.

Here's How to Crack It

Step 1: Identify the scenario.

- Age range: kindergarten

- Goal: identify the most important field trip follow-up

Step 2: Use POE to narrow down the answer choices.

A.   Maybe. This is important, but is it *most* important? Hold on to it for now.

B.   No. Kindergarten students shouldn't be expected to do that.

C.   Yes. This is a natural classroom activity that will reinforce what was learned on the trip. It also teaches students about polite and customary actions.

D.   No. Kindergarten students can't be expected to do that.

Step 3: Make a final decision.
Of choices A and C, C is better because it's a class activity that is a natural next step. The best answer is C.

88. Shortly after the students' drawings were mailed to the restaurant as a thank-you, the students received a letter from the restaurant manager thanking them for the beautiful pictures and letting them know he had displayed them in the restaurant. The teacher should share this letter with the students in order to:

A. help the students understand the value of people's time.

B. justify to the students the purpose of their artwork.

C. encourage the students to visit the restaurant to eat.

D. encourage the students to remember to thank people.

D This question tests Competency 008: The teacher provides appropriate instruction that actively engages students in the learning process.

Here's How to Crack It

Step 1: Identify the scenario.

- Age range: kindergarten

- Goal: determine why the teacher should share the letter

Step 2: Use POE to narrow down the answer choices.
Clearly, the teacher should use this opportunity to link the letter to their original thank-you pictures. Let's see what we've got:

A. No. That doesn't show the link to the thank-you note.

B. Maybe. It depends what the teacher says the purpose was.

C. No. That doesn't show the link to the thank-you note.

D. Yes. That expresses the link very well.

Step 3: Make a final decision.
Although answer choice B could be construed to achieve the teacher's purpose, choice D states it much more clearly. The best answer is D.

89. A preschool teacher sees two students playing at the water table. One child is pouring a liquid back and forth between two containers. The second child begins to mimic this behavior. This is an example of what kind of play?

A. associative

B. cooperative

C. parallel

D. solitary

C   This question tests Competency 001: The teacher understands human developmental processes and applies this knowledge to plan instruction and ongoing assessment that motivate students and are responsive to their developmental characteristics and needs.

Here's How to Crack It

Step 1: Identify the scenario.

- Age range: preschool

- Goal: identify the type of play

Step 2: Use POE to narrow down the answer choices.
Let's assume that you've forgotten the whole section on play.

A. "Associative" suggests that the children are playing with each other, interacting, somehow. They're not. Cross it out.

B. "Cooperative" suggests that the children are helping each other. They're not. Cross it out.

C. "Parallel" suggests that the children are playing side-by-side. They are. Leave it in.

D. "Solitary" suggests that the children are alone when they are playing . They're not. Cross it out.

Step 3: Make a final decision.
There's only one choice left. The best answer is C.

90. A teacher is shocked when a female student in her class announced during a discussion of airplanes that women can't be pilots. How should the teacher respond?

    A. Invite a female pilot to speak to the class.

    B. Invite both a female and male pilot to speak to the class.

    C. Invite females and males to speak to the class from many professions.

    D. Have students write a report about a famous woman who worked in a traditionally male job.

C This question tests Competency 002: The teacher understands student diversity and knows how to plan learning experiences and design assessments that are responsive to differences among students and that promote all students' learning.

Here's How to Crack It

Step 1: Identify the scenario.

- Age range: none given

- Goal: respond to a statement reflecting a gender bias

Step 2: Use POE to narrow down the answer choices.
Clearly, the teacher needs to respond to the gender bias in a meaningful, positive way.

    A. Maybe. This might be a good idea.

    B. Better than A, because it includes male pilots, too.

    C. Better than A or B, because it includes many professions.

    D. No. Students might view this as punitive, which could stifle future discussions.

Step 3: Make a final decision.
The best answer is C.

91. A new first-grade teacher is trying to decide how to arrange her classroom. What is the most important aspect for her to take into consideration?

    A. future discipline issues

    B. the furniture available to her

    C. the approach she plans to teach with in her classroom

    D. how the other first-grade teachers arrange their classrooms

C   This question tests Competency 005: The teacher knows how to establish a classroom climate that fosters learning, equity, and excellence and uses this knowledge to create a physical and emotional environment that is safe and productive.

Here's How to Crack It

Step 1: Identify the scenario.

- Age range: first grade

- Goal: decide what to take into account as she designs her classroom

Step 2: Use POE to narrow down the answer choices.
According to the SBEC, a good teacher understands that a well-designed classroom space can facilitate learning. Let's see what we've got:

   A.   No. That doesn't sound like it's focused on facilitating learning.

   B.   No. That doesn't sound like it's focused on facilitating learning, either.

   C.   Yes. That suggests that the teacher understands that the two concepts are related.

   D.   No. That sounds like the teacher has no ideas of her own.

Step 3: Make a final decision.
There's only one answer left. The best choice is C.

92.   A third-grade teacher has decided to call a class meeting for the students to deal with the problems associated with cliques that are developing in the class. Talking as a group is important because:

   A.   the students will understand the expectations of their teachers.

   B.   the students will communicate better in the future.

   C.   the students will not discuss the problem individually.

   D.   the students will be able to recognize the consequences of their actions.

D   This question tests Competency 006: The teacher understands strategies for creating an organized and productive learning environment and for managing student behavior.

Here's How to Crack It

Step 1: Identify the scenario.

- Age range: third grade

- Goal: dealing with the problems caused by cliques

Step 2: Use POE to narrow down the answer choices.
Why is it important to have a group discussion? It must be because the cliques affect the class as a whole as well as individually. Let's see what we have:

A. No. That doesn't deal with the group vs. individual idea.

B. No. That doesn't deal with the group vs. individual idea.

C. Maybe. Do we really know they won't discuss the problem outside of the class?

D. Maybe. Class discussion will allow for the expression of many ideas and perspectives.

Step 3: Make a final decision.
Choices C and D are both possible. C suggests that students won't discuss the problem one-on-one, but we have no evidence for that. Further, a group setting is better suited for the discussion. D does a better job of hinting at the individual vs. group dynamic and is therefore the best answer.

93. Two children who are playing in the same area but are not playing together are exhibiting what type of play?

A. associative

B. cooperative

C. parallel

D. solitary

A   This question tests Competency 001: The teacher understands human developmental processes and applies this knowledge to plan instruction and ongoing assessment that motivate students and are responsive to their developmental characteristics and needs.

Here's How to Crack It

Step 1: Identify the scenario.

- Age range: preschool

- Goal: identify the type of play

Step 2: Use POE to narrow down the answer choices.
As with question 94, let's assume that you've forgotten the whole section on play.

A. No. They don't seem as though they're associating

B. No. They certainly aren't cooperating.

C. No. That was the answer to question 89.

D. No. They're not alone.

Step 3: Make a final decision.
Wait. We crossed them all out. Now what? Well, choices C and D are definitely wrong. We know those definitions. B is shady, too, because they certainly aren't cooperating. Maybe there's another definition of associative, one that simply suggests that the children are in the same area. The best answer is A. (Now go review the section on play.)

94. A teacher asks the students to come up with as many ways that they can think of to recycle. This is an example of what type of thinking?

    A. convergent

    B. divergent

    C. affective

    D. associative

B This question tests Competency 008: The teacher provides appropriate instruction that actively engages students in the learning process.

Here's How to Crack It

Step 1: Identify the scenario.

- Age range: none given

- Goal: identify the type of thinking

Step 2: Use POE to narrow down the answer choices.
We've seen this before. We're looking for divergent thinking.

    A. No.

    B. Yes. This is it.

    C. No.

    D. No.

Step 3: Make a final decision.
We already did. The best answer is B.

95. Which of the following situations demonstrates solitary play?

    A. a child playing trucks with one other child

    B. a girl who is brushing her doll's hair and who will not share the brush

    C. a child copying what her friend does

    D. two boys building a sand castle together

B This question tests Competency 001: The teacher understands human developmental processes and applies this knowledge to plan instruction and ongoing assessment that motivate students and are responsive to their developmental characteristics and needs.

Here's How to Crack It

Step 1: Identify the scenario.

- Age range: none given

- Goal: identify the type of play

Step 2: Use POE to narrow down the answer choices.

   A.   No. That's not alone.

   B.   Yes. That's alone.

   C.   No. That's not alone.

   D.   No. That's not alone.

Step 3: Make a final decision.
The best answer is B.

10

TExES 4–8
Practice Test

Directions: Each question in this practice test is a multiple-choice question with four answer choices. Read each question carefully and choose the ONE best answer.

1. What is the best way for a teacher to keep parents informed about what is going on in the classroom?

   A. Call the parents at home in the evening.

   B. Call the parents at work.

   C. Email the parents.

   D. Send a monthly class newsletter home with students.

2. An art teacher divides her fifth-grade class into five groups and gives each group some feathers and art supplies. The teacher instructs each group to come up with the most creative art-work possible from the supplies available. This requires students to use:

   A. brainstorming and convergent thinking

   B. brainstorming and divergent thinking

   C. affective learning and convergent thinking

   D. affective learning and divergent thinking

3. An eighth-grade science teacher is planning to talk to his class about potential energy vs. kinetic energy. Which of the following strategies would *best* help students understand these concepts?

   A. Plan time during the lesson for a lengthy question-and-answer period.

   B. Before explaining the concept, have students discuss what they already know about energy.

   C. Give the students everyday examples of potential and kinetic energy.

   D. Pass out a list of vocabulary words relating to energy before the lesson.

4. A fourth-grade teacher is planning to conduct a science experiment about magnetism. She has a student with a visual impairment in her class. The fourth-grade teacher should ask the special education teacher:

   A. for help in developing the details of the experiment so that the student can participate in the experiment with the other students.

   B. nothing; the fourth-grade teacher is responsible for the content of her own classroom.

   C. for additional resources related to the experiment that the student can work with instead of working on the experiment.

   D. to come to the classroom and help the student participate in the experiment.

5. Which of the following situations would be considered unethical for a Texas teacher?

   A. giving students practice TAKS questions from previous TAKS exam administrations

   B. informing students about the content that will be measured on the TAKS

   C. answering content questions for students during the actual administration of the TAKS

   D. reviewing the objectives tested on the TAKS shortly before the actual administration of the TAKS

6. A teacher begins a small-group activity by saying that there is not just one correct solution to this activity but rather many good answers. By saying this, the teacher is encouraging which of the following?

   A. convergent thinking

   B. creativity

   C. time management

   D. social acceptance

7. A fourth-grade teacher is sending home a note to parents after the first week of classes of a new school year. The note asks parents to write a few sentences describing their children to help the teacher get to know the students a little better, and the note also asks the parents to write about their hopes for the new school year. This information will allow the teacher to:

   A. get a head start on classroom management.

   B. head off potential behavior problems with certain students.

   C. adapt the teaching plan to fit the needs expressed by the parents.

   D. provide a curriculum and classroom environment that meets the needs of the students.

8. A social studies teacher is concerned with the lower-than-average grades her students received on their weekly quiz. What should the teacher's *first* step now be?

   A. Review the quiz to make sure the questions did in fact measure whether or not the students had learned the content from the week.

   B. Retest the students in a different format to determine if the students really did or did not know the content.

   C. Devote additional classroom time to teach the information again.

   D. Assign homework to make sure the students spend more time with the information.

Use the information below to answer the three questions that follow.

A middle-school librarian relies heavily on parent volunteers to help staff the library and its programs. Volunteerism in the library has dropped significantly over the last year and several programs are in danger of being cut if the librarian cannot recruit more volunteers.

9. Which of the following would be a good first step for the librarian and faculty to take in order to address the problem with volunteerism in the library?

   A.   Send home a flyer to parents outlining the need for library volunteers.

   B.   Ask former volunteers why they have chosen not to return to the library to volunteer.

   C.   Send home a flyer to parents outlining what programs will be cut if there are not enough volunteers.

   D.   Analyze the school budget to see if there is enough money for additional staff.

10. Increasing the number of volunteers in the library is most likely to benefit the school by:

   A.   increasing community involvement in the school.

   B.   improving behavioral issues by increasing the number of "staff."

   C.   facilitating development of relationships between teachers.

   D.   maximizing resources.

11. Which of the following would most likely help parent volunteers feel as though they've contributed to the school in a meaningful way?

   A.   Allow volunteers to choose what they would like to do while at the school.

   B.   Allow volunteers to work in their children's classrooms.

   C.   Assign volunteers to tasks that maximize the strengths of the volunteers.

   D.   Rotate volunteers through the different volunteer positions so that each volunteer experiences a variety of tasks.

◆ ◆ ◆ ◆ ◆ ◆ ◆ ◆

12. Which of the following is legally required before a teacher can request a special education evaluation of a student?

   A. Receive written permission from a parent/guardian.

   B. Conduct a formal review of the student's records.

   C. Meet with the school counselor.

   D. Receive written permission from the principal's office.

13. Students in Mr. Brown's sixth-grade class are writing reports about continents and must do some portion of their research on the Internet in order to develop Internet skills. The computer instructor could best help the students by:

   A. setting a schedule for the students to visit the computer lab.

   B. printing out and giving students the research needed from the Internet.

   C. demonstrating how to use search engines.

   D. monitoring how much time they spend on the Internet in the computer lab.

14. Which type of software is most appropriate for tracking students' mock-portfolios during their stock exchange project?

   A. simulation

   B. word processing

   C. spreadsheet

   D. database

15. A sixth-grade teacher decides to try a new policy to improve the level of student compliance with the classroom rules. This new policy holds the entire class responsible when two or more students break a classroom rule. This new policy could be effective because:

   A. students this age want the approval of their peers.

   B. students this age want the approval of authority figures.

   C. students this age strongly support their peers.

   D. students this age prefer to work together as a team.

16. A fourth-grade teacher is preparing to start a new school year. Her new fourth-grade class will include Tom, a mainstreamed student with special needs. Tom must also spend time away from his class working with the special education teacher. Which of the following is the most important aspect of Tom's education for the fourth-grade teacher to plan for?

A. Tom should have specific time to socialize with other special needs students.

B. The teacher should make alternative arrangements when class work is too difficult for Tom.

C. Tom should have specific time to socialize with other students in the class.

D. Tom should have an area in the classroom for his needs.

17. A fifth-grade teacher has two computers in his classroom for students to use. He has noticed that students who do not have computers at home are far less likely to use the classroom computers than are students who do have computers at home. What should the teacher do to increase the classroom computer use of students who do not have computers at home?

A. Give informal basic computer lessons to these students during their regular recess time.

B. Require all students to spend a minimum amount of time on the classroom computer each week.

C. Develop a computer project with easy-to-follow instructions that will allow the students to build confidence in using the computer.

D. Talk to the students about the importance of technology in education and in the rest of their lives.

18. A new eighth-grade American history teacher is planning the upcoming school year. What would be the best first step for her to take in the planning process?

A. Determine the number of topics that can be effectively covered during the school year.

B. Make a list of the topics she would like to teach.

C. Reach out to history teachers at other schools for assistance.

D. Determine the curriculum themes required by the course and the best order in which to teach them.

19. A fourth-grade teacher has broken up her class into groups. The groups will work together on a report on a continent. Although the requirements of the group report have been very clearly defined, the teacher has noticed that a couple of the groups are having problems focusing on what needs to be done. What would be the teacher's best approach to this situation?

A. Assign each group a leader to determine the direction of the group.

B. Assign each student in the troubled groups a specific portion of the report.

C. Reassign the students having trouble to other groups.

D. Remind the students how much this report will be reflected in their final class grade.

20. A seventh-grade teacher has broken up his class into groups. The groups are to work together on a presentation and each member of the group will have specific tasks to complete. At the end of the project, each group will complete an evaluation of their own group's performance. The likely purpose of this evaluation is to:

A. help students review their own effectiveness.

B. help the teacher determine each group member's grades on the project.

C. help the teacher understand the dynamics of each group.

D. allow students to participate in determining their own grade.

21. A sixth-grade mathematics teacher is grading a paper from one of his students and sees that she has correctly multiplied all the numbers on her homework but frequently misplaced the decimal point. Which of the following comments could he leave on her paper that would be the most effective in correcting this mistake?

A. Please review these questions again.

B. Great job on the multiplication problems but be careful with your decimal points. Come see me at my desk for a quick review of placing decimal points.

C. You've missed too many questions. Please come see me for a review.

D. Good job on knowing your multiplication tables but too many answers are still wrong.

22. Mrs. Burney's fifth-grade class will begin working on their state projects soon. Prior to assigning the projects to the students, Mrs. Burney visits the librarian to ensure the availability of many different types of resources. What is the most important benefit in having various resources available to the students for their state reports?

A. ensuring there are sufficient resources overall for the students to use

B. allowing students to choose how they will research their assigned states

C. providing additional resources in case all computer terminals are full

D. giving the students time to work on their projects

23. The average fifth-grade student would be likely to have the most difficulty with which of the following?

A. understanding the written rules of the classroom

B. following verbal instructions

C. sitting quietly after finishing work while waiting for others to finish

D. understanding the dynamics of peer relationships

24. Which of the following would be correct to instruct students to do when they use information from the Internet in a report?

A. Try to locate the same information in a book or magazine.

B. Cite the website as a source.

C. Do not cite the website as a source.

D. Cite the website only when using exact words from the site.

25. Mr. Walters will be the physical education teacher for a coeducational group. To plan activities for the group, Mr. Walters should:

A. develop two distinct grading systems—one for the boys, one for the girls.

B. avoid activities the boys might consider too girlish.

C. plan activities of interest to both the boys and girls.

D. separate the boys from girls during their physical education class.

26. A new fifth-grade teacher is trying to decide how to best encourage students to follow her classroom code of conduct. Which of the following would be most effective for her?

A. Include the students in the development of the code of conduct.

B. Apply the code of conduct in a flexible manner.

C. Ensure that she lists all behavior that will NOT be accepted.

D. Occasionally offer rewards to those who follow the code of conduct.

27. What would be the best teaching plan for a middle-school teacher whose class includes students of varying levels of cognitive development?

A. group the students according to ability on a regular basis

B. experiment with the manner in which content is taught so as to target all students

C. develop instruction aimed at students with the lowest level of development

D. suggest tutoring to parents of students with lower levels of cognitive development

28. A teacher planning for a new school year can *best* use the evaluations from her students' previous teachers when:

A. determining the seating chart for the school year.

B. deciding what field trips might be appropriate.

C. scheduling assessments and testing.

D. choosing lessons that will meet the needs of the students.

29. An eighth-grade teacher starts a new chapter from the American History textbook by asking the students what they know about the Great Depression. What does the teacher probably hope to do by starting the lesson with this question?

A. Allow the students to answer freely.

B. Learn what knowledge the students already have about the subject.

C. Determine what sections of the chapter the teacher can skip.

D. Separate the students based on level of previous knowledge.

30. A seventh-grade class will prepare and give a presentation on a country they have chosen. The students have begun to prepare and are asking to be allowed to incorporate multimedia aspects into their presentation. The teacher is concerned that students will devote too much of their time to the visual aspects of the presentation instead of the written content of the presentation. What steps could the teacher take to prevent this?

A. Agree to the students' request with the provision they do not devote too much time to the visual aspects.

B. Adjust the grading scale so that only 10% of the grade is based on the look of the presentation.

C. Monitor the students' progress on their presentations.

D. Not allow the multimedia aspects as part of the presentation.

31. A teacher is meeting with Sam's parents to discuss Sam's repeated problems with finishing his homework by the due date. His parents explain that he has a very busy after-school schedule with sports practices. Which of the following would be the most appropriate action for the teacher to take?

A. Strongly recommend to the parents that they help their son develop a standard study time so that his schoolwork does not fall behind.

B. Allow Sam time during the school day to complete his homework.

C. Speak with the sports coach about Sam's problem with completing assignments.

D. Suggest to the parents that they take their son's schoolwork more seriously.

32. Mrs. Martin tries her hardest to give immediate feedback to students on their assignments. The students benefit from this practice because:

A. they will be less likely to be surprised by their final grades.

B. parents are kept aware of their student's progress.

C. they are most likely to respond favorably to feedback that is timely.

D. they know their homework score has been recorded.

33. A seventh-grade teacher has seen some of her students smoking off campus and wants to impress upon them the dangers of smoking. Which of the following would be the most effective manner of conveying this?

A. inviting a guest speaker to discuss the hazards of smoking

B. handing out pamphlets and anti-tobacco literature

C. having a fellow student speak about losing his father to lung cancer caused by cigarette smoking

D. the school hosting a "stay smoke-free" pep rally

34. A music teacher is planning to take her classes to a symphony performance. The students will travel by bus. One of the students uses a wheelchair and the teacher is unsure what she is required to do to transport this student. She should:

A. ask the parents to provide transportation.

B. make sure the student has interest in going to the symphony.

C. arrange transportation through the transportation department for this student as for all of the others.

D. make arrangements for the student to skip the field trip and listen to a taped performance at a later time.

35. A teacher has a few students in his class that require additional instruction from the reading lab teacher. Which of the following times would be best to send the students needing this extra help to the reading lab?

   A. while the rest of the students attend recess

   B. after school

   C. while the rest of the class attends art class

   D. during center time when students work individually

36. Which of the following is the most effective method for evaluating and grading group collaborations?

   A. multiple-choice testing

   B. peer evaluations

   C. group self-evaluation

   D. frequent informal observation

37. A fourth-grade teacher realizes that Patrick rushes through his seatwork making careless errors so that he can move on to group activities with his friends. What is the best step for the fourth-grade teacher to take?

   A.. Allow Patrick to redo the work during recess time if necessary.

   B. Remove Patrick from group activities until his seatwork improves.

   C. Require Patrick to work on seatwork for a set amount of time.

   D. Have Patrick's report card grades reflect his poor attention to seatwork.

38. Which type of computer software would be best to demonstrate scientific experiments not feasible for the classroom?

   A. simulation

   B. word processing

   C. spreadsheet

   D. database

39. At the beginning of the school year, a seventh-grade government teacher informs the students they will be studying their city government, and that the teacher will allow the students to choose the destination of the field trip that will be part of this unit. The teacher's probable purpose is:

   A. to create a positive attitude in the classroom.

   B. to involve the students in their own learning.

   C. to be able to come to a consensus on where the field trip will be.

   D. to research different field trip options.

40. While dropping off her daughter at school one morning, a parent asks her daughter's teacher her opinion on paying students for good grades. What would be the teacher's best response?

A. Let the parent know this goes against her educational philosophies.

B. Schedule a time to discuss the issue with the parent at a later date and give reasons for opinions.

C. Let the mother know it is inappropriate to discuss at that time.

D. Refrain from giving an opinion one way or the other.

41. Which of the following gives an example of divergent thinking?

A. memorizing a song in music class

B. reciting multiplication tables in math class

C. finding different uses for milk cartons in art class

D. reading a book in front of the rest of the class

42. A teacher just moved to Texas and would like to learn more about exactly what is tested on the TEKS. He will attend a TEKS seminar and workshop with other teachers from his new school. This teacher:

A. is dedicated to his students.

B. understands the TEKS.

C. has located local resources for teachers.

D. must first register with a professional organization.

43. The fifth-grade class has an annual competition in the spring. The students must design and make a container in which a raw egg will be dropped from atop a ladder. The student who creates a container that prevents the egg from breaking from the highest height will win the competition. When designing these containers, students use:

A. convergent thinking.

B. creativity.

C. curiosity.

D. communication skills.

44. Students in a math class are studying graphs. For homework, the teacher has assigned students to measure a phenomenon and graph the results. The students will each be allowed to choose their own phenomena and, as a result, there will be an increase in:

A. the number of students who will complete the assignment.

B. questions about how to complete the homework.

C. communication between students.

D. interest in the homework because students control its direction.

45. A relatively new teacher finds one student a particular challenge due to his behavior. This student often breaks the class rules or disrupts the classroom. The teacher would like to improve her effectiveness in dealing with this student's behavior. Which of the following would probably be most helpful to her?

A. keeping a journal in which she records how she responds to his behavior problems each day and whether or not her response was effective

B. searching for resources in the library that might help her improve her effectiveness in dealing with this student

C. attending a workshop or seminar with role-playing designed to help improve classroom management

D. observing a teacher who has taught this student in the past

46. During physical education class, a female student complains to the teacher, "It isn't fair for the whole class to have to do pull-ups; pull-ups are for boys." The teacher's *first* response should be to:

A. separate the girls from the boys and select different activities for the two groups.

B. stop class to discuss gender stereotypes.

C. examine his own behavior to make sure he is not promoting this stereotype.

D. ask other girls in the class if they agree with the statement.

47. Mrs. White is getting a computer in her classroom for the first time. Before allowing students to use it, she must first:

A. learn to use it herself.

B. install student protection software.

C. develop a way to monitor students closely while on the computer.

D. obtain permission slips from all parents.

48. A new school year is starting and a teacher should primarily consider what aspect when arranging students' desks in the classroom?

A. her teaching style in the classroom

B. the students' previous conduct grades

C. the location of windows in the classroom

D. the number of boys versus girls in the class

49. Which of the following would be an effective use of an internal network of computers in a school?

A. sharing students' grades with other teachers

B. communication between teachers and administrators

C. locating a staff member

D. student access to the Internet

50. A fourth-grade teacher's class is returning from a visit to NASA. The teacher has the students write the answer to the following two questions in their daily school journals:

1) What did I learn at NASA?

2) What did I like most that I saw at NASA?

The primary purpose of these journal entries is to:

A. allow the teacher to learn if the class enjoyed the field trip.

B. inform parents of the activities of the day.

C. help the students realize what they may have learned.

D. provide a keepsake memory for the students.

51. To motivate his middle school choral group, Mr. Songbird should consider:

A. requiring students who do not participate in class to attend detention after school.

B. allowing students the opportunity to choose one or more of the songs they will perform.

C. distributing small prizes to students who participate fully.

D. assigning failing grades to students who do not participate in class.

52. A teacher has just begun a new school year and has a recently mainstreamed student who is profoundly deaf. The teacher suspects the student should not have been mainstreamed but has a responsibility to the student to:

A. make the best of a bad situation.

B. spend significant time one-on-one with this student.

C. exhaust all resources available to the special needs student before recommending another evaluation.

D. meet with the students' parents to discuss what can and cannot be done to improve the situation.

53. A sixth-grade language arts class is reading a passage. To help develop the students' critical reading skills, the teacher could follow the reading with what exercise?

A. a class discussion about what evidence the author provided in the passage

B. a class discussion about what the students agree or disagree with in the passage

C. a multiple-choice quiz about the passage

D. an assignment to identify the main parts of the passage such as purpose, conclusion, etc.

Use the information below to answer the two questions that follow.

Mr. Smith's seventh-grade English class recently visited the local university's campus to see a play. The class was also invited to eat lunch in the student union by the director of the English department.

54. Mr. Smith has assigned his class to write a letter to the English department thanking them for their generosity. The primary purpose of this letter is:

A. to have the students use a new letter-writing style learned in class recently.

B. to have the students recognize the value of establishing long-term relationships.

C. for the teacher to evaluate the students' grammar and sentence structure.

D. to have the students practice socially acceptable behavior.

55. After receiving the letters from the students, the English department director emails Mr. Smith thanking him for the students' letters and suggesting that the field trip be repeated in future years. Mr. Smith shares this email with his students primarily so that they will:

A. value people's time.

B. understand the purpose of attending the play.

C. consider attending the university.

D. remember to thank people.

◆ ◆ ◆ ◆ ◆ ◆ ◆

56. A teacher is shocked when a boy in her class is overheard telling a friend that only girls can be dancers. The teacher should react to this situation by doing which of the following?

A. Invite a male dancer to the next career day with other men and women who speak about their professions.

B. Invite both a female and male dancer to speak to the class.

C. Rent a tape of a ballet to show to the class.

D. Have students write a report about a famous man who earned his living as a dancer.

57. The fifth-grade teachers have noticed that the students returning to the new school year are not as prepared as they should be with regard to their math skills. The fourth-grade teachers include several new teachers that, in retrospect, admit they may not have covered all topics that should have been covered. The fifth-grade teachers are working with the fourth-grade teachers this year to prevent the same thing from happening next school year. This is an example of which of the following?

A. teachers collaborating to improve their students' education

B. teachers learning better communication skills

C. teachers correcting flaws in their curriculum

D. teachers expecting too much from younger colleagues

58. Which of the following would a teacher want to make sure to avoid doing to a student who needs to develop a more positive level of self-esteem?

   A. assigning projects to the student that he will be able to accomplish

   B. offering praise to the student and others for accomplishing tasks

   C. rewarding the student with privileges for successfully completing class work

   D. praising the student for actions that he may not have completed

59. A fifth-grade math teacher will begin discussing basic geometry with his students in the next lesson. Before starting the lesson, he asks his students to identify a wide variety of shapes. His probable reason for doing this is to:

   A. determine what students already know about the lesson.

   B. know how best to arrange the seating chart for the class.

   C. eliminate the need to find examples of these shapes.

   D. determine how much of the lesson can be skipped.

60. Middle school health teachers know the importance of education for teenagers about the consequences of alcohol and drug use. It is difficult to get through to students at this age because:

   A. they don't want to be lectured to by adults who might have behaved similarly when they were teenagers.

   B. they can't imagine anything really bad happening to them; it always happens to someone else.

   C. they don't believe the information and studies on drug and alcohol use are true.

   D. they don't care about hurting themselves.

61. A sixth-grade social studies class is discussing the office of president when a student asks, "How come the president has all the power but Congress makes the laws?" The teacher writes the words "checks and balances" on the board and then asks the students for the definitions of the words in order to:

   A. keep the students involved in the class by requiring their participation.

   B. have the students think about the secondary definitions of words.

   C. turn the discussion from social studies to mathematics.

   D. determine which students have read the assigned chapter material.

62. What role should parents take regarding standardized test scores?

A. Assume the school will notify the parents if there is a problem.

B. Encourage the student to do his/her best, as the student would on any exam.

C. Meet with the teacher to address any concerns or questions about the testing.

D. Keep standardized assessment scores from the student.

63. Requiring a class to clean up its classroom after an in-school holiday party is an example of:

A. the students taking responsibility for the condition of their environment.

B. the teacher modeling respect for others' property.

C. the need for stronger parental involvement at the school.

D. punishment for inappropriate behavior.

64. A fourth-grade teacher is looking for a book to read together as a class with her students. When choosing a book to read, she should:

A. search for books the fourth-grade students would enjoy reading themselves.

B. search for books related to topics already covered in class.

C. search for books students have probably never heard of.

D. search for books without difficult vocabulary.

65. Which type of thinking would a creative writing assignment entitled, "If I had $1,000, I would..." develop?

A. convergent

B. affective

C. memory recall

D. brainstorming

66. A seventh-grade English teacher is preparing to have his class start reading a novel. Before the students start reading the novel, he first asks the students to give definitions of some vocabulary words such as *plot, climax, theme, autobiography,* etc. What is his primary purpose for asking these questions?

A. To select resources that will be used by the students.

B. To determine if the students will also watch the movie version of the book.

C. To informally assess the students' current knowledge of the parts of a novel.

D. To identify budding authors in the group.

Ms. Piper is a new teacher and is just starting her first year teaching fourth-grade students. She has developed the following set of goals for herself that she has posted on the side of her computer in her school office.

1. Be patient
2. Smile
3. Learn everyone's name quickly
4. Learn what the students are interested in personally
5. Offer words of encouragement
6. Establish a code of conduct and enforce it equally

67. If Ms. Piper is able to follow goal 4, the students are more likely to:

    A. feel free to talk during class time.

    B. develop communication skills.

    C. be motivated to participate in class activities.

    D. sit quietly while working on seatwork.

68. During art class, students are paired together. Each pair includes a more artistically inclined student and a less artistically inclined student. Students will prepare art projects while giving feedback to their partners to help them improve their art projects. Which of the following practices of Ms. Piper's is most likely to lend success to this arrangement?

    A. Goal 1, the students must be patient with each other.

    B. Goal 2, smiling at another student will lessen hurtful words.

    C. Goal 4, knowing students' interests will help them give each other suggestions.

    D. Goal 5, demonstrating encouragement has taught the students how best to respond.

69. Ms. Piper could best anticipate that students will follow the classroom's code of conduct if she first:

A. asks the students to help develop the code of conduct.

B. follows goal 1.

C. clearly outlines the punishment for each behavior in the code of conduct.

D. follows goal 2.

70. Mrs. Grant has paired up students. Each pair of students will work together for three minutes to spell new words from the letters in a word Mrs. Grant will write on the board. The team with the most new words will win a special prize. Which type of thinking does this activity require?

A. motivated

B. parallel

C. convergent

D. divergent

DECISION SET ENDS HERE

71. A music teacher explains to her class the importance of the phrase "every good boy does fine" to help them remember the location of notes written on music sheets. This information is an example of which of the following?

   A. rote memory

   B. memory trick

   C. mnemonics

   D. chunking

72. Two sixth-grade girls have been caught fighting on the school grounds. Their teacher's primary goal should be to do what?

   A. Determine which of the two students is the aggressor.

   B. Teach the girls how to work through their problems without becoming physical.

   C. Work with the school administration to transfer one of the girls to another classroom.

   D. Separate the girls from each other in as many activities as possible.

73. Before taking a field trip, a teacher must do which of the following according to Texas law?

   A. obtain written permission from a parent/guardian

   B. obtain a written release of liability from a parent/guardian

   C. verify all medical information is on file for the students

   D. arrange for students to make up work missed in other classes

74. During a parent open house evening at the school, a teacher encourages parents to ask their students what they have learned each day because remembering this information and relating it will help increase the students' understanding of the topic. By talking to the parents about this, the teacher has demonstrated that she:

   A. understands the importance family can play in a student's education.

   B. believes the families are not involved enough in the student's education.

   C. communicates openly with her students.

   D. is confident in her student's talking about her teaching ability.

75. Mrs. Sparks is meeting with Tony's parents to recommend that they consider holding Tony back a year and have him repeat the fourth grade. What should Mrs. Sparks first discuss with the parents during this difficult meeting?

   A. List the objectives that fourth graders are required to master.

   B. Relate the increase in responsibility and independence expected of students in fifth grade.

   C. Talk about the academic improvements Tony has made in the past school year.

   D. List the legal options of the parents and make sure they understand them.

The middle school's student council has decided that it would like to start a recycling project at the school. It has invited its teacher-sponsor, Ms. Greene, to a council meeting to discuss recycling at the school.

76. After the meeting is called to order, Ms. Greene begins by asking the students what they know about how to recycle. This is important because:

A. the project must allow the students to learn something new.

B. students should have already researched the project.

C. Ms. Greene wants the students to be aware of how much work may be involved.

D. Ms. Greene does not know much about recycling herself.

77. Students have developed a list of questions asking why the school does not recycle that Ms. Greene does not know the answer to. She should encourage the students to find the answers by:

A. finding a custodian right then and talking to him/her about recycling.

B. developing a committee to study the problem, meet with administrators, and return to the council with a report.

C. researching recycling on the Internet.

D. accompanying her to a meeting already scheduled with the principal the next day.

78. As one portion of the recycling project, students want to deliver newspapers they've collected to the recycling center. To arrange this, Ms. Greene *must*:

A. obtain written permission from the school office.

B. obtain written permission from the parents/guardians.

C. accompany the students to the recycling center.

D. encourage the students to ask their parents to take them.

79. Shortly before the trip to the recycling center, Ms. Greene is greeted one morning by a parent explaining that she will not allow her son, who incidentally first conceived of this project, to participate in the field trip. Ms. Greene should:

A. accept the parent's decision about her son and thank the parent for informing her.

B. try to explain to the parent the educational benefit her son would gain from the trip.

C. listen to the parent and ask her to reconsider and allow her son to complete what he has started.

D. try to determine why the parent is not allowing her son to participate.

80. Leaving the responsibility for re-searching the recycling project with the students on the student council provides what benefit?

A. The teacher is able to devote the time it would have taken her to research the project to something else.

B. The students are empowered by being in charge of their own learning process.

C. The students will be able to measure what they have learned at the end of the project.

D. The teacher will be able to see what level of dedication the students have for this project.

81. Ms. Greene has been asked to send one of the students who worked on this project to the school board meeting to discuss the findings of the project and end report. Which of the following would be the best way to decide which student will represent the group?

A. Ms. Greene will send the student she feels contributed the most to the project.

B. Ms. Greene will ask the students to select the student who can best represent the project to the school board.

C. Ms. Greene will hold a random lottery to choose a student.

D. The school principal will choose a student.

DECISION SET ENDS HERE

82. Mary comes to school one day in tears and, after much discussion, confides in you that her stepfather touched her inappropriately. What are you required to do?

   A. Report the incident to the police for investigation.

   B. Determine if there is enough truth in Mary's story to accuse the stepfather.

   C. Ask Mary's mother if she has any knowledge of the incident.

   D. Report the accusation to all involved parties.

83. If a teacher asks her students to brainstorm solutions to a problem, the teacher is asking the students to do which of the following?

   A. rapidly think through all options

   B. come up with as many ideas as possible

   C. evaluate ideas quickly

   D. think of creative solutions

84. Michelle approaches her teacher in the hallway in a very excited state and is obviously upset with the teacher. The teacher takes Michelle aside and asks her to explain clearly what she is upset about. The purpose for trying to clarify what Michelle has said is to:

   A. signal to Michelle that she is being taken seriously.

   B. calm Michelle down.

   C. provide a starting point to their discussion.

   D. give Michelle the opportunity to realize she should not approach her teacher in this way.

85. A sixth-grade class has just completed a project during which the students worked in small groups. The teacher has already assigned grades to the students but has not yet told the students their grades. The teacher would like the students to evaluate their own contributions to their group before he tells them their grades. This exercise is most likely to:

   A. identify which students did not contribute as much as others.

   B. demonstrate that sixth graders' self-evaluation skills are heavily influenced by their friends.

   C. identify who took the leadership role in each group.

   D. reveal discrepancies between the self-evaluations and the teacher's evaluation.

86. Teachers should use which of the following to help them track and compute grades for students?

   A. a grade book

   B. a calculator

   C. a computer spreadsheet

   D. a ledger

87. A teacher has noticed that Lola suddenly seems unmotivated and withdrawn. The teacher calls Lola's parents. Which of the following would most likely help Lola the most?

A. The teacher should not be the one to contact the parents.

B. The teacher asks the parents to have Lola tested.

C. The teacher shares with Lola's parents her concerns about the negative impact of Lola's home environment on her education.

D. The teacher asks for the parents' help understanding what might be going on with Lola's behavior.

88. Mrs. Graham, a fifth-grade teacher, has learned that one of her students, Alexis, is frequently shuttled between several different households. As a result, Alexis often arrives late to school and often without the items she needs for the day. To help Alexis, Mrs. Graham should:

A. have Alexis visit the school counselor.

B. notify the proper authorities.

C. provide a predictable and stable environment at school.

D. review Alexis's past years' records.

89. Mrs. McNeil is a new teacher and subscribes to professional teaching journals. The greatest value the journals provide is:

A. in supporting causes Mrs. McNeil feels are important in her field.

B. in offering additional resources to solve common teaching issues.

C. in helping Mrs. McNeil remain current on trends in education and technology.

D. they will serve as a resource for Mrs. McNeil in several years.

90. A middle school teacher will soon start a new chapter with her students about electricity. She plans to take her students to the Natural History Museum where there are hands-on exhibits for the students to "play" with. This field trip will most likely encourage the students':

A. curiosity

B. imagination

C. dependency

D. good behavior

91. Mr. Will's eighth-grade history class will be spending the next week debating battle strategies of different wars. He has rearranged the desks in the classroom into a horseshoe in order to:

    A. allow all students to see each other and encourage open discussion.

    B. allow himself to monitor the debate easily from the center of the room.

    C. pit the two sides of the horseshoe against each other for a livelier debate.

    D. ensure participation by everyone in the debates.

92. To measure the success of a new classroom procedure, the teacher should have:

    A. an unbiased observer's opinion.

    B. high expectations.

    C. defined goals before starting.

    D. a survey for students to fill out.

93. To *best* evaluate a student who suffers from severe testing anxiety, the teacher should:

    A. allow the student extra time to complete the test.

    B. allow the student to take the test home to complete.

    C. informally observe the student on several occasions.

    D. permit the student to take the test more than one time.

94. What must a teacher do if he/she learns a student may have brought a weapon to the school campus?

    A. Call the police immediately.

    B. Confront the student.

    C. Try to establish there is in fact a weapon.

    D. Notify other teachers.

11

TExES 4–8 Practice Test: Answers and Explanations

TExES PPR 4–8 PRACTICE TEST ANSWER KEY

1. D	26. A	51. B	76. C
2. A	27. B	52. C	77. B
3. C	28. D	53. A	78. B
4. A	29. B	54. D	79. C
5. C	30. B	55. D	80. B
6. B	31. A	56. A	81. B
7. D	32. C	57. A	82. A
8. A	33. C	58. D	83. B
9. B	34. C	59. A	84. C
10. A	35. D	60. B	85. D
11. C	36. D	61. B	86. C
12. A	37. C	62. C	87. D
13. C	38. A	63. A	88. C
14. C	39. B	64. A	89. B
15. A	40. B	65. D	90. A
16. C	41. C	66. C	91. A
17. C	42. C	67. C	92. C
18. D	43. B	68. D	93. C
19. B	44. D	69. A	94. A
20. A	45. A	70. D	
21. B	46. C	71. C	
22. B	47. B	72. B	
23. D	48. A	73. A	
24. B	49. B	74. A	
25. C	50. C	75. C	

1. What is the best way for a teacher to keep parents informed about what is going on in the classroom?

    A. Call the parents at home in the evening.

    B. Call the parents at work.

    C. Email the parents.

    D. Send a monthly class newsletter home with students.

D This question tests Competency 011: The teacher understands the importance of family involvement in children's education and knows how to interact and communicate effectively with families.

Here's How to Crack It

Step 1: Identify the scenario.

- Age range: none given

- Goal: identify preferred means of communication with parents

Step 2: Use POE to narrow down the answer choices.

It doesn't sound like there's a pressing issue that needs to be discussed with the parents; the question seems to be dealing with general communication.

    A. No. Every parent? Once per week? Once per month? Cross it out.

    B. No. That's even worse.

    C. No. Not all parents have access to email. That's a trap answer, because normally technology is good. Cross it out.

    D. Yes. That seems reasonable.

Step 3: Make a final decision.

Of the four choices, D is the best.

2. An art teacher divides her fifth-grade class into five groups and gives each group some feathers and art supplies. The teacher instructs each group to come up with the most creative artwork possible from the supplies available. This requires students to use:

    A. brainstorming and convergent thinking

    B. brainstorming and divergent thinking

    C. affective learning and convergent thinking

    D. affective learning and divergent thinking

A This question tests Competency 008: The teacher provides appropriate instruction that actively engages students in the learning process.

Here's How to Crack It

Step 1: Identify the scenario.

- Age range: fifth grade

- Goal: identify thought process

Step 2: Use POE to narrow down the answer choices.
The students are asked to create a creative project in groups.

A. Sure. It's likely that the groups will consider many different ideas first.

B. No. The students will need to agree on a single idea. Divergent thinking wouldn't do that.

C. No. That's not affective learning.

D. No. That's not affective learning.

Step 3: Make a final decision.
A is the best answer.

3. An eighth-grade science teacher is planning to talk to his class about potential energy vs. kinetic energy. Which of the following strategies would *best* help students understand these concepts?

   A. Plan time during the lesson for a lengthy question-and-answer period.

   B. Before explaining the concept, have students discuss what they already know about energy.

   C. Give the students everyday examples of potential and kinetic energy,

   D. Pass out a list of vocabulary words relating to energy before the lesson.

C This question tests Competency 007: The teacher understands and applies principles and strategies for communicating effectively in varied teaching and learning contexts.

Here's How to Crack It

Step 1: Identify the scenario.

- Age range: eighth grade

- Goal: identify strategy to teach science concept

Step 2: Use POE to narrow down the answer choices.

A. No. That puts the burden on the students to come up with the questions. A good teacher can do better than that. Cross it out.

B. Maybe. Putting new ideas into the context of old ideas is an effective teaching strategy.

C. Maybe. Concrete examples of scientific ideas are useful.

D. No. Vocabulary usually isn't the problem when dealing with complex concepts.

Step 3: Make a final decision.

We're down to choices B and C. The question suggests that the important concept is the contrast between two ideas rather than the introduction of new ideas. Choice B would be a good way of introducing a new chapter or unit, but choice C is a better way of clarifying the difference between two ideas. The best answer is C.

4. A fourth-grade teacher is planning to conduct a science experiment about magnetism. She has a student with a visual impairment in her class. The fourth-grade teacher should ask the special education teacher:

A. for help in developing the details of the experiment so that the student can participate in the experiment with the other students.

B. nothing; the fourth-grade teacher is responsible for the content of her own classroom.

C. for additional resources related to the experiment that the student can work with instead of working on the experiment.

D. to come to the classroom and help the student participate in the experiment.

A   This question tests Competency 012: The teacher enhances professional knowledge and skills by effectively interacting with other members of the educational community and participating in various types of professional activities.

Here's How to Crack It

Step 1: Identify the scenario.

- Age range: fourth grade

- Goal: identify the role of the special education teacher

Step 2: Use POE to narrow down the answer choices.
Students with disabilities should be included to the fullest extent possible. Let's see what we've got:

A. Maybe. That would result in the student's inclusion.

B. No. Teachers should be able to ask each other for assistance. Cross it out.

C. No. That doesn't include the student in the experiment.

D. Maybe. That would also result in the student's inclusion.

Step 3: Make a final decision.
We're down to choices A and D. Should the fourth-grade teacher ask the special education teacher to come to the classroom and help? Nothing in the question suggests that the student requires that level of assistance, and choice A suggests that the student would be able to fully participate without that level of assistance. The best answer is A.

5. Which of the following situations would be considered unethical for a Texas teacher?

A. giving students practice TAKS questions from previous TAKS exam administrations

B. informing students about the content that will be measured on the TAKS

C. answering content questions for students during the actual administration of the TAKS

D. reviewing the objectives tested on the TAKS shortly before the actual administration of the TAKS

C   This question tests Competency 013: The teacher understands and adheres to legal and ethical requirements for educators and is knowledgeable of the structure of education in Texas.

Here's How to Crack It

Step 1: Identify the scenario.

*   Age range: none given

*   Goal: identify the unethical action

Step 2: Use POE to narrow down the answer choices.
Let's see what we've got. Remember that common sense goes a long way in questions dealing with ethics.

A. No. That's not unethical. In fact, it may be a good way to prepare.

B. No. That's definitely a good way to prepare.

C. Yes. That's cheating.

D. No. That's also a good way to prepare.

Step 3: Make a final decision.
Choice C is the best answer.

6. A teacher begins a small-group activity by saying that there is not just one correct solution to this activity but rather many good answers. By saying this, the teacher is encouraging which of the following?

   A. convergent thinking

   B. creativity

   C. time management

   D. social acceptance

B This questions tests Competency 007: The teacher understands and applies principles and strategies for communicating effectively in varied teaching and learning contexts.

Here's How to Crack It

Step 1: Identify the scenario.

- Age range: none given

- Goal: determine what is being encouraged

Step 2: Use POE to narrow down the answer choices.
It sounds like the teacher is encouraging "thinking outside the box." Let's see what we've got:

   A. No. Convergent thinking implies coming up with a "best" answer.

   B. Maybe.

   C. No. Time management is irrelevant to this question.

   D. No. That's not what the teacher is encouraging in this context.

Step 3: Make a final decision.
The best answer is B.

7. A fourth-grade teacher is sending home a note to parents after the first week of classes of a new school year. The note asks parents to write a few sentences describing their children to help the teacher get to know the students a little better, and the note also asks the parents to write about their hopes for the new school year. This information will allow the teacher to:

    A.   get a head start on classroom management.

    B.   head off potential behavior problems with certain students.

    C.   adapt the teaching plan to fit the needs expressed by the parents.

    D.   provide a curriculum and classroom environment that meets the needs of the students.

D   This question tests Competency 011: The teacher understands the importance of family involvement in children's education and knows how to interact and communicate effectively with families.

Here's How to Crack It

Step 1: Identify the scenario.

- Age range: fourth grade

- Goal: identify purpose of solicitation of parental information

Step 2: Use POE to narrow down the answer choices.
Let's see what we've got. There could be many correct answers.

    A.   No. After the first week of classes is too late to get a "head start" on classroom management.

    B.   Maybe, but that doesn't sound like a great answer. Keep it for now.

    C.   Maybe, and it's better than B because it emphasizes the positive aspects of students. Cross out B.

    D.   Maybe. That's a worthy goal.

Step 3: Make a final decision.
Choices C and D seem reasonable. Choice C is not as good, though, because it suggests that the teacher will automatically modify his or her style based on parental input, which may or may not be the case. Choice D is general and vague enough to be inarguable, and is therefore the best answer.

8. A social studies teacher is concerned with the lower-than-average grades her students received on their weekly quiz. What should the teacher's *first* step now be?

    A. Review the quiz to make sure the questions did in fact measure whether or not the students had learned the content from the week.

    B. Retest the students in a different format to determine if the students really did or did not know the content.

    C. Devote additional classroom time to teach the information again.

    D. Assign homework to make sure the students spend more time with the information.

A   This question tests Competency 003: The teacher understands procedures for designing effective and coherent instruction and assessment based on appropriate learning goals and objectives.

Here's How to Crack It

Step 1: Identify the scenario.

- Age range: none given

- Goal: determine the teacher's first step

Step 2: Use POE to narrow down the answer choices.
Note that the question asks for the *first* step. Let's see what we've got:

    A. Yes. That's an appropriate first step.

    B. No. A review would happen before a retest. Cross out B.

    C. No. A review would happen before a reteach. Cross out C.

    D. No. A review would happen before assigning homework to reinforce the tested information. Cross out D.

Step 3: Make a final decision.
A is the best answer.

9. Which of the following would be a good first step for the librarian and faculty to take in order to address the problem with volunteerism in the library?

   A. Send home a flyer to parents outlining the need for library volunteers.

   B. Ask former volunteers why they have chosen not to return to the library to volunteer.

   C. Send home a flyer to parents outlining what programs will be cut if there are not enough volunteers.

   D. Analyze the school budget to see if there is enough money for additional staff.

B   This question tests Competency 011: The teacher understands the importance of family involvement in children's education and knows how to interact and communicate effectively with families.

Here's How to Crack It

Step 1: Identify the scenario.

   • Age range: none given

   • Goal: identify a first step to solve the volunteerism problem

Step 2: Use POE to narrow down the answer choices.
Note that the question is asking for the first step. Let's see what the choices are:

   A. Maybe. Let's see what else there is.

   B. That's better than A. It would help to know why the former volunteers didn't return. Perhaps some things need to change in the library in order to retain volunteers. Cross out choice A.

   C. No. That won't solve the underlying problem.

   D. No. If there were money, the district wouldn't have relied on volunteers in the first place.

Step 3: Make a final decision.
Choice B is the best answer.

10. Increasing the number of volunteers in the library is most likely to benefit the school by:

  A. increasing community involvement in the school.

  B. improving behavioral issues by increasing the number of "staff."

  C. facilitating development of relationships between teachers.

  D. maximizing resources.

A   This question tests Competency 005: The teacher knows how to establish a classroom climate that fosters learning, equity, and excellence and uses this knowledge to create a physical and emotional environment that is safe and productive.

Here's How to Crack It

Step 1: Identify the scenario.

  • Age range: none given

  • Goal: determine how volunteers help the school

Step 2: Use POE to narrow down the answer choices.
Clearly, there's a monetary value, but that's unlikely to be the correct answer on the TExES—this is an exam about education.

  A. Yes. This is an important benefit.

  B. No. That may be a benefit, but it emphasizes the negative aspects of students, and is therefore a worse answer choice than A. Cross it out.

  C. No. Increasing the number of volunteers would have no impact on that.

  D. Maybe, but that comes close to mentioning a monetary benefit. Cross it out.

Step 3: Make a final decision.
A is the best answer.

11. Which of the following would most likely help parent volunteers feel as though they've contributed to the school in a meaningful way?

    A. Allow volunteers to choose what they would like to do while at the school.

    B. Allow volunteers to work in their children's classrooms.

    C. Assign volunteers to tasks that maximize the strengths of the volunteers.

    D. Rotate volunteers through the different volunteer positions so that each volunteer experiences a variety of tasks.

C This question tests Competency 011: The teacher understands the importance of family involvement in children's education and knows how to interact and communicate effectively with families.

Here's How to Crack It

Step 1: Identify the scenario.

- Age range: none given

- Goal: help volunteers to feel as though they've contributed

Step 2: Use POE to narrow down the answer choices.

    A. No. That's not always the most effective or efficient way of using a volunteer staff. What if everyone chose to do the same thing?

    B. No. That won't necessarily make volunteers feel effective.

    C. Maybe. If volunteers do things they're good at, they're likely to feel as though they've contributed.

    D. No. Rotating through tasks volunteers are unsuited for won't make them feel as though they've contributed.

Step 3: Make a final decision.
C is the best answer.

12. Which of the following is legally required before a teacher can request a special education evaluation of a student?

   A. Receive written permission from a parent/ guardian.

   B. Conduct a formal review of the student's records.

   C. Meet with the school counselor.

   D. Receive written permission from the principal's office.

A This question tests Competency 013: The teacher understands and adheres to legal and ethical requirements for educators and is knowledgeable of the structure of education in Texas.

Here's How to Crack It

Step 1: Identify the scenario.

- Age range: none given

- Goal: identify legal requirement

Step 2: Use POE to narrow down the answer choices.
You should know this one: written permission from the parent.

   A. Yes. You must obtain permission from a parent or guardian.

   B. No. A formal review would only happen after written permission is secured.

   C. No. This may or may not happen, but it is not a legal requirement for a special education evaluation.

   D. No. This is not a legally required prerequisite for requesting a special education evaluation.

Step 3: Make a final decision.
A is the best answer.

13. Students in Mr. Brown's sixth-grade class are writing reports about continents and must do some portion of their research on the Internet in order to develop Internet skills. The computer instructor could best help the students by:

A. setting a schedule for the students to visit the computer lab.

B. printing out and giving students the research needed from the Internet.

C. demonstrating how to use search engines.

D. monitoring how much time they spend on the Internet in the computer lab.

C This question tests Competency 009: The teacher incorporates the effective use of technology to plan, organize, deliver, and evaluate instruction for all students.

Here's How to Crack It

Step 1: Identify the scenario.

- Age range: sixth grade

- Goal: identify how the computer instructor can help develop students' research skills

Step 2: Use POE to narrow down the answer choices.

A. No. That won't help students' research skills.

B. No. That won't teach the students anything.

C. Yes. That gives students a needed tool.

D. No. That won't help students' research skills.

Step 3: Make a final decision.
C is the best answer.

14. Which type of software is most appropriate for tracking students' mock-portfolios during their stock exchange project?

A. simulation

B. word processing

C. spreadsheet

D. database

C This question tests Competency 009: The teacher incorporates the effective use of technology to plan, organize, deliver, and evaluate instruction for all students.

Here's How to Crack It

Step 1: Identify the scenario.

- Age range: none given

- Goal: identify appropriate software

Step 2: Use POE to narrow down the answer choices.

Stock portfolios are likely to involve a lot of number crunching. Let's see what we've got:

A.   No. A simulator isn't likely to be able to crunch numbers.

B.   No. This won't involve writing.

C.   Yes. A spreadsheet is good tool for working with numbers.

D.   No. C is a better answer for manipulating numerical data.

Step 3: Make a final decision.

C is the best answer.

15.   A sixth-grade teacher decides to try a new policy to improve the level of student compliance with the classroom rules. This new policy holds the entire class responsible when two or more students break a classroom rule. This new policy could be effective because:

A.   students this age want the approval of their peers.

B.   students this age want the approval of authority figures.

C.   students this age strongly support their peers.

D.   students this age prefer to work together as a team.

A   This question tests Competency 006: The teacher understands strategies for creating an organized and productive learning environment and for managing student behavior.

Here's How to Crack It

Step 1: Identify the scenario.

- Age range: sixth grade

- Goal: determine why a new policy might be effective

Step 2: Use POE to narrow down the answer choices.

    A.   Maybe. That's a true statement.

    B.   No. Sixth graders don't necessarily seek the approval of authority figures.

    C.   Maybe. That's close to choice A.

    D.   No. That's not necessarily true.

Step 3: Make a final decision.

We're down to choices A and C. What's the difference between the two? Sixth graders are more likely to seek their peers' approval than to necessarily support them. Choice A is consequently the best answer.

16.   A fourth-grade teacher is preparing to start a new school year. Her new fourth-grade class will include Tom, a mainstreamed student with special needs. Tom must also spend time away from his class working with the special education teacher. Which of the following is the most important aspect of Tom's education for the fourth-grade teacher to plan for?

    A.   Tom should have specific time to socialize with other special needs students.

    B.   The teacher should make alternative arrangements when class work is too difficult for Tom.

    C.   Tom should have specific time to socialize with other students in the class.

    D.   Tom should have an area in the classroom for his needs.

    C   This question tests Competency 002: The teacher understands student diversity and knows how to plan learning experiences and design assessments that are responsive to differences among students and that promote all students' learning.

Here's How to Crack It

Step 1: Identify the scenario.

- Age range: fourth grade

- Goal: identify the most important aspect of Tom's education

Step 2: Use POE to narrow down the answer choices.
Students with special needs should be included to the fullest extent possible. Let's see what we've got:

A. No. That sounds like something the special education teacher should plan for.

B. Maybe. But, remember we're looking for the *most important* aspect of the main-stream experience.

C. Maybe. Think about what benefits Tom might get from being in the mainstream classroom as opposed to being in a separate learning environment.

D. No. That's not necessarily true, and might exclude Tom.

Step 3: Make a final decision.
We're down to choices B and C. Choice B may be an element to plan for, but it emphasizes the negative aspects of Tom's education, and therefore is a worse answer than C. C is the best answer.

17. A fifth-grade teacher has two computers in his classroom for students to use. He has noticed that students who do not have computers at home are far less likely to use the classroom computers than are students who do have computers at home. What should the teacher do to increase the classroom computer use of students who do not have computers at home?

A. Give informal basic computer lessons to these students during their regular recess time.

B. Require all students to spend a minimum amount of time on the classroom computer each week.

C. Develop a computer project with easy-to-follow instructions that will allow the students to build confidence in using the computer.

D. Talk to the students about the importance of technology in education and in the rest of their lives.

C   This question tests Competency 002: The teacher understands student diversity and knows how to plan learning experiences and design assessments that are responsive to differences among students and that promote all students' learning.

Here's How to Crack It

Step 1: Identify the scenario.

- Age range: fifth grade

- Goal: increase students' computer use

Step 2: Use POE to narrow down the answer choices.

A. No. That seems punitive.

B. No. That also seems punitive, and those students already familiar with computers don't need the required time.

C. Maybe.

D. No. A hands-on approach is better.

Step 3: Make a final decision.

Choice C is best.

18. A new eighth-grade American history teacher is planning the upcoming school year. What would be the best first step for her to take in the planning process?

A. Determine the number of topics that can be effectively covered during the school year.

B. Make a list of the topics she would like to teach.

C. Reach out to history teachers at other schools for assistance.

D. Determine the curriculum themes required by the course and the best order in which to teach them.

D This question tests Competency 003: The teacher understands procedures for designing effective and coherent instruction and assessment based on appropriate learning goals and objectives.

Here's How to Crack It

Step 1: Identify the scenario.

- Age range: eighth grade

- Goal: determine the first step in a new teacher's planning process

Step 2: Use POE to narrow down the answer choices.

A. Maybe. Let's see what else there is.

B. No. What the teacher wants to teach is irrelevant.

C. No. Not as a first step.

D. Yes. There are state requirements that a teacher should look at first.

Step 3: Make a final decision.

Choice D is the best answer.

19. A fourth-grade teacher has broken up her class into groups. The groups will work together on a report on a continent. Although the requirements of the group report have been very clearly defined, the teacher has noticed that a couple of the groups are having problems focusing on what needs to be done. What would be the teacher's best approach to this situation?

A. Assign each group a leader to determine the direction of the group.

B. Assign each student in the troubled groups a specific portion of the report.

C. Reassign the students having trouble to other groups.

D. Remind the students how much this report will be reflected in their final class grade.

B This question tests Competency 006: The teacher understands strategies for creating an organized and productive learning environment and for managing student behavior.

Here's How to Crack It

Step 1: Identify the scenario.

- Age range: fourth grade

- Goal: fix a small-group problem

Step 2: Use POE to narrow down the answer choices.

A. No. If the group couldn't figure out a direction together, there's no reason to believe an individual leader will be able to.

B. Maybe. That seems very hands-on, but let's see what else there is.

C. No. That would suggest to the students that they'd failed, and involves no teaching on the part of the teacher.

D. No. That's punitive and does nothing to help solve the problem.

Step 3: Make a final decision.

Choice B is the best answer. While it is usually better for students to work out details of who's the leader, who's doing what, how to approach the task, and so on, it is sometimes necessary for the teacher to get involved. If the group's at a standstill, the teacher will likely need to step in to get things moving again. In addition, the other three answers were clearly worse.

20. A seventh-grade teacher has broken up his class into groups. The groups are to work together on a presentation and each member of the group will have specific tasks to complete. At the end of the project, each group will complete an evaluation of their own group's performance. The likely purpose of this evaluation is to:

   A. help students review their own effectiveness.

   B. help the teacher determine each group member's grades on the project.

   C. help the teacher understand the dynamics of each group.

   D. allow students to participate in determining their own grade.

A   This question tests Competency 004: The teacher understands learning processes and factors that impact student learning and demonstrates this knowledge by planning effective, engaging instruction and appropriate assessments.

Here's How to Crack It

Step 1: Identify the scenario.

- Age range: seventh grade

- Goal: determine the purpose of students' self-evaluation

Step 2: Use POE to narrow down the answer choices.

   A. Maybe. Seventh graders should be able to do that.

   B. No. The question said that each member had specific tasks, so the teacher should be able to assess individual performance.

   C. No. The teacher could better evaluate that through informal observation while the groups are working.

   D. No. Seventh graders are too young to do that.

Step 3: Make a final decision.
The best answer is A.

21. A sixth-grade mathematics teacher is grading a paper from one of his students and sees that she has correctly multiplied all the numbers on her homework but frequently misplaced the decimal point. Which of the following comments could he leave on her paper that would be the most effective in correcting this mistake?

A. Please review these questions again.

B. Great job on the multiplication problems but be careful with your decimal points. Come see me at my desk for a quick review of placing decimal points.

C. You've missed too many questions. Please come see me for a review.

D. Good job on knowing your multiplication tables but too many answers are still wrong.

B This question tests Competency 010: The teacher monitors student performance and achievement; provides students with timely, high-quality feedback; and responds flexibly to promote learning for all students.

Here's How to Crack It

Step 1: Identify the scenario.

- Age range: sixth grade

- Goal: determine most effective comment

Step 2: Use POE to narrow down the answer choices.
We're looking for an answer that praises the good work and suggests ways of improving in those areas that need it. Let's see what we've got:

A. No. That offers no praise.

B. Yes. That sounds good.

C. No. That offers no praise.

D. No. That offers praise, but no help in correcting the errors.

Step 3: Make a final decision.
The best answer is B.

22. Mrs. Burney's fifth-grade class will begin working on their state projects soon. Prior to assigning the projects to the students, Mrs. Burney visits the librarian to ensure the availability of many different types of resources. What is the most important benefit in having various resources available to the students for their state reports?

   A. ensuring there are sufficient resources overall for the students to use

   B. allowing students to choose how they will research their assigned states

   C. providing additional resources in case all computer terminals are full

   D. giving the students time to work on their projects

B This question tests Competency 003: The teacher understands procedures for designing effective and coherent instruction and assessment based on appropriate learning goals and objectives.

Here's How to Crack It

Step 1: Identify the scenario.

- Age range: fifth grade

- Goal: identify benefit of many resources

Step 2: Use POE to narrow down the answer choices.

   A. Maybe, but the question emphasizes the variety. Keep it for now.

   B. Maybe. This answer choice addresses variety (emphasized in the question) and suggests student choice (usually a good thing).

   C. No. Computers are only one resource.

   D. No. Time is irrelevant.

Step 3: Make a final decision.
The question emphasizes the variety of resources available, and only choice B addresses the importance of variety, because that would provide a range of options for students. B is the best answer.

23. The average fifth-grade student would be likely to have the most difficulty with which of the following?

   A. understanding the written rules of the classroom

   B. following verbal instructions

   C. sitting quietly after finishing work while waiting for others to finish

   D. understanding the dynamics of peer relationships

D This question tests Competency 001: The teacher understands human developmental processes and applies this knowledge to plan instruction and ongoing assessment that motivate students and are responsive to their developmental characteristics and needs.

Here's How to Crack It

Step 1: Identify the scenario.

- Age range: fifth grade

- Goal: identify the situation that would give a student difficulty

Step 2: Use POE to narrow down the answer choices.

A. No. A fifth grader can do that.

B. No. A fifth grader can do that, too.

C. Maybe. Sitting quietly can be difficult for students of all ages.

D. More likely than answer choice C.

Step 3: Make a final decision.
Many adults have difficulty understanding the dynamics of peer relationships. While sitting quietly is difficult for some fifth graders, understanding peer relationships is more difficult. The best answer is D.

24. Which of the following would be correct to instruct students to do when they use information from the Internet in a report?

   A. Try to locate the same information in a book or magazine.

   B. Cite the website as a source.

   C. Do not cite the website as a source.

   D. Cite the website only when using exact words from the site.

B This question tests Competency 009: The teacher incorporates the effective use of technology to plan, organize, deliver, and evaluate instruction for all students.

Here's How to Crack It

Step 1: Identify the scenario.

- Age range: none given

- Goal: determine the correct instruction

Step 2: Use POE to narrow down the answer choices.
The Internet should be treated as any other source. Let's see what we've got:

A. No. The Internet is a valid source in and of itself.

B. Yes. Sources should be cited.

C. No. Again, sources should be cited.

D. No. Sources must be cited even when information is paraphrased.

Step 3: Make a final decision.
B is the best answer.

25. Mr. Walters will be the physical education teacher for a coeducational group. To plan activities for the group, Mr. Walters should:

   A. develop two distinct grading systems—one for the boys, one for the girls.

   B. avoid activities the boys might consider too girlish.

   C. plan activities of interest to both the boys and girls.

   D. separate the boys from girls during their physical education class.

C   This question tests Competency 002: The teacher understands student diversity and knows how to plan learning experiences and design assessments that are responsive to differences among students and that promote all students' learning.

Here's How to Crack It

Step 1: Identify the scenario.

- Age range: none given

- Goal: determine coed activities

Step 2: Use POE to narrow down the answer choices.

A. No. That introduces an inappropriate gender distinction.

B. No. That's also inappropriate.

C. Yes. That's a good idea.

D. No. That also introduces an inappropriate gender distinction.

Step 3: Make a final decision.
The best answer is C.

26. A new fifth-grade teacher is trying to decide how to best encourage students to follow her classroom code of conduct. Which of the following would be most effective for her?

    A.   Include the students in the development of the code of conduct.

    B.   Apply the code of conduct in a flexible manner.

    C.   Ensure that she lists all behavior that will NOT be accepted.

    D.   Occasionally offer rewards to those who follow the code of conduct.

A   This question tests Competency 006: The teacher understands strategies for creating an organized and productive learning environment and for managing student behavior.

Here's How to Crack It

Step 1: Identify the scenario.

- Age range: fifth grade

- Goal: encourage students to follow conduct guidelines

Step 2: Use POE to narrow down the answer choices.

    A. Maybe. Fifth graders could be included in that discussion.

    B. No. That's the last thing you should do with a code of conduct.

    C. No. That's impossible. There are too many unacceptable behaviors to list.

    D. Maybe. That might encourage good behavior.

Step 3: Make a final decision.

In general, motivation should be internal rather than external, so students are more likely to follow behavior guidelines if students were involved in their creation than if an external reward is occasionally offered. The best answer is A.

27. What would be the best teaching plan for a middle-school teacher whose class includes students of varying levels of cognitive development?

  A. group the students according to ability on a regular basis

  B. experiment with the manner in which content is taught so as to target all students

  C. develop instruction aimed at students with the lowest level of development

  D. suggest tutoring to parents of students with lower levels of cognitive development

B This question tests Competency 001: The teacher understands human developmental processes and applies this knowledge to plan instruction and ongoing assessment that motivate students and are responsive to their developmental characteristics and needs.

Here's How to Crack It

Step 1: Identify the scenario.

- Age range: middle school

- Goal: determine teaching plan for a developmentally wide-ranging class

Step 2: Use POE to narrow down the answer choices.

  A. Maybe. Let's see what else is there.

  B. Maybe. "Experiment" seems a little vague.

  C. No. That will bore all the other students.

  D. No. It's the teacher's responsibility to teach.

Step 3: Make a final decision.

We're down to choices A and B. Which would the SBEC prefer, to break up the class regularly, or to develop teaching skills to accommodate all students? The SBEC would prefer the latter, so the best answer is B.

28. A teacher planning for a new school year can *best* use the evaluations from her students' previous teachers when:

  A. determining the seating chart for the school year.

  B. deciding what field trips might be appropriate.

  C. scheduling assessments and testing.

  D. choosing lessons that will meet the needs of the students.

D This question tests Competency 003: The teacher understands procedures for designing effective and coherent instruction and assessment based on appropriate learning goals and objectives.

Here's How to Crack It

Step 1: Identify the scenario.

- Age range: none given

- Goal: determine best use of previous student evaluations

Step 2: Use POE to narrow down the answer choices.

A. No. That doesn't have much of an educational value.

B. No. That doesn't sound like a "best" use.

C. Maybe. Let's leave it in.

D. Maybe. Hold onto this one, too.

Step 3: Make a final decision.

It seems a bit early to schedule assessments, but previous evaluations might be useful in planning lessons. The best answer is D.

29. An eighth-grade teacher starts a new chapter from the American History textbook by asking the students what they know about the Great Depression. What does the teacher probably hope to do by starting the lesson with this question?

    A. Allow the students to answer freely.

    B. Learn what knowledge the students already have about the subject.

    C. Determine what sections of the chapter the teacher can skip.

    D. Separate the students based on level of previous knowledge.

B This question tests Competency 005: The teacher knows how to establish a classroom climate that fosters learning, equity, and excellence and uses this knowledge to create a physical and emotional environment that is safe and productive.

Here's How to Crack It

Step 1: Identify the scenario.

- Age range: eighth grade

- Goal: determine why a teacher asks about previous knowledge

Step 2: Use POE to narrow down the answer choices.

    A. No. That doesn't have anything to do with beginning a new chapter.

    B. Maybe.

    C. No. That makes things easier on the teacher.

    D. No. There's nothing to suggest that the teacher is going to use small-group instruction.

Step 3: Make a final decision.
The best answer is B.

30. A seventh-grade class will prepare and give a presentation on a country they have chosen. The students have begun to prepare and are asking to be allowed to incorporate multimedia aspects into their presentation. The teacher is concerned that students will devote too much of their time to the visual aspects of the presentation instead of the written content of the presentation. What steps could the teacher take to prevent this?

    A. Agree to the students' request with the provision they do not devote too much time to the visual aspects.

    B. Adjust the grading scale so that only 10% of the grade is based on the look of the presentation.

    C. Monitor the students' progress on their presentations.

    D. Not allow the multimedia aspects as part of the presentation.

B   This question tests Competency 009: The teacher incorporates the effective use of technology to plan, organize, deliver, and evaluate instruction for all students.

Here's How to Crack It

Step 1: Identify the scenario.

- Age range: seventh grade

- Goal: prevent overemphasis on visual aspects of a presentation

Step 2: Use POE to narrow down the answer choices.

    A. Maybe.

    B. Maybe.

    C. No. That wouldn't be effective.

    D. No. That's rigid and inflexible.

Step 3: Make a final decision.
We're down to choices A and B. Seventh grade is a bit too young to allow students to be wholly responsible for structuring their own time. Choice B provides an effective incentive for them to spend most of their time on the nonvisual aspects of their presentation. The best answer is B.

31. A teacher is meeting with Sam's parents to discuss Sam's repeated problems with finishing his homework by the due date. His parents explain that he has a very busy after-school schedule with sports practices. Which of the following would be the most appropriate action for the teacher to take?

   A. Strongly recommend to the parents that they help their son develop a standard study time so that his schoolwork does not fall behind.

   B. Allow Sam time during the school day to complete his homework.

   C. Speak with the sports coach about Sam's problem with completing assignments.

   D. Suggest to the parents that they take their son's schoolwork more seriously.

A   This question tests Competency 011: The teacher understands the importance of family involvement in children's education and knows how to interact and communicate effectively with families.

Here's How to Crack It

Step 1: Identify the scenario.

- Age range: none given

- Goal: deal with Sam's time management troubles

Step 2: Use POE to narrow down the answer choices.
When dealing with parents, a teacher needs to be polite but still address the concerns that need to be addressed.

   A. Maybe. That seems polite, and it certainly addresses the issue.

   B. No. That's unwarranted.

   C. No. This is a problem that Sam, his parents, and his teacher should solve.

   D. No. That sounds harsh and impolite.

Step 3: Make a final decision.
The best answer is A.

32. Mrs. Martin tries her hardest to give immediate feedback to students on their assignments. The students benefit from this practice because:

    A.   they will be less likely to be surprised by their final grades.

    B.   parents are kept aware of their student's progress.

    C.   they are most likely to respond favorably to feedback that is timely.

    D.   they know their homework score has been recorded.

C   This question tests Competency 008: The teacher provides appropriate instruction that actively engages students in the learning process.

Here's How to Crack It

Step 1: Identify the scenario.

- Age range: none given

- Goal: determine why students benefit from immediate feedback

Step 2: Use POE to narrow down the answer choices.

    A.   No. That wouldn't require immediate feedback.

    B.   No. That's not a benefit for the students.

    C.   Maybe.

    D.   That's not as strong as choice C.

Step 3: Make a final decision.
C is the best answer.

33. A seventh-grade teacher has seen some of her students smoking off campus and wants to impress upon them the dangers of smoking. Which of the following would be the most effective manner of conveying this?

    A.   inviting a guest speaker to discuss the hazards of smoking

    B.   handing out pamphlets and anti-tobacco literature

    C.   having a fellow student speak about losing his father to lung cancer caused by cigarette smoking

    D.   the school hosting a "stay smoke-free" pep rally

C This question tests Competency 001: The teacher understands human developmental processes and applies this knowledge to plan instruction and ongoing assessment that motivate students and are responsive to their developmental characteristics and needs.

Here's How to Crack It

Step 1: Identify the scenario.

- Age range: seventh grade

- Goal: effectively communicate the dangers of smoking

Step 2: Use POE to narrow down the answer choices.

A. Maybe, but don't you remember tuning those people out when you were in school?

B. No. That won't have much of an effect.

C. Maybe. That could be very powerful.

D. No. That does nothing to address the dangers of smoking.

Step 3: Make a final decision.
Choice C is the best answer.

34. A music teacher is planning to take her classes to a symphony performance. The students will travel by bus. One of the students uses a wheelchair and the teacher is unsure what she is required to do to transport this student. She should:

    A. ask the parents to provide transportation.

    B. make sure the student has interest in going to the symphony.

    C. arrange transportation through the transportation department for this student as for all of the others.

    D. make arrangements for the student to skip the field trip and listen to a taped performance at a later time.

C This question tests Competency 002: The teacher understands student diversity and knows how to plan learning experiences and design assessments that are responsive to differences among students and that promote all students' learning.

Here's How to Crack It

Step 1: Identify the scenario.

- Age range: none given

- Goal: accommodate a student's transportation needs

Step 2: Use POE to narrow down the answer choices.
Students with special needs should be accommodated to the fullest extent possible.

A. No. Transportation is the school's responsibility.

B. No. Are other students being asked if they want to go?

C. Yes.

D. No. The student's needs can be accommodated.

Step 3: Make a final decision.
The best answer is C.

35. A teacher has a few students in his class that require additional instruction from the reading lab teacher. Which of the following times would be best to send the students needing this extra help to the reading lab?

A. while the rest of the students attend recess

B. after school

C. while the rest of the class attends art class

D. during center time when students work individually

D This question tests Competency 002: The teacher understands student diversity and knows how to plan learning experiences and design assessments that are responsive to differences among students and that promote all students' learning.

Here's How to Crack It

Step 1: Identify the scenario.

- Age range: none given

- Goal: determine the best time to send students to the reading lab

Step 2: Use POE to narrow down the answer choices.

    A. No. That makes the reading lab seem like a punishment.

    B. No. That also makes the reading lab seem like a punishment.

    C. No. Missing art class is not an acceptable solution.

    D. Yes. Because students are working on individual activities, this would be a good time.

Step 3: Make a final decision.
The best answer is D.

> 36. Which of the following is the most effective method for evaluating and grading group collaborations?
>
>   A.   multiple-choice testing
>
>   B.   peer evaluations
>
>   C.   group self-evaluation
>
>   D.   frequent informal observation

D   This question tests Competency 010: The teacher monitors student performance and achievement; provides students with timely, high-quality feedback; and responds flexibly to promote learning for all students.

Here's How to Crack It

Step 1: Identify the scenario.

- Age range: none given

- Goal: identify the most effective method of assessing group collaborations

Step 2: Use POE to narrow down the answer choices.

    A. No. Part of what needs to be graded is the group interaction. Cross out A.

    B. No. The grade range isn't specified, but it is unlikely that students in the fourth- to eighth-grade range would possess the maturity needed for peer evaluation.

    C. Maybe, but fourth–eighth still seems young.

    D. Yes. Informal observation would be most effective.

Step 3: Make a final decision.
The best choice is D.

37. A fourth-grade teacher realizes that Patrick rushes through his seatwork making careless errors so that he can move on to group activities with his friends. What is the best step for the fourth-grade teacher to take?

A. Allow Patrick to redo the work during recess time if necessary.

B. Remove Patrick from group activities until his seatwork improves.

C. Require Patrick to work on seatwork for a set amount of time.

D. Have Patrick's report card grades reflect his poor attention to seatwork.

C This question tests Competency 006: The teacher understands strategies for creating an organized and productive learning environment and for managing student behavior.

Here's How to Crack It

Step 1: Identify the scenario.

- Age range: fourth grade

- Goal: stop Patrick from rushing through his seatwork

Step 2: Use POE to narrow down the answer choices.

A. No. That doesn't address the underlying time management issue.

B. Maybe, but it seems punitive. Is there something better?

C. Maybe, but it doesn't seem to offer a real solution.

D. No. That is punitive, and offers no solution.

Step 3: Make a final decision.
Neither of the remaining answer choices offer a real solution to the problem, but choice C isn't punitive, and is therefore the best answer.

38. Which type of computer software would be best to demonstrate scientific experiments not feasible for the classroom?

A. simulation

B. word processing

C. spreadsheet

D. database

A This question tests Competency 009: The teacher incorporates the effective use of technology to plan, organize, deliver, and evaluate instruction for all students.

Here's How to Crack It

Step 1: Identify the scenario.

- Age range: none given

- Goal: identify appropriate software

Step 2: Use POE to narrow down the answer choices.

A. Yes, that sounds right.

B. No. Word-processing software is most often used to write and edit documents.

C. No. This is best used to store and manipulate numbers.

D. No. Databases are most often used to store and sort information.

Step 3: Make a final decision.

Even if you don't know what simulation software is, you could eliminate the other three choices. The best answer is A.

39. At the beginning of the school year, a seventh-grade government teacher informs the students they will be studying their city government, and that the teacher will allow the students to choose the destination of the field trip that will be part of this unit. The teacher's probable purpose is:

   A. to create a positive attitude in the classroom.

   B. to involve the students in their own learning.

   C. to be able to come to a consensus on where the field trip will be.

   D. to research different field trip options.

B This question tests Competency 005: The teacher knows how to establish a classroom climate that fosters learning, equity, and excellence and uses this knowledge to create a physical and emotional environment that is safe and productive.

Here's How to Crack It

Step 1: Identify the scenario.

- Age range: seventh grade

- Goal: identify teacher's purpose in allowing students to determine their own field trip destination

Step 2: Use POE to narrow down the answer choices.

    A. Maybe.

    B. Maybe.

    C. No. That's not the purpose, although that's a step the students will take.

    D. No. That's not the purpose, although that's also a step the students will take.

Step 3: Make a final decision.

We're down to two possible answer choices. One mentions an educational objective, and the other doesn't. The best answer is B.

40. While dropping off her daughter at school one morning, a parent asks her daughter's teacher her opinion on paying students for good grades. What would be the teacher's best response?

    A. Let the parent know this goes against her educational philosophies.

    B. Schedule a time to discuss the issue with the parent at a later date and give reasons for opinions.

    C. Let the mother know it is inappropriate to discuss at that time.

    D. Refrain from giving an opinion one way or the other.

B This question tests Competency 011: The teacher understands the importance of family involvement in children's education and knows how to interact and communicate effectively with families.

Here's How to Crack It

Step 1: Identify the scenario.

- Age range: none given

- Goal: respond to a parent's question

Step 2: Use POE to narrow down the answer choices.
When dealing with parents, address the concern without offense.

A. No. We don't know if that's the case. And even if it were, it would be difficult for the teacher to fully explain her position on a complicated issue through a rolled-down car window.

B. Yes. The issue warrants a discussion.

C. No. That doesn't address the parent's concern, and might offend.

D. No. The parent asked for an opinion.

Step 3: Make a final decision.
The best answer is B.

41. Which of the following gives an example of divergent thinking?

    A. memorizing a song in music class

    B. reciting multiplication tables in math class

    C. finding different uses for milk cartons in art class

    D. reading a book in front of the rest of the class

C This question tests Competency 007: The teacher understands and applies principles and strategies for communicating effectively in varied teaching and learning contexts.

Here's How to Crack It

Step 1: Identify the scenario.

- Age range: none given

- Goal: identify the example of divergent thinking

Step 2: Use POE to narrow down the answer choices.

A. No. Memorization doesn't involve divergent thinking.

B. No. That's also rote memorization and recall.

C. Yes. That involves multiple solutions.

D. No. That's a learnable skill, not divergent thinking.

Step 3: Make a final decision.
The best answer is C.

42. A teacher just moved to Texas and would like to learn more about exactly what is tested on the TEKS. He will attend a TEKS seminar and workshop with other teachers from his new school. This teacher:

A. is dedicated to his students.

B. understands the TEKS.

C. has located local resources for teachers.

D. must first register with a professional organization.

C This question tests Competency 012: The teacher enhances professional knowledge and skills by effectively interacting with other members of the educational community and participating in various types of professional activities.

Here's How to Crack It

Step 1: Identify the scenario.

- Age range: none given

- Goal: identify what the teacher has done

Step 2: Use POE to narrow down the answer choices.

A. Perhaps, but that's not proven with information in the question.

B. No. That's why he's taking the seminar.

C. Yes. That's definitely true.

D. No. There's no such requirement.

Step 3: Make a final decision.
C is the best answer.

43. The fifth-grade class has an annual competition in the spring. The students must design and make a container in which a raw egg will be dropped from atop a ladder. The student who creates a container that prevents the egg from breaking from the highest height will win the competition. When designing these containers, students use:

A. convergent thinking.

B. creativity.

C. curiosity.

D. communication skills.

B   This question tests Competency 004: The teacher understands learning processes and factors that impact student learning and demonstrates this knowledge by planning effective, engaging instruction and appropriate assessments.

Here's How to Crack It

Step 1: Identify the scenario.

- Age range: fifth grade

- Goal: identify students' thought processes

Step 2: Use POE to narrow down the answer choices.

    A. Maybe. A student might have decided upon one plan from multiple choices.

    B. Yes. Whatever solution a student came up with would have involved creativity.

    C. No. Students wouldn't necessarily have to be curious.

    D. No. Students were working alone.

Step 3: Make a final decision.
Although it's possible that a student's decision-making strategy involved the use of convergent thinking, the question doesn't definitively say so. The best answer is B.

44.   Students in a math class are studying graphs. For homework, the teacher has assigned students to measure a phenomenon and graph the results. The students will each be allowed to choose their own phenomena and, as a result, there will be an increase in:

    A. the number of students who will complete the assignment.

    B. questions about how to complete the homework.

    C. communication between students.

    D. interest in the homework because students control its direction.

D   This question tests Competency 008: The teacher provides appropriate instruction that actively engages students in the learning process.

Here's How to Crack It

Step 1: Identify the scenario.

- Age range: none given

- Goal: identify the result of letting students choose their own phenomena

Step 2: Use POE to narrow down the answer choices.

    A.   Maybe. Let's see what else there is.

    B.   No. If anything, this should reduce questions.

    C.   No. There's no need for the students to communicate.

    D.   Maybe. Offering choices to students often increases interest.

Step 3: Make a final decision.

There's no proof offered for answer choice A, but choice D gives a compelling rationale, and is therefore the best answer.

45.   A relatively new teacher finds one student a particular challenge due to his behavior. This student often breaks the class rules or disrupts the classroom. The teacher would like to improve her effectiveness in dealing with this student's behavior. Which of the following would probably be most helpful to her?

    A.   keeping a journal in which she records how she responds to his behavior problems each day and whether or not her response was effective

    B.   searching for resources in the library that might help her improve her effectiveness in dealing with this student

    C.   attending a workshop or seminar with role-playing designed to help improve classroom management

    D.   observing a teacher who has taught this student in the past

A   This question tests Competency 012: The teacher enhances professional knowledge and skills by effectively interacting with other members of the educational community and participating in various types of professional activities.

Here's How to Crack It

Step 1: Identify the scenario.

- Age range: none given

- Goal: identify most helpful action when dealing with recalcitrant student

Step 2: Use POE to narrow down the answer choices.

    A. Maybe. That would give the teacher an opportunity for self-analysis.

    B. Maybe. The teacher might find useful information there.

    C. No. That would take too long.

    D. No. Observing the teacher now wouldn't make a difference unless the teacher happened to have an equivalently difficult student.

Step 3: Make a final decision.

This one's tough. But because choice B is unlikely to provide specific information about the student and choice A would force the teacher to look for patterns of behavior and response, it's likely that the teacher would get more benefit out of choice A.

46. During physical education class, a female student complains to the teacher, "It isn't fair for the whole class to have to do pull-ups; pull-ups are for boys." The teacher's *first* response should be to:

    A. separate the girls from the boys and select different activities for the two groups.

    B. stop class to discuss gender stereotypes.

    C. examine his own behavior to make sure he is not promoting this stereotype.

    D. ask other girls in the class if they agree with the statement.

C   This question tests Competency 002: The teacher understands student diversity and knows how to plan learning experiences and design assessments that are responsive to differences among students and that promote all students' learning.

Here's How to Crack It

Step 1: Identify the scenario.

- Age range: none given

- Goal: identify the teacher's first response to gender-bias-related comment

Step 2: Use POE to narrow down the answer choices.

    A. No. That would reinforce the stereotype.

    B. No. That's an overreaction.

    C. Maybe.

    D. No. That's lending credence to the stereotype.

Step 3: Make a final decision.
Notice that the question asks what the teacher's *first* response should be. In that context, stopping to examine his own behavior is the best response. The best answer is C.

47. Mrs. White is getting a computer in her classroom for the first time. Before allowing students to use it, she must first:

    A.   learn to use it herself.

    B.   install student protection software.

    C.   develop a way to monitor students closely while on the computer.

    D.   obtain permission slips from all parents.

B   This question tests Competency 009: The teacher incorporates the effective use of technology to plan, organize, deliver, and evaluate instruction for all students.

Here's How to Crack It

Step 1: Identify the scenario.

- Age range: none given

- Goal: identify what a teacher must do

Step 2: Use POE to narrow down the answer choices.
Notice that the question says must, so this must be a legal requirements question. You should already know the answer.

    A.   No. Of course this would be helpful, but it is not a legal requirement.

    B.   Yes. This is a legal requirement.

    C.   No. This is something the teacher might, in fact, do, but it is not a legal requirement.

    D.   No. This is not necessary.

Step 3: Make a final decision.
The best answer is B.

48. A new school year is starting and a teacher should primarily consider what aspect when arranging students' desks in the classroom?

    A.   her teaching style in the classroom

    B.   the students' previous conduct grades

    C.   the location of windows in the classroom

    D.   the number of boys versus girls in the class

A This question tests Competency 005: The teacher knows how to establish a classroom climate that fosters learning, equity, and excellence and uses this knowledge to create a physical and emotional environment that is safe and productive.

Here's How to Crack It

Step 1: Identify the scenario.

- Age range: none given

- Goal: identify what the teacher should think about when arranging desks

Step 2: Use POE to narrow down the answer choices.

A. Maybe. Teaching style might impact classroom setup.

B. No. That's not giving students the chance to improve.

C. Maybe. This might be a consideration.

D. No. That's not relevant.

Step 3: Make a final decision.

Although choices A and C could both be correct, A goes directly to an educational concern, and is therefore the best answer.

49. Which of the following would be an effective use of an internal network of computers in a school?

  A. sharing students' grades with other teachers

  B. communication between teachers and administrators

  C. locating a staff member

  D. student access to the Internet

B This question tests Competency 009: The teacher incorporates the effective use of technology to plan, organize, deliver, and evaluate instruction for all students.

Here's How to Crack It

Step 1: Identify the scenario.

- Age range: none given

- Goal: identify effective use of an internal network

Step 2: Use POE to narrow down the answer choices.

    A. No. That's inappropriate.

    B. Maybe.

    C. No. A paging system would work well for that, but not a computer network.

    D. No. An internal network isn't connected to the Internet.

Step 3: Make a final decision.
The best answer is B.

50. A fourth-grade teacher's class is returning from a visit to NASA. The teacher has the students write the answer to the following two questions in their daily school journals:

> 1) What did I learn at NASA?
>
> 2) What did I like most that I saw at NASA?

The primary purpose of these journal entries is to:

    A. allow the teacher to learn if the class enjoyed the field trip.

    B. inform parents of the activities of the day.

    C. help the students realize what they may have learned.

    D. provide a keepsake memory for the students.

C   This question tests Competency 004: The teacher understands learning processes and factors that impact student learning and demonstrates this knowledge by planning effective, engaging instruction and appropriate assessments.

Here's How to Crack It

Step 1: Identify the scenario.

- Age range: fourth grade

- Goal: identify the purpose of journal entries

Step 2: Use POE to narrow down the answer choices.
The purpose of journal entries is to allow students to reflect on the day's activities. Let's see what the choices are:

    A. No. That's not the primary purpose.

    B. No. Journals wouldn't do that.

    C. Yes. That's close to the idea of reflection.

    D. No. That's not the primary purpose.

Step 3: Make a final decision.
C is the best answer.

51.   To motivate his middle school choral group, Mr. Song-bird should consider:

    A. requiring students who do not participate in class to attend detention after school.

    B. allowing students the opportunity to choose one or more of the songs they will perform.

    C. distributing small prizes to students who participate fully.

    D. assigning failing grades to students who do not participate in class.

B   This question tests Competency 008: The teacher provides appropriate instruction that actively engages students in the learning process.

Here's How to Crack It

Step 1: Identify the scenario.

- Age range: middle school

- Goal: motivate the choir

Step 2: Use POE to narrow down the answer choices.
Motivation should be internal. Let's see what the choices are:

    A. No. That's punitive.

    B. Yes. That would create internal motivation.

    C. No. That's external motivation.

    D. No. That's also punitive.

Step 3: Make a final decision.
B is the best answer.

52. A teacher has just begun a new school year and has a recently mainstreamed student who is profoundly deaf. The teacher suspects the student should not have been mainstreamed but has a responsibility to the student to:

A. make the best of a bad situation.

B. spend significant time one-on-one with this student.

C. exhaust all resources available to the special needs student before recommending another evaluation.

D. meet with the student's parents to discuss what can and cannot be done to improve the situation.

C   This question tests Competency 013: The teacher understands and adheres to legal and ethical requirements for educators and is knowledgeable of the structure of education in Texas.

Here's How to Crack It

Step 1: Identify the scenario.

- Age range: none given

- Goal: determine the teacher's responsibility to a deaf student

Step 2: Use POE to narrow down the answer choices.

A. No. The SBEC would not approve of that answer.

B. Maybe. This is something the teacher might do.

C. Maybe. This is broader than B and, as such, sounds like a better answer.

D. No. That's not the responsibility the teacher has to the student.

Step 3: Make a final decision.
Although the teacher may spend significant time with the student, the primary responsibility is to actively pursue all available avenues to help teach the student. The best answer is C.

53. A sixth-grade language arts class is reading a passage. To help develop the students' critical reading skills, the teacher could follow the reading with what exercise?

A. a class discussion about what evidence the author provided in the passage

B. a class discussion about what the students agree or disagree with in the passage

C. a multiple-choice quiz about the passage

D. an assignment to identify the main parts of the passage such as purpose, conclusion, etc.

A   This question tests Competency 007: The teacher understands and applies principles and strategies for communicating effectively in varied teaching and learning contexts.

Here's How to Crack It

Step 1: Identify the scenario.

- Age range: sixth grade

- Goal: develop critical reading skills

Step 2: Use POE to narrow down the answer choices.

- A.   Maybe. This would directly address the students' understanding of the author's work and critical reading skills.

- B.   Maybe. This might work, but we really want to know if the students understand what the author has written.

- C.   No. That would test recall.

- D.   No. That doesn't involve reading critically.

Step 3: Make a final decision.

Notice that the goal is to improve critical reading skills. While a class discussion about what students agree or disagree with might prove beneficial, only answer choice A specifically deals with critical reading skills. The best answer is A.

54.   Mr. Smith has assigned his class to write a letter to the English department thanking them for their generosity. The primary purpose of this letter is:

- A.   to have the students use a new letter-writing style learned in class recently.

- B.   to have the students recognize the value of establishing long-term relationships.

- C.   for the teacher to evaluate the students' grammar and sentence structure.

- D.   to have the students practice socially acceptable behavior.

D   This question tests Competency 001: The teacher understands human developmental processes and applies this knowledge to plan instruction and ongoing assessment that motivate students and are responsive to their developmental characteristics and needs.

Here's How to Crack It

Step 1: Identify the scenario.

- Age range: seventh grade

- Goal: identify primary purpose of a thank-you letter

Step 2: Use POE to narrow down the answer choices.
You write thank-you notes because it's polite. Let's see what the choices are:

A. No. This might be a good exercise to reinforce a newly learned letter-writing style, but it is not the primary purpose for writing the thank-you notes.

B. Maybe, but this is unlikely to be a long-term relationship.

C. No. In context, that's not the primary purpose.

D. Yes. That matches our initial idea about politeness.

Step 3: Make a final decision.
The best answer is D.

55. After receiving the letters from the students, the English department director emails Mr. Smith thanking him for the students' letters and suggesting that the field trip be repeated in future years. Mr. Smith shares this email with his students primarily so that they will:

A. value people's time.

B. understand the purpose of attending the play.

C. consider attending the university.

D. remember to thank people.

D This question tests Competency 008: The teacher provides appropriate instruction that actively engages students in the learning process.

Here's How to Crack It

Step 1: Identify the scenario.

- Age range: seventh grade

- Goal: identify why Mr. Smith shared the letter with his students

Step 2: Use POE to narrow down the answer choices.
He did it to show that people are polite to you when you're polite to them.

A. No. This has nothing to do with the question.

B. No. That wasn't the purpose of attending the play.

C. No. Attending the university or not is not the focus of this lesson.

D. Yes. That comes closest to what we're looking for.

Step 3: Make a final decision.
D is the best answer.

56. A teacher is shocked when a boy in her class is over-heard telling a friend that only girls can be dancers. The teacher should react to this situation by doing which of the following?

    A. Invite a male dancer to the next career day with other men and women who speak about their professions.

    B. Invite both a female and male dancer to speak to the class.

    C. Rent a tape of a ballet to show to the class.

    D. Have students write a report about a famous man who earned his living as a dancer.

A This question tests Competency 002: The teacher understands student diversity and knows how to plan learning experiences and design assessments that are responsive to differences among students and that promote all students' learning.

Here's How to Crack It

Step 1: Identify the scenario.

- Age range: none given

- Goal: react to a gender-biased situation

Step 2: Use POE to narrow down the answer choices.

    A. Maybe. This would address the gender bias both as it relates to professional dance and other professions.

    B. No. A is a better choice because it involves more professions than dance.

    C. No. The more diverse choice is better.

    D. No. That's punitive.

Step 3: Make a final decision.
A is the best answer.

57. The fifth-grade teachers have noticed that the students returning to the new school year are not as prepared as they should be with regard to their math skills. The fourth-grade teachers include several new teachers that, in retrospect, admit they may not have covered all topics that should have been covered. The fifth-grade teachers are working with the fourth-grade teachers this year to prevent the same thing from happening next school year. This is an example of which of the following?

    A. teachers collaborating to improve their students' education

    B. teachers learning better communication skills

    C. teachers correcting flaws in their curriculum

    D. teachers expecting too much from younger colleagues

A This question tests Competency 012: The teacher enhances professional knowledge and skills by effectively interacting with other members of the educational community and participating in various types of professional activities.

Here's How to Crack It

Step 1: Identify the scenario.

- Age range: fourth and fifth grades

- Goal: identify the type of communication

Step 2: Use POE to narrow down the answer choices.

    A. Maybe. The teachers are communicating and addressing a goal.

    B. Maybe. This involves improving communication.

    C. No. It wasn't a flaw in the curriculum, just its execution.

    D. No. They weren't expecting too much.

Step 3: Make a final decision.

Of choices A and B, choice A discusses a tangible educational advantage and is therefore the best answer.

58. Which of the following would a teacher want to make sure to avoid doing to a student who needs to develop a more positive level of self-esteem?

    A. assigning projects to the student that he will be able to accomplish

    B. offering praise to the student and others for accomplishing tasks

    C. rewarding the student with privileges for successfully completing class work

    D. praising the student for actions that he may not have completed

D This question tests Competency 005: The teacher knows how to establish a classroom climate that fosters learning, equity, and excellence and uses this knowledge to create a physical and emotional environment that is safe and productive.

Here's How to Crack It

Step 1: Identify the scenario.

- Age range: none given

- Goal: identify the action to avoid

Step 2: Use POE to narrow down the answer choices.

    A. No. That's a good thing for the teacher to do.

    B. No. That's also a good thing for the teacher to do.

    C. No. That's also a good thing for the teacher to do.

    D. Yes. That won't develop self-esteem. Self-esteem comes from successfully accomplishing things.

Step 3: Make a final decision.
The best answer is D.

59. A fifth-grade math teacher will begin discussing basic geometry with his students in the next lesson. Before starting the lesson, he asks his students to identify a wide variety of shapes. His probable reason for doing this is to:

   A. determine what students already know about the lesson.

   B. know how best to arrange the seating chart for the class.

   C. eliminate the need to find examples of these shapes.

   D. determine how much of the lesson can be skipped.

A The question tests Competency 003: The teacher understands procedures for designing effective and coherent instruction and assessment based on appropriate learning goals and objectives.

Here's How to Crack It

Step 1: Identify the scenario.

- Age range: fifth grade

- Goal: determine why the teacher asks students to identify shapes

Step 2: Use POE to narrow down the answer choices.

   A. Yes. If he's going to introduce a new unit, he should find out what students already know.

   B. No. The seating chart is irrelevant.

   C. No. Examples might still prove useful.

   D. No. That makes life easier for the teacher.

Step 3: Make a final decision.
The best answer is A.

60. Middle school health teachers know the importance of education for teenagers about the consequences of alcohol and drug use. It is difficult to get through to students at this age because:

   A. they don't want to be lectured to by adults who might have behaved similarly when they were teenagers.

   B. they can't imagine anything really bad happening to them; it always happens to someone else.

   C. they don't believe the information and studies on drug and alcohol use are true.

   D. they don't care about hurting themselves.

B The question tests Competency 001: The teacher understands human developmental processes and applies this knowledge to plan instruction and ongoing assessment that motivate students and are responsive to their developmental characteristics and needs.

Here's How to Crack It

Step 1: Identify the scenario.

- Age range: none given

- Goal: identify why students are not receptive to anti-drug messages

Step 2: Use POE to narrow down the answer choices.

   A. Maybe. Middle school students might feel this way.

   B. Maybe. This answer identifies an aspect of psychological development, making it a good possibility.

   C. No. We don't know what they believe.

   D. No. That's not likely to be true.

Step 3: Make a final decision.
Although choice A might be correct, choice B is more consistent with common psychological patterns among middle school students. The best answer is B.

61. A sixth-grade social studies class is discussing the office of president when a student asks, "How come the president has all the power but Congress makes the laws?" The teacher writes the words "checks and balances" on the board and then asks the students for the definitions of the words in order to:

   A. keep the students involved in the class by requiring their participation.

   B. set up the link between their forthcoming knowledge of the U.S. system of government and their previous understanding of the words "checks" and "balances."

   C. turn the discussion from social studies to mathematics.

   D. determine which students have read the assigned chapter material.

B   The question tests Competency 007: The teacher understands and applies principles and strategies for communicating effectively in varied teaching and learning contexts.

Here's How to Crack It

Step 1: Identify the scenario.

- Age range: sixth grade

- Goal: identify the teacher's purpose in writing words on the board

Step 2: Use POE to narrow down the answer choices.

   A. Maybe, but that doesn't seem like it has much to do with the lesson.

   B. Yes. That's likely.

   C. No. The words are relevant to the discussion at hand.

   D. No. That's not the purpose.

Step 3: Make a final decision.

Although choice A might be one reason the teacher asks for the definitions, choice B is a better answer in the context of the scenario.

62. What role should parents take regarding standardized test scores?

    A.   Assume the school will notify the parents if there is a problem.

    B.   Encourage the student to do his/her best, as the student would on any exam.

    C.   Meet with the teacher to address any concerns or questions about the testing.

    D.   Keep standardized assessment scores from the student.

C   This question tests Competency 010: The teacher monitors student performance and achievement; provides students with timely, high-quality feedback; and responds flexibly to promote learning for all students.

Here's How to Crack It

Step 1: Identify the scenario.

- Age range: none given

- Goal: identify the role parents should take regarding standardized test scores

Step 2: Use POE to narrow down the answer choices.

    A.   No. Parents should take a more active role than that.

    B.   Maybe. This seems like a good idea.

    C.   Maybe. This is a positive, proactive role.

    D.   No. Students should have access to their scores.

Step 3: Make a final decision.
Although parents might want to take the action described in choice B, the question asks about the parents' role regarding the scores. Choice C is therefore the best answer.

63. Requiring a class to clean up its classroom after an in-school holiday party is an example of:

    A.   the students taking responsibility for the condition of their environment.

    B.   the teacher modeling respect for others' property.

    C.   the need for stronger parental involvement at the school.

    D.   punishment for inappropriate behavior.

A This question tests Competency 006: The teacher understands strategies for creating an organized and productive learning environment and for managing student behavior.

Here's How to Crack It

Step 1: Identify the scenario.

- Age range: none given

- Goal: identify the example

Step 2: Use POE to narrow down the answer choices.

A. Maybe. This looks good.

B. Maybe. This might work.

C. No. Students should be expected to clean up after themselves.

D. No. There has been no inappropriate behavior.

Step 3: Make a final decision.
The question specified that the students were cleaning up, so choice B is incorrect. The best answer is A.

64. A fourth-grade teacher is looking for a book to read together as a class with her students. When choosing a book to read, she should:

    A. search for books the fourth-grade students would enjoy reading themselves.

    B. search for books related to topics already covered in class.

    C. search for books students have probably never heard of.

    D. search for books without difficult vocabulary.

A This question tests Competency 003: The teacher understands procedures for designing effective and coherent instruction and assessment based on appropriate learning goals and objectives.

Here's How to Crack It

Step 1: Identify the scenario.

- Age range: fourth grade

- Goal: identify characteristics of a book

Step 2: Use POE to narrow down the answer choices.

A. Maybe, but then why would they need the book read aloud?

B. Maybe, but why would that be important?

C. No. There's no reason the students shouldn't have heard of the books.

D. No. That's one way for students to learn vocabulary.

Step 3: Make a final decision.
We're down to choices A and B. In the absence of any other information, the teacher should be trying to inculcate a love of reading, so A is the best answer.

65. Which type of thinking would a creative writing assignment entitled, "If I had $1,000, I would…" develop?

A. convergent

B. affective

C. memory recall

D. brainstorming

D This question tests Competency 007: The teacher understands and applies principles and strategies for communicating effectively in varied teaching and learning contexts.

Here's How to Crack It

Step 1: Identify the scenario.

- Age range: none given

- Goal: identify a type of thinking

Step 2: Use POE to narrow down the answer choices.

A. No. That involves picking the best of many responses.

B. No. Affective thinking deals with emotional response to an action.

C. No. It's unlikely that many students have a memory of spending $1,000.

D. Yes. Students would likely think of many ways of spending the $1,000.

Step 3: Make a final decision.
D is the best answer.

66. A seventh-grade English teacher is preparing to have his class start reading a novel. Before the students start reading the novel, he first asks the students to give definitions of some vocabulary words such as *plot, climax, theme, autobiography,* etc. What is his primary purpose for asking these questions?

   A. To select resources that will be used by the students.

   B. To determine if the students will also watch the movie version of the book.

   C. To informally assess the students' current knowledge of the parts of a novel.

   D. To identify budding authors in the group.

C This question tests Competency 003: The teacher understands procedures for designing effective and coherent instruction and assessment based on appropriate learning goals and objectives.

Here's How to Crack It

Step 1: Identify the scenario.

- Age range: seventh grade

- Goal: determine the purpose of a vocabulary quiz

Step 2: Use POE to narrow down the answer choices.
It sounds as if the teacher is preparing the students to analyze the novel. Let's see what the choices are:

   A. No. How would that help determine the resources?

   B. No. That's irrelevant.

   C. Yes. That's possible.

   D. No. That's irrelevant.

Step 3: Make a final decision.
Even though it's not exactly what we were looking for, C is the best answer.

67. If Ms. Piper is able to follow goal 4, the students are more likely to:

    A.   feel free to talk during class time.

    B.   develop communication skills.

    C.   be motivated to participate in class activities.

    D.   sit quietly while working on seatwork.

C   This question tests Competency 008: The teacher provides appropriate instruction that actively engages students in the learning process.

Here's How to Crack It

Step 1: Identify the scenario.

- Age range: fourth grade

- Goal: identify what students will do if their teacher learns what they are interested in personally

Step 2: Use POE to narrow down the answer choices.

    A. No. That would be a negative consequence.

    B. No. There's no link to communication skills.

    C. Maybe.

    D. No. That wouldn't help students sit quietly.

Step 3: Make a final decision.
C is the best answer.

68. During art class, students are paired together. Each pair includes a more artistically inclined student and a less artistically inclined student. Students will prepare art projects while giving feedback to their partners to help them improve their art projects. Which of the following practices of Ms. Piper's is most likely to lend success to this arrangement?

    A.   Goal 1, the students must be patient with each other.

    B.   Goal 2, smiling at another student will lessen hurtful words.

    C.   Goal 4, knowing students' interests will help them give each other suggestions.

    D.   Goal 5, demonstrating encouragement has taught the students how best to respond.

D   This question tests Competency 010: The teacher monitors student performance and achievement; provides students with timely, high-quality feedback; and responds flexibly to promote learning for all students.

Here's How to Crack It

Step 1: Identify the scenario.

- Age range: fourth grade

- Goal: determine which of Ms. Piper's goals will transfer to the students to help this project succeed

Step 2: Use POE to narrow down the answer choices.

A.   No. Patience won't help the project succeed.

B.   No. This project requires constructive criticism.

C.   No. Knowing each other's interests won't necessarily help the project.

D.   Maybe. Encouragement is probably important.

Step 3: Make a final decision.
This seems like a strange question, but D is the best answer.

69.   Ms. Piper could best anticipate that students will follow the classroom's code of conduct if she first:

A.   asks the students to help develop the code of conduct.

B.   follows goal 1.

C.   clearly outlines the punishment for each behavior in the code of conduct.

D.   follows goal 2.

A   This question tests Competency 006: The teacher understands strategies for creating an organized and productive learning environment and for managing student behavior.

Here's How to Crack It

Step 1: Identify the scenario.

- Age range: fourth grade

- Goal: determine the circumstances under which students will be most likely to follow the code of conduct

Step 2: Use POE to narrow down the answer choices.

A. Yes. Students at this age are just starting to be able to develop their own rules of conduct.

B. No. Too much patience might actually have an adverse effect.

C. No. This takes a negative view.

D. No. Relying on smiling is not a good way to manage a classroom.

Step 3: Make a final decision.
A is the best answer.

70. Mrs. Grant has paired up students. Each pair of students will work together for three minutes to spell new words from the letters in a word Mrs. Grant will write on the board. The team with the most new words will win a special prize. Which type of thinking does this activity require?

A. motivated

B. parallel

C. convergent

D. divergent

D This question tests Competency 008: The teacher provides appropriate instruction that actively engages students in the learning process.

Here's How to Crack It

Step 1: Identify the scenario.

- Age range: none given

- Goal: identify a type of thinking

Step 2: Use POE to narrow down the answer choices.

A. No. There's no such thing as motivated thinking.

B. No. There's parallel play, but not parallel thinking.

C. No. That involves deciding on one best solution.

D. Yes. That's divergent thinking.

Step 3: Make a final decision.
D is the best answer.

71. A music teacher explains to her class the importance of the phrase "every good boy does fine" to help them remember the location of notes written on music sheets. This information is an example of which of the following?

   A. rote memory

   B. memory trick

   C. mnemonics

   D. chunking

C   This question tests Competency 004: The teacher understands learning processes and factors that impact student learning and demonstrates this knowledge by planning effective, engaging instruction and appropriate assessments.

Here's How to Crack It

Step 1: Identify the scenario.

- Age range: none given

- Goal: categorize the given information

Step 2: Use POE to narrow down the answer choices.
The question says we're looking for a memory aid of some kind. Let's see what we've got:

   A. No. That's repetition.

   B. Maybe, but that doesn't sound like a real name.

   C. Yes. That's what this sort of memory aid is called.

   D. No. That's splitting up ideas into small pieces.

Step 3: Make a final decision.
C is the best answer.

72. Two sixth-grade girls have been caught fighting on the school grounds. Their teacher's primary goal should be to do what?

   A. Determine which of the two students is the aggressor.

   B. Teach the girls how to work through their problems without becoming physical.

   C. Work with the school administration to transfer one of the girls to another classroom.

   D. Separate the girls from each other in as many activities as possible.

B   This question tests Competency 006: The teacher understands strategies for creating an organized and productive learning environment and for managing student behavior.

Here's How to Crack It

Step 1: Identify the scenario.

- Age range: sixth grade

- Goal: identify the teacher's primary goal

Step 2: Use POE to narrow down the answer choices.
Clearly, the teacher's goal should be to keep them from fighting.

A.   No. That won't keep them from fighting.

B.   Yes. That might work.

C.   No. The teacher should be able to solve his or her own problems.

D.   Maybe. Physical separation might stop the girls from fighting, but it doesn't teach them how to respond differently to each other or to resolve problems in a more acceptable manner. They'll undoubtedly come into contact with each other at some point, and then what?

Step 3: Make a final decision.
Although choice D might stop the girls from fighting, it's a temporary solution at best, and doesn't address the real issue. Choice B describes the teacher's primary goal, and is therefore the best answer.

73.   Before taking a field trip, a teacher must do which of the following according to Texas law?

A.   obtain written permission from a parent/guardian

B.   obtain a written release of liability from a parent/ guardian

C.   verify all medical information is on file for the students

D.   arrange for students to make up work missed in other classes

A   This question tests Competency 013: The teacher understands and adheres to legal and ethical requirements for educators and is knowledgeable of the structure of education in Texas.

Here's How to Crack It

Step 1: Identify the scenario.

- Age range: none given

- Goal: identify legal requirement

Step 2: Use POE to narrow down the answer choices.
You should know this one: written permission from the parent or guardian is required.

A. Yes. This is it.

B. No. Permission, not release from liability, is legally required.

C. No. This is a good idea, but not legally required.

D. No. This may or may not be necessary, but it is not legally required.

Step 3: Make a final decision.
A is the best answer.

74. During a parent open house evening at the school, a teacher encourages parents to ask their students what they have learned each day because remembering this information and relating it will help increase the students' understanding of the topic. By talking to the parents about this, the teacher has demonstrated that she:

    A. understands the importance family can play in a student's education.

    B. believes the families are not involved enough in the student's education.

    C. communicates openly with her students.

    D. is confident in her student's talking about her teaching ability.

A This question tests Competency 011: The teacher understands the importance of family involvement in children's education and knows how to interact and communicate effectively with families.

Here's How to Crack It

Step 1: Identify the scenario.

- Age range: none given

- Goal: identify the importance of talking to parents

Step 2: Use POE to narrow down the answer choices.
According to the SBEC, teachers and parents should be equal partners in students' education. Let's see what the choices are:

A. Yes. That suggests equal partnership.

B. No. That might antagonize the parents.

C. No. That doesn't deal with the parent/teacher partnership.

D. No. That doesn't deal with the parent/teacher partnership.

Step 3: Make a final decision.
The best answer is A.

75. Mrs. Sparks is meeting with Tony's parents to recommend that they consider holding Tony back a year and have him repeat the fourth grade. What should Mrs. Sparks first discuss with the parents during this difficult meeting?

   A. List the objectives that fourth graders are required to master.

   B. Relate the increase in responsibility and independence expected of students in fifth grade.

   C. Talk about the academic improvements Tony has made in the past school year.

   D. List the legal options of the parents and make sure they understand them.

C This question tests Competency 011: The teacher understands the importance of family involvement in children's education and knows how to interact and communicate effectively with families.

Here's How to Crack It

Step 1: Identify the scenario.

- Age range: fourth grade

- Goal: identify first topic of discussion with parents

Step 2: Use POE to narrow down the answer choices.
Remember the rule: address the issue without offending the parents.

   A. Maybe. Leave it in.

   B. Maybe, but this seems like the flip side of choice A.

   C. Maybe. It's a good idea to start with the positives.

   D. No. That's offensive and cold.

Step 3: Make a final decision.
If the teacher does choice A or B first, then the teacher is in the uncomfortable position of then explaining how Tony doesn't measure up. If the teacher begins with explaining some good things, then parents may be more receptive to the bad news later. The best answer is C.

76. After the meeting is called to order, Ms. Greene begins by asking the students what they know about how to recycle. This is important because:

   A. the project must allow the students to learn something new.

   B. students should have already researched the project.

   C. Ms. Greene wants the students to be aware of how much work may be involved.

   D. Ms. Greene does not know much about recycling herself.

C This question tests Competency 004: The teacher understands learning processes and factors that impact student learning and demonstrates this knowledge by planning effective, engaging instruction and appropriate assessments.

Here's How to Crack It

Step 1: Identify the scenario.

- Age range: middle school

- Goal: identify why the question is important

Step 2: Use POE to narrow down the answer choices.

We're looking for something that suggests that Ms. Greene wants to make sure that the students are organized and have a plan worked out.

   A. No. There's no evidence to support that.

   B. Maybe. This might be helpful in assessing what the students know about recycling.

   C. Maybe. This might help the students understand what will be involved in the project.

   D. No. The students are not responsible for educating Ms. Greene.

Step 3: Make a final decision.

We're down to choices B and C, and neither one exactly matches what we are looking for. There's nothing to suggest that the students should have already researched the project—researching is probably a good first step—so the best answer is C.

77. Students have developed a list of questions asking why the school does not recycle that Ms. Greene does not know the answer to. She should encourage the students to find the answers by:

    A. finding a custodian right then and talking to him/her about recycling.

    B. developing a committee to study the problem, meet with administrators, and return to the council with a report.

    C. researching recycling on the Internet.

    D. accompanying her to a meeting already scheduled with the principal the next day.

B   This question tests Competency 008: The teacher provides appropriate instruction that actively engages students in the learning process.

Here's How to Crack It

Step 1: Identify the scenario.

- Age range: middle school

- Goal: determine how Ms. Greene should help

Step 2: Use POE to narrow down the answer choices.

It sounds like Ms. Greene should help the students organize their thoughts and approach the administration. Let's see what the choices are:

    A. No. A custodian is unlikely to be able to answer the administrative questions. In addition the words *right then* suggest that this answer choice is unlikely.

    B. Yes. That's very close to what we're looking for.

    C. No. That wouldn't answer questions specific to the school.

    D. No. The previously scheduled meeting wouldn't be about recycling. Besides, the students should be in charge of scheduling the time.

Step 3: Make a final decision.

B is the best answer.

78. As one portion of the recycling project, students want to deliver newspapers they've collected to the recycling center. To arrange this, Ms. Greene *must*:

    A.   obtain written permission from the school office.

    B.   obtain written permission from the parents/guardians.

    C.   accompany the students to the recycling center.

    D.   encourage the students to ask their parents to take them.

B   This question tests Competency 013: The teacher understands and adheres to legal and ethical requirements for educators and is knowledgeable of the structure of education in Texas.

Here's How to Crack It

Step 1: Identify the scenario.

- Age range: middle school

- Goal: identify what the teacher must do

Step 2: Use POE to narrow down the answer choices.
This sounds like a legal requirements question. The teacher must obtain written parental permission.

    A.   No. This may be part of the school's procedure for planning field trips, but it is not a legal requirement.

    B.   Yes. This is a legal requirement.

    C.   No. This is not necessary or legally required.

    D.   No. This is not a good answer. The class is working together on the project and should be encouraged to work together on each aspect of the project.

Step 3: Make a final decision.
B is the best answer.

79. Shortly before the trip to the recycling center, Ms. Greene is greeted one morning by a parent explaining that she will not allow her son, who incidentally first conceived of this project, to participate in the field trip. Ms. Greene should:

   A. accept the parent's decision about her son and thank the parent for informing her.

   B. try to explain to the parent the educational benefit her son would gain from the trip.

   C. listen to the parent and ask her to reconsider and allow her son to complete what he has started.

   D. try to determine why the parent is not allowing her son to participate.

C This question tests Competency 011: The teacher understands the importance of family involvement in children's education and knows how to interact and communicate effectively with families.

Here's How to Crack It

Step 1: Identify the scenario.

- Age range: middle school

- Goal: deal with parent

Step 2: Use POE to narrow down the answer choices.
As always, the teacher should address the issue without upsetting the parent.

   A. No. The teacher doesn't address the issue.

   B. No. That doesn't acknowledge the parent's control.

   C. Maybe. "Listening" is usually a good way to start.

   D. Maybe. Determining why the parent doesn't want the student to go may or may not help.

Step 3: Make a final decision.
We're down to choices C and D. Choice C explicitly says that the teacher should listen to the parent, so it better fits our general notion of not upsetting parents. The best answer is C.

80. Leaving the responsibility for researching the recy-cling project with the students on the student council provides what benefit?

A. The teacher is able to devote the time it would have taken her to research the project to something else.

B. The students are empowered by being in charge of their own learning process.

C. The students will be able to measure what they have learned at the end of the project.

D. The teacher will be able to see what level of dedication the students have for this project.

B This question tests Competency 003: The teacher understands procedures for designing effective and coherent instruction and assessment based on appropriate learning goals and objectives.

Here's How to Crack It

Step 1: Identify the scenario.

- Age range: middle school

- Goal: identify the benefit of letting the student council research its own activity

Step 2: Use POE to narrow down the answer choices.
Students learn better and enjoy learning more if they have appropriate control over their education. Let's see what we've got:

A. No. That's an advantage for the teacher.

B. Maybe. Answers that involve empowering students are usually good.

C. No. Planning the activity wouldn't necessarily give students that benefit.

D. No. That's an advantage for the teacher.

Step 3: Make a final decision.
B is the best answer.

81. Ms. Greene has been asked to send one of the students who worked on this project to the school board meeting to discuss the findings of the project and end report. Which of the following would be the best way to decide which student will represent the group?

   A.   Ms. Greene will send the student she feels contributed the most to the project.

   B.   Ms. Greene will ask the students to select the student who can best represent the project to the school board.

   C.   Ms. Greene will hold a random lottery to choose a student.

   D.   The school principal will choose a student.

B   This question tests Competency 006: The teacher understands strategies for creating an organized and productive learning environment and for managing student behavior.

Here's How to Crack It

Step 1: Identify the scenario.

- Age range: middle school

- Goal: determine the best way to choose a student representative

Step 2: Use POE to narrow down the answer choices.

   A.   Maybe. Having the teacher select the representative would work, but it wouldn't reinforce the student-centered control that the project promoted.

   B.   Maybe. This is better than A, because it empowers the students.

   C.   No. That's arbitrary.

   D.   No. Ms. Greene doesn't need to involve the principal.

Step 3: Make a final decision.

In the absence of any compelling reason why faculty should make a decision such as this, it's best to let the students make their own decisions. The best answer is B.

82. Mary comes to school one day in tears and, after much discussion, confides in you that her stepfather touched her inappropriately. What are you required to do?

A. Report the incident to the police for investigation.

B. Determine if there is enough truth in Mary's story to accuse the stepfather.

C. Ask Mary's mother if she has any knowledge of the incident.

D. Report the accusation to all involved parties.

A This question tests Competency 013: The teacher understands and adheres to legal and ethical requirements for educators and is knowledgeable of the structure of education in Texas.

Here's How to Crack It

Step 1: Identify the scenario.

- Age range: none given

- Goal: identify a requirement

Step 2: Use POE to narrow down the answer choices.
This must be a legal requirements question, and you should already know the answer.

A. Yes. That's a legal requirement.

B. No. You must report an accusation of this nature to the proper authorities.

C. No. You must report an accusation of this nature to the proper authorities.

D. No. You must report an accusation of this nature to the proper authorities.

Step 3: Make a final decision.
A is the best answer.

83. If a teacher asks her students to brainstorm solutions to a problem, the teacher is asking the students to do which of the following?

A. rapidly think through all options

B. come up with as many ideas as possible

C. evaluate ideas quickly

D. think of creative solutions

B This question tests Competency 007: The teacher understands and applies principles and strategies for communicating effectively in varied teaching and learning contexts.

Here's How to Crack It

Step 1: Identify the scenario.

- Age range: none given

- Goal: define *brainstorming*

Step 2: Use POE to narrow down the answer choices.

A. No. Evaluating the options isn't brainstorming.

B. Maybe. This sounds good.

C. No. That's similar to choice A.

D. Maybe. Possible.

Step 3: Make a final decision.

Be careful here. Although brainstorming can be used to stimulate creative thinking, each solution itself needn't be creative. Brainstorming is just the process of coming up with possible solutions. The best answer is B.

84. Michelle approaches her teacher in the hallway in a very excited state and is obviously upset with the teacher. The teacher takes Michelle aside and asks her to explain clearly what she is upset about. The purpose for trying to clarify what Michelle has said is to:

    A. signal to Michelle that she is being taken seriously.

    B. calm Michelle down.

    C. provide a starting point to their discussion.

    D. give Michelle the opportunity to realize she should not approach her teacher in this way.

C This question tests Competency 007: The teacher understands and applies principles and strategies for communicating effectively in varied teaching and learning contexts.

Here's How to Crack It

Step 1: Identify the scenario.

- Age range: none given

- Goal: determine why the teacher asked Michelle for clarification

Step 2: Use POE to narrow down the answer choices.

    A. No. Michelle expects to be taken seriously.

    B. Maybe. This might defuse the situation and help Michelle articulate her concerns.

    C. Maybe. It is important to establish a starting point for the discussion.

    D. No. Michelle might be too upset to realize that.

Step 3: Make a final decision.

Although calming Michelle down might be a side benefit and allow a conversation to proceed, the teacher asks Michelle to explain in an effort to determine what the matter is and begin to address it. The best answer is C.

85. A sixth-grade class has just completed a project during which the students worked in small groups. The teacher has already assigned grades to the students but has not yet told the students their grades. The teacher would like the students to evaluate their own contributions to their group before he tells them their grades. This exercise is most likely to:

    A. identify which students did not contribute as much as others.

    B. demonstrate that sixth graders' self-evaluation skills are heavily influenced by their friends.

    C. identify who took the leadership role in each group.

    D. reveal discrepancies between the self-evaluations and the teacher's evaluation.

D   This question tests Competency 010: The teacher monitors student performance and achievement; provides students with timely, high-quality feedback; and responds flexibly to promote learning for all students.

Here's How to Crack It

Step 1: Identify the scenario.

- Age range: sixth grade

- Goal: determine why the teacher asked students to evaluate themselves

Step 2: Use POE to narrow down the answer choices.
The question referred to the teacher's grades several times. We can expect that the right answer will link two ideas.

A. No. Self-evaluation wouldn't necessarily reveal which students contributed less than others.

B. No. That doesn't relate to the material in the question.

C. No. The teacher would have determined that through informal observation.

D. Yes. That would be a good use of the self-evaluations.

Step 3: Make a final decision.
The best answer is D.

86. Teachers should use which of the following to help them track and compute grades for students?

A. a grade book

B. a calculator

C. a computer spreadsheet

D. a ledger

C   This question tests Competency 009: The teacher incorporates the effective use of technology to plan, organize, deliver, and evaluate instruction for all students.

Here's How to Crack It

Step 1: Identify the scenario.

- Age range: none given

- Goal: choose the best tool for tracking and computing grades

Step 2: Use POE to narrow down the answer choices.

A. Maybe, but unlikely.

B. No. That couldn't track grades.

C. Yes. Spreadsheets are good tools for organizing and storing information.

D. No, and we can cross out choice A now, too.

Step 3: Make a final decision.
The best answer is C.

87. A teacher has noticed that Lola suddenly seems unmotivated and withdrawn. The teacher calls Lola's parents. Which of the following would most likely help Lola the most?

   A. The teacher should not be the one to contact the parents.

   B. The teacher asks the parents to have Lola tested.

   C. The teacher shares with Lola's parents her concerns about the negative impact of Lola's home environment on her education.

   D. The teacher asks for the parents' help understanding what might be going on with Lola's behavior.

D   This question tests Competency 010: The teacher monitors student performance and achievement; provides students with timely, high-quality feedback; and responds flexibly to promote learning for all students.

Here's How to Crack It

Step 1: Identify the scenario.

- Age range: none given

- Goal: determine what would best help Lola

Step 2: Use POE to narrow down the answer choices.

   A. No. It's appropriate for the teacher to contact the parents.

   B. No. There's no evidence that Lola needs to be tested.

   C. No. We're not told anything about Lola's home life, and even if we were, that would be an antagonistic opening for a discussion.

   D. Yes. This addresses the problem and is respectful of the parents.

Step 3: Make a final decision.
D is the best answer.

88. Mrs. Graham, a fifth-grade teacher, has learned that one of her students, Alexis, is frequently shuttled between several different households. As a result, Alexis often arrives late to school and often without the items she needs for the day. To help Alexis, Mrs. Graham should:

    A.   have Alexis visit the school counselor.

    B.   notify the proper authorities.

    C.   provide a predictable and stable environment at school.

    D.   review Alexis's past years' records.

C   This question tests Competency 002: The teacher understands student diversity and knows how to plan learning experiences and design assessments that are responsive to differences among students and that promote all students' learning.

Here's How to Crack It

Step 1: Identify the scenario.

- Age range: fifth grade

- Goal: help Alexis

Step 2: Use POE to narrow down the answer choices.

    A. No. There's nothing to suggest that Alexis is facing any psychological problems.

    B. No. There's no suspicion of abuse.

    C. Maybe.

    D. No. That's irrelevant.

Step 3: Make a final decision.
C is the best answer.

89. Mrs. McNeil is a new teacher and subscribes to professional teaching journals. The greatest value the journals provide is:

    A.   in supporting causes Mrs. McNeil feels are important in her field.

    B.   in offering additional resources to solve common teaching issues.

    C.   in helping Mrs. McNeil remain current on trends in education and technology.

    D.   they will serve as a resource for Mrs. McNeil in several years.

B This question tests Competency 012: The teacher enhances professional knowledge and skills by effectively interacting with other members of the educational community and participating in various types of professional activities.

Here's How to Crack It

Step 1: Identify the scenario.

- Age range: none given

- Goal: determine the greatest benefit of subscribing to journals

Step 2: Use POE to narrow down the answer choices.
Teachers subscribe to journals to get new information. Let's see what the choices are:

A. No. That's not relevant to getting new information.

B. Maybe.

C. Maybe.

D. No. That's not about getting new information.

Step 3: Make a final decision.
Choices B and C both are compelling reasons to subscribe to journals. In light of Mrs. McNeil's relative inexperience, it is likely that she will find practical day-to-day information in her journals that may be useful. The best answer is B.

90. A middle school teacher will soon start a new chapter with her students about electricity. She plans to take her students to the Natural History Museum where there are hands-on exhibits for the students to "play" with. This field trip will most likely encourage the students':

A. curiosity

B. imagination

C. dependency

D. good behavior

A This question tests Competency 004: The teacher understands learning processes and factors that impact student learning and demonstrates this knowledge by planning effective, engaging instruction and appropriate assessments.

Here's How to Crack It

Step 1: Identify the scenario.

- Age range: middle school

- Goal: determine result of field trip

Step 2: Use POE to narrow down the answer choices.

A. Maybe.

B. Maybe.

C. No. If anything, the exhibits should encourage independence.

D. No. That doesn't address the idea of the hands-on experiments.

Step 3: Make a final decision.

Choices A and B could both be correct. Because the question specifically deals with science experiments, it is more likely that students' curiosity would be encouraged more than their imaginations. The best answer is A.

91. Mr. Will's eighth-grade history class will be spending the next week debating battle strategies of different wars. He has rearranged the desks in the classroom into a horseshoe in order to:

A. allow all students to see each other and encourage open discussion.

B. allow himself to monitor the debate easily from the center of the room.

C. pit the two sides of the horseshoe against each other for a livelier debate.

D. ensure participation by everyone in the debates.

A This question tests Competency 005: The teacher knows how to establish a classroom climate that fosters learning, equity, and excellence and uses this knowledge to create a physical and emotional environment that is safe and productive.

Here's How to Crack It

Step 1: Identify the scenario.

- Age range: eighth grade

- Goal: determine why Mr. Will rearranged the desks

Step 2: Use POE to narrow down the answer choices.

A. Maybe.

B. No. That makes life easier for the teacher.

C. No. There may be more than two sides.

D. Maybe. How would this desk arrangement ensure participation?

Step 3: Make a final decision.

Choices A and D could both be correct, but choice D uses very strong language. Would arranging the desks necessarily ensure total participation? No. A is the best answer.

92. To measure the success of a new classroom procedure, the teacher should have:

    A.   an unbiased observer's opinion.

    B.   high expectations.

    C.   defined goals before starting.

    D.   a survey for students to fill out.

C   This question tests Competency 003: The teacher understands procedures for designing effective and coherent instruction and assessment based on appropriate learning goals and objectives.

Here's How to Crack It

Step 1: Identify the scenario.

- Age range: none given

- Goal: determine the requirements to measure the success of a new procedure

Step 2: Use POE to narrow down the answer choices.

We're given no information regarding the nature of the procedure, so the answer must be very general.

    A. Maybe. An open mind is important.

    B. No. Measuring the success of a new procedure wouldn't require high expectations.

    C. Maybe. To measure success, there must be established goals.

    D. No. We're not sure of the nature of the procedure.

Step 3: Make a final decision.

Upon further reflection, it makes sense that measuring success would require a benchmark to measure it against. The best answer is C.

93. To *best* evaluate a student who suffers from severe testing anxiety, the teacher should:

    A.   allow the student extra time to complete the test.

    B.   allow the student to take the test home to complete.

    C.   informally observe the student on several occasions.

    D.   permit the student to take the test more than one time.

C   This question tests Competency 010: The teacher monitors student performance and achievement; provides students with timely, high-quality feedback; and responds flexibly to promote learning for all students.

Here's How to Crack It

Step 1: Identify the scenario.

- Age range: none given

- Goal: evaluate a student who suffers from testing anxiety

Step 2: Use POE to narrow down the answer choices.
We're looking for a supplemental assessment method.

    A.   No. That's not a different method.

    B.   No. That's not a different method.

    C.   Yes. That's a different method.

    D.   No. That's not a different method.

Step 3: Make a final decision.
C is the best answer.

94.   What must a teacher do if he/she learns a student may have brought a weapon to the school campus?

    A.   Call the police immediately.

    B.   Confront the student.

    C.   Try to establish there is in fact a weapon.

    D.   Notify other teachers.

A   This question tests Competency 013: The teacher understands and adheres to legal and ethical requirements for educators and is knowledgeable of the structure of education in Texas.

Here's How to Crack It

Step 1: Identify the scenario.

- Age range: none given

- Goal: identify a teacher's action

Step 2: Use POE to narrow down the answer choices.
This is a legal requirements question since it uses the word *must*.

    A.   Yes. A teacher is, indeed, required to call the authorities if a student is suspected of bringing a weapon to school.

    B.   No. This could be dangerous.

    C.   No. This is for the authorities to determine.

    D.   No. The teacher might, in fact, do this, but it is not legally required.

Step 3: Make a final decision.
Choice A is the only legal requirement.

12

TExES 8–12
Practice Test

Directions: Each question in this practice test is a multiple-choice question with four answer choices. Read each question carefully and choose the ONE best answer.

1. Students in a high school speech class have begun using technology in their presentations. The teacher wants to continue to allow students to do so but is concerned that the look of the presentation is becoming more important to the students than the substance of their speech. The best way to motivate the students to continue to incorporate technology without compromising content would be to do which of the following?

A. Give the students on outline of how much time they should spend at home on each aspect of their speeches.

B. Let the students know that 90% of their grade will be based on content, 10% on the use of technology.

C. Require that the students complete the content of their speeches before beginning to work on how to present them.

D. Allow the students to work with a partner where one works on content and the other works on using technology.

2. A high school Spanish teacher has several beginning classes that include both students who speak only English as well as students who speak Spanish regularly at home. The students who already speak Spanish tend not to participate in the class. What would be the best option for the teacher to motivate all students to participate?

A. Rearrange the classroom to create groups that include both types of students.

B. Separate the groups and give each group its own assignment.

C. Increase the importance of class participation in the final grade.

D. Include a variety of activities that would provide information that would be new to all students.

3. The most important benefit to be gained from a teacher's planning which science units will be covered and in what order in her class is to:

A. allow parents to know what their children are studying.

B. ensure there will be enough time during the school year to cover the required units.

C. remove the stress of determining this later in the school year when teachers are busier.

D. teach the information in a logical or natural sequence to help improve retention.

4. A high school chemistry teacher requires all students to carefully follow the safety rules even when the students are not working with dangerous chemicals because:

A. establishing a standard of behavior in the lab creates a safer, more efficient learning environment.

B. it allows the teacher to spend less time checking to make sure the safety rules have been followed.

C. one set of rules is easier for the teacher to follow than multiple sets of rules.

D. all chemicals can be dangerous.

5. When asking parents to participate in a project with their chidren, the teacher should make sure to give the parents which of the following pieces of information to ensure the success of the collaboration?

A. the amount of time the teacher expects the project will take

B. the method by which the project will be graded

C. the teacher's expectations of both the student and the parents

D. an example of what the project should end up looking like

Use the information below to answer the two questions that follow.

An eighth-grade science class is studying what effects conditions such as music or talking have on plants. Each student is first asked to give his opinion as to what will make the plant grow best. Then each student is given a small plant equal in size to those given to the other students and assigned a condition that he will need to replicate at home.

6. Including the students in the discussion prior to the experiment will help them learn to do which of the following?

    A. Develop a hypothesis and then test it.

    B. Understand the purpose of this experiment.

    C. Choose conditions for their portion of the experiment.

    D. Understand the importance of starting with equal-sized plants.

7. The teacher sends the plants home with the students and includes notes for both the students and parents explaining the importance of replicating conditions so that the experiment will be valid. This exercise is most likely intended to teach the students:

    A. how each student's work relates to that of the other students.

    B. the importance of having objective data.

    C. that one student's work, done incorrectly, can void the entire class's experiment.

    D. responsibility for themselves.

◆ ◆ ◆ ◆ ◆ ◆ ◆ ◆

8. A teacher's primary responsibility after witnessing a fight between two students is to:

A. determine which student started the fight.

B. act as a judge in settling the argument in a fair manner.

C. help the students work through their problem without violence.

D. report the incident to the school administration.

9. Which of the following is the most important aspect of designing a system used to evaluate students?

A. testing students in a variety of ways to accommodate different learning styles

B. developing test questions difficult enough to determine the highest level of retention

C. aligning test questions with the educational goals of the unit or chapter

D. ensuring that each test question can have only one possible answer

10. Mrs. Cole has requested a parent/teacher conference to discuss what she feels is an unfair punishment given to her son for his showing up 20 minutes late to class. The teacher should do which of the following at this conference?

A. Listen to Mrs. Cole and explain the reasons for the punishment.

B. Listen to Mrs. Cole and agree to lessen the punishment slightly.

C. Explain the seriousness of the problem and let the parent know how much of a problem this creates for a teacher.

D. Include a member of the school administration for support against the parent.

11. A high school physics teacher wants his students to study bridge construction as part of the class. Which of the following technologies would be best suited to doing this?

A. a video about the Brooklyn Bridge

B. viewing PDF illustrations of a bridge

C. a simulation of stress effects on a bridge

D. reading word documents about bridges

Tim Miller is a first-year high school mathematics teacher. Early in the first semester of the school year, another teacher inquires about a student of Mr. Miller's, Teddy DeWitt. The other teacher tells Mr. Miller that Teddy is wearing an unusual hairstyle and sporting different, edgier clothing than he did last year, and that he seemed unusually withdrawn and distant when the other teacher spoke to him in the hallway.

Although Mr. Miller had recognized that Teddy's demeanor was odd, he hadn't known that this was a marked change from the year before. Further, Teddy tends to sit in class with two other similarly dressed students, Aaron Dupree and Jay Efron, and Mr. Miller had assumed that the students were simply unmotivated. Mr. Miller decides to review the three students' academic records.

12. While looking at Teddy's file, he notices that Teddy's grades in mathematics had been fairly stable in past school years, with only minor variations. What explanation is most likely for the presence of the minor variations?

   A. a major change in Teddy's home environment, such as a parental divorce or the birth of a sibling

   B. slight differences in grading standards among different teachers

   C. widely different levels of difficulty of subject matter

   D. Teddy's largely poor performance in his science classes

Mr. Miller reviews all three student files and decides to have a meeting with the three of them regarding their poor performance. The following is a portion of their conversation:

> Mr. Miller: I believe that all of you could be doing better work than you currently are. I looked through your academic records, and you were all good students in mathematics last year. This year, though, you're all in danger of failing. Jay, you're currently getting a C-minus, and Aaron, you and Teddy are earning D-pluses. You're not even doing any of your homework. Can you tell me why?
>
> (*The students remain silent.*)
>
> Mr. Miller: Look, if you can't help me, I can't help you. If you want to improve at all, your attitude is really going to have to change. Please think about what I've said.

13. As a result of the conversation, the students will be most likely to:

    A. become more diligent in their schoolwork.

    B. perform poorly in other subjects besides mathematics.

    C. have negative feelings toward Mr. Miller.

    D. increase their rate of classroom participation in Mr. Miller's class.

14. The biggest error Mr. Miller made during the meeting was:

    A. not starting the meeting on a more positive note.

    B. not ending the meeting on a more positive note.

    C. not forcing the students to respond to his question.

    D. revealing each student's grades in the presence of the other students.

During the meeting, Mr. Miller noticed that Jay was particularly withdrawn. Jay had been an excellent student the year before. From speaking to other teachers, Mr. Miller learned that Jay had had few friends and spent most of his time working on schoolwork. Jay now spends most of his time with Aaron and Teddy, and Jay's current demeanor and attitude suggest that he may be under the influence of drugs.

15. Which of the following would be the most appropriate step for Mr. Miller to take first?

A. Notify the local law enforcement authorities.

B. Call Jay's parents, express his concerns, and suggest ways in which Jay's parents could help Jay to modify his own behavior.

C. Work with Jay and appropriate school staff to identify and treat Jay's problems.

D. Talk with Jay after school and confront him directly.

16. Aaron later approaches Mr. Miller individually and tells him that an overcommitted schedule has prevented him from doing his homework. In addition to maintaining a full academic load, Aaron has recently starting dating a girl, working a part-time job, and practicing guitar. Mr. Miller suggests that Aaron prioritize his responsibilities by making a chart listing the approximate number of hours that he spends on each activity, and then listing the positives and negatives associated with each activity. One benefit of applying this process is that:

A. Aaron will learn exactly how to solve his current dilemma.

B. Aaron will learn a strategy that he can apply to similar problems in the future.

C. Aaron will understand that problems can have more than one solution.

D. Aaron will realize that schoolwork is more important than a social life.

DECISION SET ENDS HERE

17. What is the best way for a teacher to inform parents about an upcoming field trip to an art museum?

    A. Call the parents at home in the evening.

    B. Call the parents at work.

    C. Email parents.

    D. Send a flyer home with students.

18. Which of the following is legally required when a teacher suspects the need for special education for one of her students?

    A. written permission from a parent/guardian

    B. review of the student's records

    C. meeting with the student to discuss the problem

    D. written permission from the school board

19. The proper manner in which to cite sources when writing a report:

    A. is optional for information found on the Internet.

    B. requires citing the source only when exact wording is used.

    C. does not include citing websites as sources.

    D. involves citing websites in the same way as citing any other source.

20. Mr. Magee has organized his students into groups of four or five in which to discuss the characters in a book his class is reading. Which of the following is the most effective method for assigning grades for group participation?

    A. allowing a group leader to grade the students

    B. informal observation

    C. group self-evaluation

    D. asking the group to write up what they have discussed

21. A tenth-grade art teacher has been told that her class can only take one field trip this year and must decide between the modern art museum and the fine art museum. The teacher is considering allowing her students to vote on which trip they prefer. The art teacher's probable purpose is:

    A. to create a positive attitude in the classroom.

    B. to involve the students in their own learning.

    C. to be able to come to a consensus about where the field trip will be.

    D. to research different field trip options.

22. Mrs. Snow, a French teacher, has invited a teacher who just transferred in from out of state to attend a TEKS seminar and workshop with other teachers from the school. This new teacher:

    A. has found an important resource for teachers.

    B. probably knows little about the TEKS.

    C. must attend in order to complete certification.

    D. must first register with a professional organization.

23. A Government teacher will start a new chapter this week on the branches of the government. The best way to begin this chapter is to:

    A. discuss key vocabulary.

    B. watch a video about checks and balances.

    C. learn what the students already know during a class discussion.

    D. assign prework and chapter reading to prepare the students.

24. A high school teacher accidentally overhears a girl talking with her boyfriend. The couple is discussing the boy's father and the fact that he had hit the boy. The teacher notices that the boy has a few large bruises. The teacher is required do which of the following?

    A. Report the encounter to authorities within 48 hours.

    B. Talk to the boy directly before making a report.

    C. Ask the school administration to investigate the report.

    D. Speak with both the boy and girl before making a report.

25. An eighth-grade teacher probably has the greatest effect on which of the following?

    A. her students' behavior

    B. her students' choice of friends

    C. her students' academic improvement

    D. her students' level of confidence

26. A high school teacher of gifted students should expect which of the following behaviors from the students?

    A. the ability to handle peer relationships easily

    B. the ability to stay self-motivated in the classroom

    C. the ability to work well in groups of mixed ability

    D. the ability to evaluate each other fairly

27. Which of the following would be the most effective way to encourage students to become more interested in literature?

    A. offering extra credit to the students for reading works of literature

    B. publishing students' names in the school newsletter

    C. increasing the percentage of the final grade based on reading literature

    D. allowing the students to be involved in choosing the literature that they are required to read

28. A biology teacher assigns students to groups, each of which includes students of varying abilities, to study and dissect a frog. The purpose of having students at different levels in each group is:

    A. to prevent students working at a lower level from getting lost in the process.

    B. to allow more advanced students to further their understanding of the material by teaching it to others.

    C. to make sure that each group will be able to arrive at the same conclusions if the same steps are followed.

    D. to allow students to meet other students who they might not know as well.

29. Which of the following would be most helpful to a teacher tracking grades for more than 100 students?

    A. presentation software

    B. computer database

    C. word-processing program

    D. computer spreadsheet

30. During a parent/teacher conference, the parent of a junior in high school asks the teacher for her opinion about where the junior should apply to college. The teacher should respond by:

A. referring the parent to the school guidance counselor.

B. informing the parent that this is not something teachers do.

C. asking what schools the parent prefers and then suggesting one of those as the best option.

D. giving the parent a few examples based on the student's interests, if possible, and encouraging the parent to do more research.

31. Mrs. Rouse has a bright student in her class who often finishes early but makes careless mistakes on tests. To help the student, Mrs. Rouse asks the student to spend the extra time double-checking his work. This is an example of which of the following?

A. preferential treatment toward a student

B. self-motivation techniques

C. use of meta-cognitive techniques

D. proper pacing

32. It has been brought to the attention of the English department that many of the students who were in a class taught by a new teacher, Mr. Timmons, have not read all of the required selections of that class. To ensure this does not continue to be a problem, Mrs. Schupe has agreed to help Mr. Timmons structure his class differently so that there will be time for all required reading selections. This is an example of which of the following?

A. teachers collaborating to improve their students' education

B. teachers learning better communication skills

C. teachers correcting flaws in their curriculum

D. teachers expecting too much from younger colleagues

33. A high school computer teacher has noticed that some students who are not as familiar with computers rely on other students to help them complete computer assignments. What should the teacher do to increase these less advanced students' classroom computer use?

A. Give informal basic computer lessons to these students during their regular lunch period.

B. Require all students to spend a minimum amount of time on the classroom computer each week.

C. Develop a computer project with easy-to-follow instructions that will allow the students to build confidence.

D. Talk to the students about the importance of technology in education as well as in other aspects of their lives.

Use the comment below that a teacher wrote on a student's essay to answer the two questions that follow.

> Good job! Nice work! B+

34. The biggest problem with the above comment is that:

    A.   the student isn't given any reason why the essay was worth a B+.

    B.   the student will believe that all work is worthy of a B+.

    C.   the student isn't given any specific information to help her improve on future essays.

    D.   the student will believe that this teacher grades arbitrarily.

35. The comment could have a counterproductive effect on the student's self-esteem for which of the following reasons?

    A.   A B+ is a substandard grade.

    B.   Undeserved praise provides no incentive for actually performing well.

    C.   Such high praise for a less-than-perfect grade will make future praise for potentially better work less meaningful.

    D.   Praise from a teacher may earn her enmity from her peer group.

◆ ◆ ◆ ◆ ◆ ◆ ◆ ◆

36. One reason why the driver's education program at the high school includes information about the consequences of drinking and driving is because:

    A.   students are required to learn this information before they can obtain a drivers license.

    B.   teenagers probably do not understand why they should not drink.

    C.   parents do not teach their children about driving responsibly.

    D.   many young people take risks, feeling that nothing bad will happen to them.

37. An eighth-grade teacher has broken her class up into small groups. The groups will work together on a budget for a pretend company and each member of the group will have specific tasks to complete. At the end of the project, each group will complete an evaluation of their own group's performance. The likely purpose of this evaluation is:

    A.   to help students review their own effectiveness.

    B.   to help the teacher determine the individual group members' grades on the project.

    C.   to help the teacher understand the dynamics of each group.

    D.   to allow the students to participate in determining their own grade.

38. A high school has an internal email system in which every teacher, administrator, and other type of employee has an email account. The school strongly suggests everyone check their email daily. The reasoning for this is probably to:

A. be able to transfer sensitive information quickly.

B. share urgent information with appropriate parties.

C. make the job of the front office administrators easier.

D. communicate information that used to be contained in daily memos.

39. David is repeatedly late to school and when asked about it, David says that his father is not always able to drive him to school and so sometimes he must walk. The teacher's best response would be to:

A. encourage David to wake up earlier and not rely on his father.

B. offer to pick up David on these mornings.

C. ask the mother of one of David's friends to pick up David each morning.

D. be supportive and ask if there is something the teacher can do.

Use the information below to answer the two questions that follow.

Students in Ms. Myers' economics class have been discussing the impact of new construction that is currently under way near the school. Students are divided about the issue because some have parents that are directly involved in the construction, but others are wary of the increased traffic the construction will cause, and mourn the loss of the open space that used to be there.

40. Tensions have been running high enough that students are raising their voices in class. To reduce the tension in a productive manner, Ms. Myers should:

   A. ban the topic from further discussion and move on to another topic.

   B. have students write research papers on the economic impact of suburban growth in general.

   C. have students objectively measure their level of support and chart the information on a graph.

   D. have students research the likely implications of this project and have them present their findings in a structured debate format.

41. Focusing on an issue of direct relevance to the students is most likely to produce which of the following educational benefits?

   A. It will teach students to more easily apply the same economic principles to other, less familiar situations.

   B. It will spark a lifelong interest in economics.

   C. It will result in higher economic grades for the students.

   D. It will ensure that students understand the fundamental principles of economics.

◆ ◆ ◆ ◆ ◆ ◆ ◆

42. Allowing students to help plan their own field trip:

A. allows students to feel they can exercise some control over their own education.

B. allows teachers to evaluate the leadership qualities of their students.

C. helps teachers identify students who are self-motivated.

D. demonstrates the principles of the democratic process.

43. Where is the best location in the classroom to seat a student with a hearing problem?

A. away from any source of background noise

B. close to where the teacher stands when lecturing

C. at the front of the classroom

D. next to a friend who can help the student keep up with what is going on

44. A high school drama teacher has developed a skit for the students that depicts two boys who decide to drive home after drinking at a friend's party. The skit demonstrates the horrible effects of their decision by showing a victim's family at the funeral, one boy in jail, and another one wracked with guilt. The primary purpose of this skit is to:

A. promote awareness about how the law treats convicted drunk drivers.

B. make parents aware of their teenagers' behavior.

C. show students the possibly devastating effects of what may seem like harmless behavior.

D. show students alternatives to drinking and driving.

45. It becomes obvious to a high school teacher that her students have some gender stereotypes about certain professions. To combat this stereotyping, the teacher could do which of the following?

A. Use the opposite of the stereotype in all classroom activities.

B. Require students to write a paper on the first woman elected to Congress.

C. Invite a woman astronaut to be a guest speaker in the class.

D. Ask the students why they think women cannot do some jobs.

46. Which of the following situations should most concern a teacher?

    A. Matthew suffers from anxiety in situations such as testing.

    B. Aaron has memorized all of his math formulas but does not understand how to apply them.

    C. Lynn doesn't like science and often does not complete her science homework.

    D. Mary is typically the last student in her class to understand difficult concepts.

47. Which of the following behaviors should lead to Travis's being permanently removed from class?

    A. falling asleep in class

    B. starting a fight with another student who had never been in trouble before

    C. interrupting the class to such a degree that all required subjects are not able to be covered

    D. continually using foul language toward the teacher and other students

48. Which of the following would be the most efficient tool a teacher could provide to a deaf interpreter working with one of her students?

    A. copies of all textbooks that will be used in the classroom

    B. a list of required content for the course

    C. a daily copy of the teacher's lesson plan

    D. a permanent small area in the classroom

49. A French teacher could most effectively instill in students a sense appreciation of French culture through which of the following methods?

    A. teaching students about French celebrations

    B. discussing what foods Americans eat that are French in origin

    C. showing students a French movie

    D. celebrating French holidays or celebrations in the classroom

50. A special education student who is transferring from another state will be joining a ninth-grade classroom. The teacher is concerned about how the other students will receive this new student. Which of the following would most help to ease this transition for everyone?

    A. Encourage the students to treat this student the same way they do everyone else.

    B. Always demonstrate patience and acceptance when problems arise during the transition.

    C. Assign students a research project about special education needs.

    D. Establish clear rules for the other students to follow before the new student arrives about how to treat this new student.

51. High school students are more likely to respond to constructive criticism when it is offered:

A. one-on-one.

B. during a meeting the student has scheduled about a different topic.

C. equally to each student in a small group of students.

D. anonymously.

52. What must a teacher do if he or she hears a rumor about a student who may have brought a weapon to the school campus?

A. Call the police immediately.

B. Try to determine the source of the rumor.

C. Try to establish if there is in fact a weapon.

D. Notify other teachers.

53. Mrs. Peters has been asked how effective her new classroom policies have been. Measuring the success of these new policies requires:

A. an unbiased observer's opinion.

B. students to give their opinions through a survey.

C. a veteran teacher to observe the classroom.

D. a comparison between the classroom before and after the new policies were established.

54. A high school art teacher will soon begin to study contemporary art with her students. She would like to take her students on a field trip to the Contemporary Art Museum to see a special display there on interactive art. The purpose of this field trip is most likely to:

A. develop students' interest in contemporary art.

B. reward students with a field trip.

C. show students a type of art they are not familiar with.

D. experience a change of scenery.

55. A teacher with over 20 years of teaching experience is returning to teaching after several years outside the profession. He is concerned about his lack of computer experience. He would benefit the most from which of the following options?

A. relying on help from other teachers in his field.

B. enrolling in a community college computer course.

C. attending a computer workshop at a teachers' convention.

D. reading about new computer trends in a professional publication.

56. Which of the following tools would most effectively compute grades that are weighted differently?

   A. a grade book

   B. a calculator

   C. a computer spreadsheet

   D. a ledger

57. Maria asks to speak to her teacher, Ms. Voss. During the conversation Maria expresses concerns about her best friend. She claims that her best friend has confided in her that her father is molesting her. What is Ms. Voss required to do?

   A. Report the incident to the police for investigation.

   B. Determine if there is enough truth in Maria's story to contact authorities.

   C. Speak to Maria's best friend before contacting any authorities.

   D. Report the accusation to all involved parties.

58. Before leaving on a field trip, the teacher must:

   A. count the number of students on each bus.

   B. arrange for eating lunch off campus.

   C. verify that all medical information is on file for the students.

   D. have written permission from each student's parent/guardian.

59. Giving students a picture and asking them all to discuss what they each see in the picture is an example of:

   A. convergent thinking

   B. divergent thinking

   C. memory recall

   D. brainstorming

60. A science teacher is planning a lesson on weather phenomena. The class could best be prepared for this lesson by first:

   A. talking about the weather patterns of the area.

   B. discussing the types of weather phenomena that they already know about.

   C. watching the weather on the TV news.

   D. measuring rainfall.

61. To motivate his tenth-grade government class, Mr. Bernard should consider:

   A. requiring students who do not participate in class to attend detention after school.

   B. assigning failing grades to students who do not participate in class.

   C. distributing small prizes to students who participate fully in class discussions.

   D. rewarding students who participate or have high grade averages by allowing them to skip a test.

62. An eighth-grade teacher is taking her class on a guided tour at the state capitol building. The teacher must make special arrangements for a boy in her class who is still learning English and may not be able to understand everything the guide will say. What should the teacher do to accommodate the needs of this student?

 A. Make arrangements for the boy to spend the day at the school with another eighth-grade class.

 B. Contact the guide service ahead of time to arrange for a tour on tape in the student's language.

 C. Pair the student with a friend during the tour who can help him follow what the tour guide is saying.

 D. Ask the student's parents to accompany their son on the field trip.

63. A tenth-grade teacher has a student, Tammy, who has recently started performing poorly in class and also seems uninterested in school. Tammy's teacher is concerned that she may be using drugs. What is the first step Tammy's teacher should take?

 A. Talk with the school counselor.

 B. Talk with the parents.

 C. Talk with Tammy.

 D. Talk with Tammy's friends.

64. During the school's open house, the music teacher asks parents who play an instrument to come and volunteer a bit of time to play for the students during music class. The music teacher's motivation for this is:

 A. to expose students to types of music they would not hear outside of school.

 B. to allow parents the opportunity to see their children in a classroom setting while they are volunteering.

 C. to meaningfully include parents in their children's formal education.

 D. to allow parents to see what resources the school has in contrast to what is needed.

65. Critical thinking is an important skill for students to develop. Which of the following exercises would be best to have the students do in order to help them develop their critical thinking ability?

 A. Identify the tone of a newspaper article.

 B. Research the meaning of unfamiliar words found in a story.

 C. Imagine what might occur after the end of a story.

 D. Identify the main idea and conclusion of an article.

66. Which of the following math exercises requires higher-order thinking than the others?

   A. converting fractions to decimals

   B. reducing a fraction

   C. recognizing a shape as a larger version of a 5-12-13 triangle

   D. converting a decimal to a percentage

67. Ms. Delta believes Tony is not living up to his potential. What is the best way for her to communicate her higher expectations for Tony?

   A. Praise Tony's work in front of others.

   B. Challenge Tony and let him know she believes he is capable.

   C. Have Tony work with students who have routinely challenged themselves.

   D. Remove the emphasis on tasks that would be challenging for Tony.

68. The parents of a high school senior are concerned that their daughter's science classes are not preparing her well enough for college. What is the most appropriate response from the teacher?

   A. Try to reassure the parents by listing the teacher's credentials and experience.

   B. Listen to the parents' concern and explain how the curriculum does meet requirements.

   C. Solicit the parents' ideas as to how the curriculum could be improved.

   D. Suggest the parents meet with a college science professor to learn what is really expected.

69. Allowing students to grade their own essays based on specific criteria would provide the teacher with:

   A. specific information about which students worked the hardest.

   B. no real usable information.

   C. a glimpse into what criteria are more important to the student than others.

   D. information about how the students perceive their own work.

70. Two students, Jack and Conner, often resort to fighting physically with each other. Their teacher's primary goal should be to do what?

   A. Separate the boys from each other in as many activities as possible.

   B. Involve school administrators in the situation as additional resources.

   C. Determine if there is a pattern of aggressive behavior by one of the students.

   D. Teach the students how to work through their problems without becoming physical.

71. A history teacher is preparing to start a section about D-Day. To best prepare, the teacher should:

   A. try to find out if the students have a family member who served in WWII.

   B. have students map the invasion on an atlas.

   C. study the history that led up to D-Day.

   D. have a class discussion about D-Day and encourage students to share stories they might know from that day.

72. A teacher must call the parents of a student. Their daughter has been caught skipping school. The teacher should start the conversation by:

   A. explaining the attendance policy of the school.

   B. informing the parents of the consequences of this action.

   C. putting the parents at ease by saying something positive.

   D. assuring the parents of the validity of the charge against the student.

73. Josh's parents have decided to get divorced. As a result, Josh is now shuttled back and forth between two homes, often forgets needed school items at the other parent's house, and has become distracted at school. The best response from Josh's teacher would be to:

   A. send Josh to visit the school counselor.

   B. let Josh's friends know he needs their support.

   C. speak with the parents about making a stronger effort to help their son.

   D. provide a regular, stable school environment and be supportive.

74. Mrs. Laurel spends the first few days of class getting to know her students. This practice has:

    A. allowed students to feel free to talk during class time.

    B. helped develop students' communication skills.

    C. increased students' participation and interest in the class.

    D. let students learn more about Mrs. Laurel.

75. At the end of each school day, Ms. Lee has her students write one new thing learned that day in their journals. This benefits the students because it:

    A. aids Ms. Lee in grading the students' comprehension.

    B. helps cement new knowledge the students have just acquired.

    C. allows the teacher to see what the students are able to recall.

    D. is a tool for the students as well as the parents.

76. Teachers in the math department work together to ensure that students learn the needed skills in one class before advancing to the next. This is an example of:

    A. communication between all involved parties.

    B. tracking students from grade level to grade level.

    C. teachers working together for the best results for their students.

    D. the math department's strict policies for advancement.

77. A teacher borrows a VCR from the library after the librarian has left for the day. He uses the VCR that night at home to tape something he plans to discuss in class. His actions are:

    A. ethical because he used the VCR for school purposes.

    B. ethical because he returned the VCR before the librarian missed it.

    C. unethical because school property should not be removed from the school.

    D. unethical because the librarian did not have knowledge of what he did.

78. Mrs. Kobbs has assigned her government students a report on the impact of the Supreme Court case of *Brown vs. the Board of Education*. Students will be allowed to research the topic at the school library or at home via the Internet. Allowing students to make use of different resources is most important because it:

A. enables a number of students to search for resources simultaneously.

B. makes it more difficult for students who are not as comfortable using computers.

C. provides different options for students to research their topic.

D. puts a great deal of pressure on the librarian.

79. The most important advantage gained by a veteran teacher from subscribing to professional teachers' journals is:

A. being able to have access to such a resource at any time.

B. remaining apprised of the activities of the professional organization.

C. staying current on trends in education and technology.

D. building a resource center for new teachers to use.

80. A new teacher has been invited to sit in on the class of a fellow English teacher. While observing, the new teacher sees several things she would like to try in her own classroom. After the class ends, the two teachers talk about some of these new ideas. This is an example of:

A. peer interaction.

B. professional mentoring.

C. on-the-job training.

D. informal mentoring.

81. Eastville High School's dropout rate due to teenage pregnancies has tripled in the past ten years. To combat this, the school has decided to show a movie depicting the consequences of having a baby as a teenager. This type of education is important because:

A. students don't want to be lectured by adults who might have had similar teenage behavior.

B. many teenagers don't think about the consequences of their actions.

C. there are many false rumors about how to avoid becoming pregnant.

D. many students have been given incorrect information about teenage pregnancy.

82. Mrs. Evans has learned that the uncle of one of her students, Terrell, has died. Which of the following could Mrs. Evans do to help Terrell the most?

   A. Provide a safe, caring and predictable classroom environment for the student.

   B. Suggest to Terrell's mother that he take some time away from school.

   C. Insist Terrell meet with the school counselor.

   D. Monitor Terrell's behavior with his friends and in the classroom.

83. A teacher is concerned when she hears some students making fun of a male student who has elected to take a cooking class populated almost exclusively by female students. The teacher should react to this situation by doing which of the following?

   A. Invite male chefs to the next career day event at the school.

   B. Express disappointment over their behavior and explain how their words can affect others.

   C. Assign the offending students an essay on famous male chefs as punishment.

   D. Talk to the home economics teacher about the incident.

84. A teacher realizes that students are not enjoying her lecture during their world history class. What can the teacher do to increase students' interest in the content?

   A. Create a game out of the information the students must learn.

   B. Allow students who participate to leave class early.

   C. Deduct points for lack of enthusiasm.

   D. Postpone the lecture until another day.

85. A computer teacher should provide her students with which of the following types of software to keep their daily computer journals?

   A. simulation

   B. word processing

   C. database

   D. design

86. Which of the following best describes a situation in which students have different ideas but come together in a compromise that they all agree upon?

   A. convergent thinking

   B. divergent thinking

   C. brainstorming

   D. objective thinking

87. When choosing which supplemental materials the students will work with for the upcoming school year, the teacher should give primary importance to which of the following?

A. materials used in previous years

B. the content that the teacher intends to cover with the materials

C. the durability of the materials

D. the cost of the materials

88. A teacher has noticed that Danny often carelessly rushes through his classwork so that he can spend the rest of the class time drawing in his notebook. How should the teacher deal with this problem?

A. Move Danny away from his friends.

B. Take Danny's notebook away from him.

C. Encourage Danny to double-check his work before moving on.

D. Suggest to Danny's mother that she enroll Danny in art classes.

89. Mrs. Davidson's English class partnered with a kindergarten class at a school nearby and answered their letters to Santa. The principal at the school then wrote a thank-you letter to Mrs. Davidson's students, which Mrs. Davidson displayed in her classroom and which she read to her students. Her likely educational purpose is to:

A. show students a new letter-writing style.

B. have students recognize the value of establishing long-term relationships.

C. allow the students to feel proud of their accomplishment.

D. have students learn socially acceptable behavior.

90. Several parents have agreed to help chaperone the senior field trip to Washington, D.C. The teacher and students will be accompanied by several parents who will serve as group leaders. To ensure the success of the field trip, the teacher should make sure to:

A. share the goals of the field trip with the group leaders/parents.

B. ask the parents to sign waivers for the field trip.

C. inform the group leaders of the daily schedules ahead of time.

D. balance the small groups with equal numbers of boys and girls.

91. Before allowing students to use the new computers in the computer lab, the teacher must first:

   A. learn to use them herself.

   B. install student protection software.

   C. catalog the ID numbers of the computers with the administration.

   D. load email software onto each machine.

92. Which of the following assignments would likely require higher-order thinking than the others?

   A. memorizing the elements on the periodic table

   B. reading a passage

   C. composing a letter

   D. interpreting a graph

93. Introducing a new chapter by asking students what they already know about the general topic:

   A. helps the students process the new information more efficiently.

   B. allows the students to recognize the pattern of learning.

   C. brings the community into the classroom.

   D. helps the students develop critical reading skills.

94. Which of the following is an example of divergent thinking?

   A. singing in the school choir

   B. playing the flute in the school orchestra

   C. composing a new song

   D. interpreting sheet music in a new manner

95. A group of girlfriends are arguing in the hallway. The teacher is able to sort out that one of the girls has had her feelings hurt by her friend. The teacher's primary goal in having the two girls sit down together to talk about what was said was to help the girls:

   A. understand this is not how they should solve disagreements.

   B. communicate better in the future.

   C. discuss the problem without feedback from others.

   D. see the consequences that their actions have on others.

13

TExES 8–12 Practice Test: Answers and Explanations

TExES PPR 8–12 PRACTICE TEST ANSWER KEY

1. B	26. B	51. A	76. C
2. D	27. D	52. A	77. A
3. D	28. B	53. D	78. C
4. A	29. D	54. A	79. C
5. C	30. D	55. C	80. D
6. A	31. C	56. C	81. B
7. B	32. A	57. A	82. A
8. C	33. C	58. D	83. B
9. C	34. C	59. B	84. A
10. A	35. C	60. B	85. B
11. C	36. D	61. D	86. A
12. B	37. A	62. B	87. B
13. C	38. D	63. C	88. C
14. D	39. D	64. C	89. D
15. C	40. D	65. A	90. A
16. B	41. A	66. C	91. B
17. D	42. A	67. B	92. D
18. A	43. B	68. B	93. A
19. D	44. C	69. D	94. D
20. B	45. D	70. D	95. B
21. B	46. B	71. D	
22. A	47. C	72. C	
23. C	48. C	73. D	
24. A	49. D	74. C	
25. C	50. B	75. B	

1. Students in a high school speech class have begun using technology in their presentations. The teacher wants to continue to allow students to do so but is concerned that the look of the presentation is becoming more important to the students than the substance of their speech. The best way to motivate the students to continue to incorporate technology without compromising content would be to do which of the following?

   A. Give the students on outline of how much time they should spend at home on each aspect of their speeches.

   B. Let the students know that 90% of their grade will be based on content, 10% on the use of technology.

   C. Require that the students complete the content of their speeches before beginning to work on how to present them.

   D. Allow the students to work with a partner where one works on content and the other works on using technology.

B The item above measures Competency 009: The teacher incorporates the effective use of technology to plan, organize, deliver, and evaluate instruction for all students.

Here's How to Crack It

Step 1: Identify the scenario.

- Age range: high school

- Goal: motivate students to use technology, yet emphasize substance over appearance

Step 2: Use POE to narrow down the answer choices.

Our goal is clearly defined, but this is a tough question to predict an answer for. Let's see what the answers look like:

A. That sets a guideline, but does it motivate? Let's keep it for now.

B. That would certainly be a motivating factor, but it seems a little heavy-handed. Let's keep it, too.

C. Like choice A, that sets a guideline, but doesn't provide a motivation. Cross out both A and C.

D. No. That's wouldn't solve the problem at all.

Step 3: Make a final decision.

None of the answers is great, but choice B best satisfies the conditions of the question, and is therefore the best answer.

2. A high school Spanish teacher has several beginning classes that include both students who speak only English as well as students who speak Spanish regularly at home. The students who already speak Spanish tend not to participate in the class. What would be the best option for the teacher to motivate all students to participate?

A. Rearrange the classroom to create groups that include both types of students.

B. Separate the groups and give each group its own assignment.

C. Increase the importance of class participation in the final grade.

D. Include a variety of activities that would provide information that would be new to all students.

D The item above measures Competency 002: The teacher understands student diversity and knows how to plan learning experiences and design assessments that are responsive to differences among students and that promote all students' learning.

Here's How to Crack It

Step 1: Identify the scenario.

- Age range: high school

- Goal: Motivate equal participation among all students

Step 2: Use POE to narrow down the answer choices.
We're looking for something that will get all students to participate.

A. How would smaller groups motivate class participation? Cross it out.

B. No. The goal was to motivate equal participation among all students. Cross it out.

C. Perhaps. That would be an external motivator.

D. Yes. That would likely be an internal motivator.

Step 3: Make a final decision.
Answers C and D would both motivate students, but intrinsic motivation is preferred over extrinsic motivation. The best answer is D.

3. The most important benefit to be gained from a teacher's planning which science units will be covered and in what order in her class is to:

   A. allow parents to know what their children are studying.

   B. ensure there will be enough time during the school year to cover the required units.

   C. remove the stress of determining this later in the school year when teachers are busier.

   D. teach the information in a logical or natural sequence to help improve retention.

D   The item above measures Competency 003: The teacher understands procedures for designing effective and coherent instruction and assessment based on appropriate learning goals and objectives.

Here's How to Crack It

Step 1: Identify the scenario.

- Age range: none specified

- Goal: identify the most important benefit of advance planning

Step 2: Use POE to narrow down the answer choices.
There could be many benefits, but we're looking for the most important one.

   A. Maybe, but only if the other choices are very bad. Keep it for the moment.

   B. Better. We can cross out choice A now.

   C. No. B is a better answer than this. Cross it out.

   D. Yes. This is clearly a benefit.

Step 3: Make a final decision.
We're down to choices B and D. D is a better answer because it directly relates to students' learning, which is always a fundamental goal.

4. A high school chemistry teacher requires all students to carefully follow the safety rules even when the students are not working with dangerous chemicals because:

A. establishing a standard of behavior in the lab creates a safer, more efficient learning environment.

B. it allows the teacher to spend less time checking to make sure the safety rules have been followed.

C. one set of rules is easier for the teacher to follow than multiple sets of rules.

D. all chemicals can be dangerous.

A   The item above measures Competency 006: The teacher understands strategies for creating an organized and productive learning environment and for managing student behavior.

Here's How to Crack It

Step 1: Identify the scenario.

- Age range: high school

- Goal: determine why a chemistry teacher adheres to standard safety procedures

Step 2: Use POE to narrow down the answer choices.

Why would the teacher do that? So that students will get used to the procedure so they won't hurt themselves when they do use dangerous chemicals. Let's see what we've got:

A. Yes. That's close to what we said.

B. No. That makes things easier for the teacher, which is almost never a correct answer.

C. No. That also makes things easier for the teacher.

D. That may be true, but it's irrelevant to the question.

Step 3: Make a final decision.

Common sense dictated a probable answer, which proved to be the best one because we crossed out all the others. The best answer is A.

5. When asking parents to participate in a project with their children, the teacher should make sure to give the parents which of the following pieces of information to ensure the success of the collaboration?

    A. the amount of time the teacher expects the project will take

    B. the method by which the project will be graded

    C. the teacher's expectations of both the student and the parents

    D. an example of what the project should end up looking like

C   The item above measures Competency 011: The teacher understands the importance of family involvement in children's education and knows how to interact and communicate effectively with families.

Here's How to Crack It

Step 1: Identify the scenario.

- Age range: none given

- Goal: ensure the success of the collaboration

Step 2: Use POE to narrow down the answer choices.
Notice the question asks about the collaboration, not the end result of the project itself. If you were the parent, wouldn't you want to know what you were supposed to do and what your child was supposed to do?

    A. No. That's got nothing to do with the collaboration. Cross it out.

    B. No. Again, that's got nothing to do with the collaboration. Cross it out.

    C. Yes. That would help with the collaboration.

    D. No. Again, that's not the collaboration.

Step 3: Make a final decision.
We had to read carefully, but the choices A, B, and D actually had little to do with the stated goal of the question. The best answer is C.

6. Including the students in the discussion prior to the experiment will help them learn to do which of the following?

   A. Develop a hypothesis and then test it.

   B. Understand the purpose of this experiment.

   C. Choose conditions for their portion of the experiment.

   D. Understand the importance of starting with equal-sized plants.

A   The item above measures Competency 001: The teacher understands human developmental processes and applies this knowledge to plan instruction and ongoing assessment that motivate students and are responsive to their developmental characteristics and needs.

Here's How to Crack It

Step 1: Identify the scenario.

- Age range: eighth grade

- Goal: determine the point of including students in the discussion

Step 2: Use POE to narrow down the answer choices.

Why would we include students in the discussion? To get them to understand the process they'll be going through as they conduct the experiment. Let's see what we've got:

   A. Perhaps. That's a good paraphrase of the scientific process.

   B. Maybe. It will help their understanding of the experiment.

   C. No. According to the question, the conditions will be assigned.

   D. Perhaps, although this sounds more like a subset of choice B.

Step 3: Make a final decision.

The question suggests that the discussion is intended to teach them how to do something in the future, not just in the context of this assignment. Of the three remaining choices, only choice A suggests a general skill that students could apply in many situations. A is therefore the best answer.

7. The teacher sends the plants home with the students and includes notes for both the students and parents explaining the importance of replicating conditions so that the experiment will be valid. This exercise is most likely intended to teach the students:

   A. how each student's work relates to that of the other students.

   B. the importance of having objective data.

   C. that one student's work, done incorrectly, can void the entire class's experiment.

   D. responsibility for themselves.

B The item above measures Competency 008: The teacher provides appropriate instruction that actively engages students in the learning process.

Here's How to Crack It

Step 1: Identify the scenario.

- Age range: none given

- Goal: determine why the teacher emphasizes the importance of replicating conditions

Step 2: Use POE to narrow down the answer choices.
The conditions must be the same so that data are reliable overall.

   A. Maybe, but that's a bit general. Is there a better choice?

   B. Yes. That's better said. Cross out A now.

   C. No. There's no support for a statement that extreme.

   D. No. That's too general, and worse than choice B.

Step 3: Make a final decision.
B is the only choice remaining, and is therefore the best answer.

8. A teacher's primary responsibility after witnessing a fight between two students is to:

   A. determine which student started the fight.

   B. act as a judge in settling the argument in a fair manner.

   C. help the students work through their problem without violence.

   D. report the incident to the school administration.

C   The item above measures Competency 006: The teacher understands strategies for creating an organized and productive learning environment and for managing student behavior.

Here's How to Crack It

Step 1: Identify the scenario.

- Age range: none given

- Goal: determine teacher's responsibility after seeing a fight

Step 2: Use POE to narrow down the answer choices.
Primary responsibility? Let's see what the choices are:

A.   No. Why would that be the teacher's responsibility? Cross it out.

B.   No. The teacher shouldn't need to settle the argument. Cross it out.

C.   Maybe. That sounds like a teacher's job.

D.   Maybe. Is that a responsibility?

Step 3: Make a final decision.
Choice D may be tempting, but suspicion of abuse is the only thing that teachers are legally required to report. In fact, involving the administration usually signifies a wrong answer because it suggests that the teacher can't handle the situation on his own. The best answer is C.

9.   Which of the following is the most important aspect of designing a system used to evaluate students?

A.   testing students in a variety of ways to accommodate different learning styles

B.   developing test questions difficult enough to determine the highest level of retention

C.   aligning test questions with the educational goals of the unit or chapter

D.   ensuring that each test question can have only one possible answer

C   The item above measures Competency 010: The teacher monitors student performance and achievement; provides students with timely, high-quality feedback; and responds flexibly to promote learning for all students.

Here's How to Crack It

Step 1: Identify the scenario.

- Age range: none given

- Goal: identify the most important aspect of an evaluation mechanism

Step 2: Use POE to narrow down the answer choices.

You should know this one: the most important aspect is that the evaluation method measures what it's supposed to measure. Let's see what the choices are:

A. No. That's not what we're looking for.

B. No. That's not what we're looking for.

C. Yes. That's close to what we said.

D. No. That's not what we're looking for.

Step 3: Make a final decision.

There's only one choice left. The best answer is C.

10. Mrs. Cole has requested a parent/teacher conference to discuss what she feels is an unfair punishment given to her son for his showing up 20 minutes late to class. The teacher should do which of the following at this conference?

   A. Listen to Mrs. Cole and explain the reasons for the punishment.

   B. Listen to Mrs. Cole and agree to lessen the punishment slightly.

   C. Explain the seriousness of the problem and let the parent know how much of a problem this creates for a teacher.

   D. Include a member of the school administration for support against the parent.

A The item above measures Competency 011: The teacher understands the importance of family involvement in children's education and knows how to interact and communicate effectively with families.

Here's How to Crack It

Step 1: Identify the scenario.

- Age range: none given

- Goal: determine teacher action at parent conference

Step 2: Use POE to narrow down the answer choices.
The golden rule is: explain your position without angering the parents. Let's see what we have to choose from:

    A.   This sounds okay. We'll keep it for now.

    B.   Why would the teacher lessen the punishment? Keep this, too, just in case.

    C.   No. The last half of this makes it wrong.

    D.   No. Teachers should be able to handle conferences by themselves.

Step 3: Make a final decision.
We have it down to choices A and B. In the absence of compelling evidence suggesting that the teacher reduce the punishment, we should go with choice A. A is the best answer.

11.   A high school physics teacher wants his students to study bridge construction as part of the class. Which of the following technologies would be best suited to doing this?

    A.   a video about the Brooklyn Bridge

    B.   viewing PDF illustrations of a bridge

    C.   a simulation of stress effects on a bridge

    D.   reading word documents about bridges

C   The item above measures Competency 009: The teacher incorporates the effective use of technology to plan, organize, deliver, and evaluate instruction for all students.

Here's How to Crack It

Step 1: Identify the scenario.

- Age range: high school

- Goal: use technology to study bridges

Step 2: Use POE to narrow down the answer choices.

    A.   Watching a video is passive. Is there anything better? Keep it for now.

    B.   Why would looking at pictures on a computer screen be using technology well? Cross it out.

    C.   Yes. This is likely. It's a unique use of technology.

    D.   No, for the same reasons we got rid of choice C.

Step 3: Make a final decision.
Choice C is better than choice A, so the best answer is C.

12. While looking at Teddy's file, he notices that Teddy's grades in mathematics had been fairly stable in past school years, with only minor variations. What explanation is most likely for the presence of the minor variations?

A. a major change in Teddy's home environment, such as a parental divorce or the birth of a sibling

B. slight differences in grading standards among different teachers

C. widely different levels of difficulty of subject matter

D. Teddy's largely poor performance in his science classes

B This question measures Competency 010: The teacher monitors student performance and achievement; provides students with timely, high-quality feedback; and responds flexibly to promote learning for all students.

Here's How to Crack It

Step 1: Identify the scenario.

- Age range: high school

- Goal: identify the reason for Teddy's grade variations

Step 2: Use POE to narrow down the answer choices.

A. No. That would likely lead to very wide fluctuations.

B. Maybe. That corresponds to a small variation.

C. No. That would also lead to wide fluctuations.

D. No. That would be irrelevant to his performance in math class.

Step 3: Make a final decision.

The best answer is B because it's the only one that would account for minor fluctuations.

13. As a result of the conversation, the students will be most likely to:

    A. become more diligent in their schoolwork.

    B. perform poorly in other subjects besides mathematics.

    C. have negative feelings toward Mr. Miller.

    D. increase their rate of classroom participation in Mr. Miller's class.

C This question measures Competency 005: The teacher knows how to establish a classroom climate that fosters learning and excellence and uses this knowledge to create a physical and emotional environment that is safe and productive.

Here's How to Crack It

Step 1: Identify the scenario.

- Age range: high school

- Goal: determine likely result of student meeting

Step 2: Use POE to narrow down the answer choices.
The answer is most likely to be negative. It doesn't sound like the meeting went all that well.

    A. No. A positive result is unlikely.

    B. No. Although that's negative, it's unlikely that the conversation would impact other courses.

    C. Maybe. That's a possible result.

    D. No. That's a positive result, and therefore unlikely.

Step 3: Make a final decision.
It's quite likely that the students will feel resentful and mistrustful of Mr. Miller in the future. The best answer is C.

14. The biggest error Mr. Miller made during the meeting was:

    A. not starting the meeting on a more positive note.

    B. not ending the meeting on a more positive note.

    C. not forcing the students to respond to his question.

    D. revealing each student's grades in the presence of the other students.

D This question measures Competency 013: The teacher understands and adheres to legal and ethical requirements for educators and is knowledgeable of the structure of education in Texas.

Here's How to Crack It

Step 1: Identify the scenario.

- Age range: high school

- Goal: determine the teacher error

Step 2: Use POE to narrow down the answer choices.
There were many things that Mr. Miller did wrong. Let's see what the choices are:

A. Maybe. The meeting started off badly.

B. Maybe. The meeting ended badly.

C. No. He was heavy-handed enough.

D. Yes. That's a big problem.

Step 3: Make a final decision.
Although he did many things badly, the most egregious was revealing grade information to other students. That's an ethical violation, and therefore the best answer is D.

15. Which of the following would be the most appropriate step for Mr. Miller to take first?

A. Notify the local law enforcement authorities.

B. Call Jay's parents, express his concerns, and suggest ways in which Jay's parents could help Jay to modify his own behavior.

C. Work with Jay and appropriate school staff to identify and treat Jay's problems.

D. Talk with Jay after school and confront him directly.

C This question measures Competency 012: The teacher enhances professional knowledge and skills by effectively interacting with other members of the educational community and participating in various types of professional activities.

Here's How to Crack It

Step 1: Identify the scenario.

- Age range: high school

- Goal: determine the appropriate action

Step 2: Use POE to narrow down the answer choices.

    A. No. There's no evidence the student was involved in a crime.

    B. No. The first half of the solution is possible, but the second half is condescending toward the parents.

    C. Maybe. It might be appropriate to involve others.

    D. Maybe. That might be a good approach, too.

Step 3: Make a final decision.

Although confronting Jay directly might prove beneficial, it's unlikely that the teacher has the counseling training to deal effectively with the situation. It's better to bring in extra support. The best answer is C.

16. Aaron later approaches Mr. Miller individually and tells him that an overcommitted schedule has prevented him from doing his homework. In addition to maintaining a full academic load, Aaron has recently starting dating a girl, working a part-time job, and practicing guitar. Mr. Miller suggests that Aaron prioritize his responsibilities by making a chart listing the approximate number of hours that he spends on each activity, and then listing the positives and negatives associated with each activity. One benefit of applying this process is that:

    A. Aaron will learn exactly how to solve his current dilemma.

    B. Aaron will learn a strategy that he can apply to similar problems in the future.

    C. Aaron will understand that problems can have more than one solution.

    D. Aaron will realize that schoolwork is more important than a social life.

B   This question measures Competency 010: The teacher monitors student performance and achievement; provides students with timely, high-quality feedback; and responds flexibly to promote learning for all students.

Here's How to Crack It

Step 1: Identify the scenario.

- Age range: high school

- Goal: determine the educational benefit

Step 2: Use POE to narrow down the answer choices.
There could be lots of good reasons to do that analysis.

    A. Unlikely. This is an analytical tool, but it won't necessarily lead to an exact conclusion.

    B. Maybe. This is a cross-applicable analysis tool.

    C. No. This technique is used for analysis.

    D. No. That's one possible outcome, but there's nothing in the scenario that suggests it's the conclusion that Aaron will come to.

Step 3: Make a final decision.
The best answer is B.

17. What is the best way for a teacher to inform parents about an upcoming field trip to an art museum?

    A. Call the parents at home in the evening.

    B. Call the parents at work.

    C. Email parents.

    D. Send a flyer home with students.

D   The item above measures Competency 011: The teacher understands the importance of family involvement in children's education and knows how to interact and communicate effectively with families.

Here's How to Crack It

Step 1: Identify the scenario.

- Age range: none given

- Goal: choose the best way to communicate with all parents in a class

Step 2: Use POE to narrow down the answer choices.
Let's see what our choices are:

    A. No. Some parents may work at night.

    B. No. That's inappropriate, except in the case of an emergency.

    C. No. Not all parents have access to email.

    D. Yes. That's better than the other three.

Step 3: Make a final decision.
Be careful that you don't assume that the answer that cites advanced technology is automatically correct. Of course, if the question asks about technology, that's a different matter, but in this case advanced technology does not mean "correct answer." Here, the best answer is D.

18. Which of the following is legally required when a teacher suspects the need for special education for one of her students?

    A.   written permission from a parent/guardian

    B.   review of the student's records

    C.   meeting with the student to discuss the problem

    D.   written permission from the school board

A   The item above measures Competency 013: The teacher understands and adheres to legal and ethical requirements for educators and is knowledgeable of the structure of education in Texas.

Here's How to Crack It

Step 1: Identify the scenario.

- Age range: none given

- Goal: identify the legal requirement

Step 2: Use POE to narrow down the answer choices.
You should know this one, too: you need parental permission to test a child for a learning disability.

    A.   Yes. That's correct.

    B.   No. That's not a legal requirement.

    C.   No. That's not a legal requirement.

    D.   No. That's not a legal requirement.

Step 3: Make a final decision.
A is the best answer.

19. The proper manner in which to cite sources when writing a report:

    A.   is optional for information found on the Internet.

    B.   requires citing the source only when exact wording is used.

    C.   does not include citing websites as sources.

    D.   involves citing websites in the same way as citing any other source.

D   The item above measures Competency 009: The teacher incorporates the effective use of technology to plan, organize, deliver and evaluate instruction for all students.

Here's How to Crack It

Step 1: Identify the scenario.

- Age range: none given

- Goal: identify the proper way to cite sources

Step 2: Use POE to narrow down the answer choices.

A good basic rule is: don't plagiarize. Let's see what we've got:

A. Why would it be optional? Cross it out.

B. No. It's still plagiarism if it's a paraphrase. Cross it out.

C. No. It's still plagiarism.

D. Yes. That's correct.

Step 3: Make a final decision.

D is the best answer.

20. Mr. Magee has organized his students into groups of four or five in which to discuss the characters in a book his class is reading. Which of the following is the most effective method for assigning grades for group participation?

    A. allowing a group leader to grade the students

    B. informal observation

    C. group self-evaluation

    D. asking the group to write up what they have discussed

B   The item above measures Competency 010: The teacher monitors student performance and achievement; provides students with timely, high-quality feedback; and responds flexibly to promote learning for all students.

Here's How to Crack It

Step 1: Identify the scenario.

- Age range: none given

- Goal: pick an effective assessment method for a collaborative learning project

Step 2: Use POE to narrow down the answer choices.

    A.   No. Grading is the teacher's responsibility.

    B.   Maybe. It's tough to grade participation formally.

    C.   No. These are individual grades for participation within a group.

    D.   No. Again, these are participation grades.

Step 3: Make a final decision.

There's only one answer that even merited a "maybe." The best answer is B.

21.   A tenth-grade art teacher has been told that her class can only take one field trip this year and must decide between the modern art museum and the fine art museum. The teacher is considering allowing her students to vote on which trip they prefer. The art teacher's probable purpose is:

    A.   to create a positive attitude in the classroom.

    B.   to involve the students in their own learning.

    C.   to be able to come to a consensus about where the field trip will be.

    D.   to research different field trip options.

B   The item above measures Competency 005: The teacher knows how to establish a classroom climate that fosters learning, equity, and excellence and uses this knowledge to create a physical and emotional environment that is safe and productive.

Here's How to Crack It

Step 1: Identify the scenario.

- Age range: tenth grade

- Goal: determine why a teacher allows students to choose their own field trip destination

Step 2: Use POE to narrow down the answer choices.

    A.   Maybe. Keep it for now.

    B.   Maybe. Keep it for now.

    C.   No. Voting doesn't make a consensus.

    D.   No. Voting should happen after the options have been explored.

Step 3: Make a final decision.

Which answer do you think the SBEC would prefer, A or B? Remember that a teacher's job is fundamentally about promoting learning. The best answer is B.

22. Mrs. Snow, a French teacher, has invited a teacher who just transferred in from out of state to attend a TEKS seminar and workshop with other teachers from the school. This new teacher:

   A. has found an important resource for teachers.

   B. probably knows little about the TEKS.

   C. must attend in order to complete certification.

   D. must first register with a professional organization.

A The item above measures Competency 012: The teacher enhances professional knowledge and skills by effectively interacting with other members of the educational community and participating in various types of professional activities.

Here's How to Crack It

Step 1: Identify the scenario.

  • Age range: not given

  • Goal: none given

Step 2: Use POE to narrow down the answer choices.

We're asked to comment on the new teacher. We'd better look at the answer choices:

   A. Maybe. That's a true statement, but it's very vague. We'll keep it for now.

   B. That might be true, but it's not necessarily true. Besides, how much is "little?" Cross it out.

   C. No. That's not a requirement for certification.

   D. No. That's not a requirement.

Step 3: Make a final decision.

Even if you didn't know whether choices C and D were requirements or not, A is still a true answer, even if it's very vague. The best choice is A.

23. A Government teacher will start a new chapter this week on the branches of the government. The best way to begin this chapter is to:

   A.   discuss key vocabulary.

   B.   watch a video about checks and balances.

   C.   learn what the students already know during a class discussion.

   D.   assign prework and chapter reading to prepare the students.

C   The item above measures Competency 007: The teacher understands and applies principles and strategies for communicating effectively in varied teaching and learning contexts.

Here's How to Crack It

Step 1: Identify the scenario.

- Age range: none given

- Goal: determine the best way to begin a new chapter

Step 2: Use POE to narrow down the answer choices.

How should any teacher start a new topic? By determining how new knowledge should be integrated with previous knowledge. Let's see what we have:

   A.   No. That won't tell the teacher anything about previous knowledge.

   B.   No. That mentions specific subject matter, which can't be the right answer on a TExES PPR exam.

   C.   Maybe. That would give the teacher information about previous knowledge.

   D.   No. Again, there's no reference to previous knowledge.

Step 3: Make a final decision.

We only had one answer left. The best answer is C.

24. A high school teacher accidentally overhears a girl talking with her boyfriend. The couple is discussing the boy's father and the fact that he had hit the boy. The teacher notices that the boy has a few large bruises. The teacher is required do which of the following?

    A. Report the encounter to authorities within 48 hours.

    B. Talk to the boy directly before making a report.

    C. Ask the school administration to investigate the report.

    D. Speak with both the boy and girl before making a report.

A The item above measures Competency 013: The teacher understands and adheres to legal and ethical requirements for educators and is knowledgeable of the structure of education in Texas.

Here's How to Crack It

Step 1: Identify the scenario.

- Age range: high school

- Goal: determine a teacher's requirement

Step 2: Use POE to narrow down the answer choices.
You should know this one: a teacher is required to report the suspicion of abuse.

    A. Yes. This is required.

    B. No. That's not required.

    C. No. That's not required.

    D. No. That's not required.

Step 3: Make a final decision.
There's only one answer left. A is the best answer.

25. An eighth-grade teacher probably has the greatest effect on which of the following?

    A. her students' behavior

    B. her students' choice of friends

    C. her students' academic improvement

    D. her students' level of confidence

C   The item above measures Competency 001: The teacher understands human developmental processes and applies this knowledge to plan instruction and ongoing assessment that motivate students and are responsive to their developmental characteristics and needs.

Here's How to Crack It

Step 1: Identify the scenario.

- Age range: eighth grade

- Goal: determine what effect a teacher might have

Step 2: Use POE to narrow down the answer choices.
This is tough. What do we know about eighth graders? They are searching for identity and typically are entering puberty.

A.   Maybe, but unlikely. Leave it in until we find something better.

B.   No. That's virtually impossible at this age.

C.   Possibly. That's better than choice A, so we can cross A out now.

D.   No. Confidence is determined by a student's peers at this age.

Step 3: Make a final decision.
C is the only choice left, and is therefore the best answer.

26.   A high school teacher of gifted students should expect which of the following behaviors from the students?

A.   the ability to handle peer relationships easily

B.   the ability to stay self-motivated in the classroom

C.   the ability to work well in groups of mixed ability

D.   the ability to evaluate each other fairly

B   The item above measures Competency 001: The teacher understands human developmental processes and applies this knowledge to plan instruction and ongoing assessment that motivate students and are responsive to their developmental characteristics and needs.

Here's How to Crack It

Step 1: Identify the scenario.

- Age range: high school

- Goal: determine expected abilities of gifted students

Step 2: Use POE to narrow down the answer choices.

    A. No. This is not a predominant characteristic of gifted students. Cross it out.

    B. Maybe. Keep it for now.

    C. No. This, in fact, is usually not the case with gifted students. Cross it out.

    D. No. This is not usually characteristic of any high school students. Cross it out.

Step 3: Make a final decision.
We gave answer choice B a "maybe," but it's the only choice left, and is therefore the best answer.

27. Which of the following would be the most effective way to encourage students to become more interested in literature?

    A. offering extra credit to the students for reading works of literature

    B. publishing students' names in the school newsletter

    C. increasing the percentage of the final grade based on reading literature

    D. allowing the students to be involved in choosing the literature that they are required to read

D   The item above measures Competency 008: The teacher provides appropriate instruction that actively engages students in the learning process.

Here's How to Crack It

Step 1: Identify the scenario.

- Age range: none given

- Goal: motive students' interest in literature.

Step 2: Use POE to narrow down the answer choices.

    A. Maybe. That would motivate students.

    B. No. That's not much of a motivation, and depending on the age range, could make students less inclined to read.

    C. Maybe. That would motivate students, too.

    D. Maybe. That would also motivate students.

Step 3: Make a final decision.
When answering a question regarding motivation, remember that internal motivation is preferred over external motivation. The best answer, therefore, is D.

28. A biology teacher assigns students to groups, each of which includes students of varying abilities, to study and dissect a frog. The purpose of having students at different levels in each group is:

A. to prevent students working at a lower level from getting lost in the process.

B. to allow more advanced students to further their understanding of the material by teaching it to others.

C. to make sure that each group will be able to arrive at the same conclusions if the same steps are followed.

D. to allow students to meet other students who they might not know as well.

B The item above measures Competency 005: The teacher knows how to establish a classroom climate that fosters learning, equity, and excellence and uses this knowledge to create a physical and emotional environment that is safe and productive.

Here's How to Crack It

Step 1: Identify the scenario.

- Age range: none given

- Goal: determine the purpose of mixed-ability groups

Step 2: Use POE to narrow down the answer choices.
In general, mixed-ability groups allow students to learn from each other.

A. No. That wouldn't be a unique advantage of mixed-ability groups.

B. Yes. That's one purpose of mixed-ability groups.

C. No. There's no guarantee that would happen.

D. No. That's not a unique advantage of mixed-ability groups.

Step 3: Make a final decision.
B is the best answer.

29. Which of the following would be most helpful to a teacher tracking grades for more than 100 students?

A. presentation software

B. computer database

C. word-processing program

D. computer spreadsheet

D   The item above measures Competency 009: The teacher incorporates the effective use of technology to plan, organize, deliver, and evaluate instruction for all students.

Here's How to Crack It

Step 1: Identify the scenario.

- Age range: none given

- Goal: identify appropriate technology to track grades

Step 2: Use POE to narrow down the answer choices.

A. No, not for tracking grades.

B. Maybe. Keep it for now.

C. No, not for tracking grades.

D. Maybe.

Step 3: Make a final decision.
You could use a database, but because numerical calculations with those grades are likely, the best answer is D.

30. During a parent/teacher conference, the parent of a junior in high school asks the teacher for her opinion about where the junior should apply to college. The teacher should respond by:

A. referring the parent to the school guidance counselor.

B. informing the parent that this is not something teachers do.

C. asking what schools the parent prefers and then suggesting one of those as the best option.

D. giving the parent a few examples based on the student's interests, if possible, and encouraging the parent to do more research.

D   The item above measures Competency 011: The teacher understands the importance of family involvement in children's education and knows how to interact and communicate effectively with families.

Here's How to Crack It

Step 1: Identify the scenario.

- Age range: high school junior

- Goal: reply to parent about college ideas

Step 2: Use POE to narrow down the answer choices.

A. No. The teacher will have valuable insight that would complement the counselor's work.

B. No. Teachers do that all the time.

C. No. The parent is coming to the teacher for expertise.

D. Yes. This way, the teacher gives valuable insight.

Step 3: Make a final decision.
Choice D is the best answer.

31. Mrs. Rouse has a bright student in her class who often finishes early but makes careless mistakes on tests. To help the student, Mrs. Rouse asks the student to spend the extra time double-checking his work. This is an example of which of the following?

    A. preferential treatment toward a student

    B. self-motivation techniques

    C. use of meta-cognitive techniques

    D. proper pacing

C   The item above measures Competency 007: The teacher understands and applies principles and strategies for communicating effectively in varied teaching and learning contexts.

Here's How to Crack It

Step 1: Identify the scenario.

- Age range: none given

- Goal: identify the type of help the teacher is offering

Step 2: Use POE to narrow down the answer choices.

A. No. That's not preferential treatment.

B. Maybe, but it doesn't seem like a motivating technique.

C. That's better, even if you're not sure what "meta" means.

D. No. Telling the student to spend time double-checking answers isn't an example of pacing.

Step 3: Make a final decision.
The best answer is C. Meta-cognition refers to having students be aware of their learning strengths and weaknesses.

32. It has been brought to the attention of the English department that many of the students who were in a class taught by a new teacher, Mr. Timmons, have not read all of the required selections of that class. To ensure this does not continue to be a problem, Mrs. Schupe has agreed to help Mr. Timmons structure his class differently so that there will be time for all required reading selections. This is an example of which of the following?

   A. teachers collaborating to improve their students' education

   B. teachers learning better communication skills

   C. teachers correcting flaws in their curriculum

   D. teachers expecting too much from younger colleagues

A The item above measures Competency 012: The teacher enhances professional knowledge and skills by effectively interacting with other members of the educational community and participating in various types of professional activities.

Here's How to Crack It

Step 1: Identify the scenario.

- Age range: none given

- Goal: categorize teacher interaction

Step 2: Use POE to narrow down the answer choices.

   A. Maybe. Keep it for now.

   B. No. Teachers aren't learning better skills; they're fixing a problem.

   C. Maybe. Keep it for now.

   D. No. The more experienced teacher is helping out, not expecting too much.

Step 3: Make a final decision.
Choices A and C are left. While the teachers are correcting a flaw, it doesn't sound like it's a flaw in the curriculum as much as a flaw in the implementation. A is therefore the best answer.

33. A high school computer teacher has noticed that some students who are not as familiar with computers rely on other students to help them complete computer assignments. What should the teacher do to increase these less advanced students' classroom computer use?

A. Give informal basic computer lessons to these students during their regular lunch period.

B. Require all students to spend a minimum amount of time on the classroom computer each week.

C. Develop a computer project with easy-to-follow instructions that will allow the students to build confidence.

D. Talk to the students about the importance of technology in education as well as in other aspects of their lives.

C   The item above measures Competency 002: The teacher understands student diversity and knows how to plan learning experiences and design assessments that are responsive to differences among students and that promote all students' learning.

Here's How to Crack It

Step 1: Identify the scenario.

- Age range: high school

- Goal: increase less advanced students' computer use

Step 2: Use POE to narrow down the answer choices

A. No. Taking away students' free time is unlikely to be a motivator.

B. Maybe. Keep it for now.

C. Maybe. Keep it for now.

D. No. That won't help the students learn about computers.

Step 3: Make a final decision.

We're down to choices B and C. Requiring time may solve the problem, but it would help if the less advanced students had a project they could complete independently. C is a better answer than B.

Good job! Nice work! B+

34. The biggest problem with the above comment is that:

    A.   the student isn't given any reason why the essay was worth a B+.

    B.   the student will believe that all work is worthy of a B+.

    C.   the student isn't given any specific information to help her improve on future essays.

    D.   the student will believe that this teacher grades arbitrarily.

C   This question measures Competency 010: The teacher monitors student performance and achievement; provides students with timely, high-quality feedback; and responds flexibly to promote learning for all students.

Here's How to Crack It

Step 1: Identify the scenario.

- Age range: high school

- Goal: analyze a poor comment

Step 2: Use POE to narrow down the answer choices.

    A.   That's true, and is a problem.

    B.   No. That's unlikely to happen based on this one comment.

    C.   That's true, and is also a problem.

    D.   Perhaps, but one comment is unlikely to lead the student to that conclusion.

Step 3: Make a final decision.

While both choices A and C are problems, choice C is a bigger problem because feedback is supposed to promote learning, and here the student is given nothing to learn from. The best answer is C.

35. The comment could have a counterproductive effect on the student's self-esteem for which of the following reasons?

   A.   A B+ is a substandard grade.

   B.   Undeserved praise provides no incentive for actually performing well.

   C.   Such high praise for a less-than-perfect grade will make future praise for potentially better work less meaningful.

   D.   Praise from a teacher may earn her enmity from her peer group.

C   This question measures Competency 005: The teacher knows how to establish a classroom climate that fosters learning and excellence and uses this knowledge to create a physical and emotional environment that is safe and productive.

Here's How to Crack It

Step 1: Identify the scenario.

- Age range: high school

- Goal: identify a potential self-esteem issue

Step 2: Use POE to narrow down the answer choices.

   A.   No. That's not true.

   B.   Maybe, but that's not a self-esteem issue.

   C.   Yes. If there are no firm standards, then achievement will become meaningless. Because self-esteem derives from achievement, this could have a detrimental impact.

   D.   No. It's unlikely that the teacher praises only this student.

Step 3: Make a final decision.
The best answer is C.

36. One reason why the driver's education program at the high school includes information about the consequences of drinking and driving is because:

    A.   students are required to learn this information before they can obtain a drivers license.

    B.   teenagers probably do not understand why they should not drink.

    C.   parents do not teach their children about driving responsibly.

    D.   many young people take risks, feeling that nothing bad will happen to them.

D The item above measures Competency 001: The teacher understands human developmental processes and applies this knowledge to plan instruction and ongoing assessment that motivate students and are responsive to their developmental characteristics and needs.

Here's How to Crack It

Step 1: Identify the scenario.

- Age range: high school

- Goal: determine why alcohol education is included in driver's education classes

Step 2: Use POE to narrow down the answer choices.

    A.   Unlikely. They're required to pass an examination that might include that information, though. Keep it for now.

    B.   No. Teenagers are likely to understand why they shouldn't, but are also likely to ignore the dangers.

    C.   No. There's no evidence for that statement.

    D.   Yes. That's characteristic of teenage behavior in general.

Step 3: Make a final decision.
Although choice A was a plausible answer, D is better.

37. An eighth-grade teacher has broken her class up into small groups. The groups will work together on a budget for a pretend company and each member of the group will have specific tasks to complete. At the end of the project, each group will complete an evaluation of their own group's performance. The likely purpose of this evaluation is:

A. to help students review their own effectiveness.

B. to help the teacher determine the individual group members' grades on the project.

C. to help the teacher understand the dynamics of each group.

D. to allow the students to participate in determining their own grade.

A The item above measures Competency 004: The teacher understands learning processes and factors that impact student learning and demonstrates this knowledge by planning effective, engaging instruction and appropriate assessments.

Here's How to Crack It

Step 1: Identify the scenario.

- Age range: eighth grade

- Goal: identify purpose of group self-evaluation

Step 2: Use POE to narrow down the answer choices.
Let's see what we have:

A. Yes. This is a possible purpose.

B. No. A group self-evaluation wouldn't help determine individual grades.

C. Maybe, but a teacher could better understand group dynamics through informal observation.

D. No. Eighth graders are too young to help determine their own grades.

Step 3: Make a final decision.
A seems to be the best answer.

38. A high school has an internal email system in which every teacher, administrator, and other type of employee has an email account. The school strongly suggests everyone check their email daily. The reasoning for this is probably to:

   A. be able to transfer sensitive information quickly.

   B. share urgent information with appropriate parties.

   C. make the job of the front office administrators easier.

   D. communicate information that used to be contained in daily memos.

D The item above measures Competency 009: The teacher incorporates the effective use of technology to plan, organize, deliver, and evaluate instruction for all students.

Here's How to Crack It

Step 1: Identify the scenario.

- Age range: none given

- Goal: determine reasoning behind school's use of email

Step 2: Use POE to narrow down the answer choices.
Why does anyone use email? Because it's convenient. Let's see what we've got:

   A. Unlikely, because of the word *sensitive*.

   B. Also unlikely, because of the word *urgent*.

   C. Perhaps, but that doesn't sound like a correct answer.

   D. Yes! That makes life easier for everyone.

Step 3: Make a final decision.
D is the best answer.

39. David is repeatedly late to school and when asked about it, David says that his father is not always able to drive him to school and so sometimes he must walk. The teacher's best response would be to:

    A.   encourage David to wake up earlier and not rely on his father.

    B.   offer to pick up David on these mornings.

    C.   ask the mother of one of David's friends to pick up David each morning.

    D.   be supportive and ask if there is something the teacher can do.

D   The item above measures Competency 004: The teacher understands learning processes and factors that impact student learning and demonstrates this knowledge by planning effective, engaging instruction and appropriate assessments.

Here's How to Crack It

Step 1: Identify the scenario.

- Age range: none given

- Goal: identify the appropriate teacher response

Step 2: Use POE to narrow down the answer choices.

    A.   Maybe. Let's keep it.

    B.   No. That oversteps student/teacher boundaries.

    C.   No. That also oversteps student/teacher boundaries.

    D.   Maybe. Let's keep it.

Step 3: Make a final decision.
This is tough. Choice D won't necessarily solve the problem, but choice A seems to intrude on the father/son relationship. In a situation such as this, it's better to err on the side of caution, so the best answer is D.

40. Tensions have been running high enough that students are raising their voices in class. To reduce the tension in a productive manner, Ms. Myers should:

A. ban the topic from further discussion and move on to another topic.

B. have students write research papers on the economic impact of suburban growth in general.

C. have students objectively measure their level of support and chart the information on a graph.

D. have students research the likely implications of this project and have them present their findings in a structured debate format.

D This question tests Competency 007: The teacher understands and applies principles and strategies for communicating effectively in varied teaching and learning contexts.

Here's How to Crack It

Step 1: Identify the scenario.

- Age range: high school

- Goal: reduce class tension in a productive manner

Step 2: Use POE to narrow down the answer choices.

A. No. That wouldn't be productive.

B. Maybe, but it doesn't seem relevant to the issue at hand.

C. No. How would that resolve the tension?

D. Maybe. That would be productive.

Step 3: Make a final decision.

It would take a good teacher to channel that much energy, but choice D is most likely to produce positive results. The best answer is D.

41. Focusing on an issue of direct relevance to the students is most likely to produce which of the following educational benefits?

  A. It will teach students to more easily apply the same economic principles to other, less familiar situations.

  B. It will spark a lifelong interest in economics.

  C. It will result in higher economic grades for the students.

  D. It will ensure that students understand the fundamental principles of economics.

A   This question tests Competency 008: The teacher provides appropriate instruction that actively engages students in the learning process.

Here's How to Crack It

Step 1: Identify the scenario.

- Age range: high school

- Goal: determine an educational benefit

Step 2: Use POE to narrow down the answer choices.

  A. Maybe. That could be a benefit.

  B. No. That's unlikely.

  C. No. That's not necessarily true.

  D. No. That's not necessarily true.

Step 3: Make a final decision.

The question asks for the most likely benefit. Choice A is the best-supported answer because studying this topic will definitely make it easier for students to study similar topics later. The other choices are not as easily supported.

42. Allowing students to help plan their own field trip:

  A. allows students to feel they can exercise some control over their own education.

  B. allows teachers to evaluate the leadership qualities of their students.

  C. helps teachers identify students who are self-motivated.

  D. demonstrates the principles of the democratic process.

A   The item above measures Competency 003: The teacher understands procedures for designing effective and coherent instruction and assessment based on appropriate learning goals and objectives.

Here's How to Crack It

Step 1: Identify the scenario.

- Age range: none given

- Goal: determine why students should be allowed to help plan their own field trip

Step 2: Use POE to narrow down the answer choices.
A teacher should give students as much responsibility for their own education as they are able to handle.

A.   Maybe. This looks like a good answer.

B.   No. Choice A is a better answer.

C.   No. Choice A is a better answer.

D.   No. The planning isn't necessarily democratic.

Step 3: Make a final decision.
Although a teacher might be able to derive the benefits described in choices B and C, choice A is what the SBEC is looking for. Remember the primary responsibility is to the students' education.

43.   Where is the best location in the classroom to seat a student with a hearing problem?

A.   away from any source of background noise

B.   close to where the teacher stands when lecturing

C.   at the front of the classroom

D.   next to a friend who can help the student keep up with what is going on

B   The item above measures Competency 005: The teacher knows how to establish a classroom climate that fosters learning, equity, and excellence and uses this knowledge to create a physical and emotional environment that is safe and productive.

Here's How to Crack It

Step 1: Identify the scenario.

- Age range: none given

- Goal: to best place a hearing-impaired student

Step 2: Use POE to narrow down the answer choices.
Let's see what we've got.

A.   Maybe. Let's keep it.

B.   That's also a possibility. Keep it.

C.   Not necessarily. B is a better answer. Cross out C.

D.   No. That's not a student's responsibility.

Step 3: Make a final decision.
We're down to A and B. Is it really possible to position a student away from any background noise? Probably not. The best answer is B.

44.   A high school drama teacher has developed a skit for the students that depicts two boys who decide to drive home after drinking at a friend's party. The skit demonstrates the horrible effects of their decision by showing a victim's family at the funeral, one boy in jail, and another one wracked with guilt. The primary purpose of this skit is to:

A.   promote awareness about how the law treats convicted drunk drivers.

B.   make parents aware of their teenagers' behavior.

C.   show students the possibly devastating effects of what may seem like harmless behavior.

D.   show students alternatives to drinking and driving.

C   The item above measures Competency 006: The teacher understands strategies for creating an organized and productive learning environment and for managing student behavior.

Here's How to Crack It

Step 1: Identify the scenario.

- Age range: high school

- Goal: identify the primary purpose of a skit

Step 2: Use POE to narrow down the answer choices.
We're looking for an answer that says, "scare tactics." Let's see what we have:

A.   Maybe, but there's more to it than that.

B.   No. We don't know if the parents are involved, and there's no evidence that the students are engaged in that sort of behavior.

C. Yes. That's close to "scare tactics."

D. No. No alternatives were presented.

Step 3: Make a final decision.
C is a better answer than A, because A is one component of C.

45. It becomes obvious to a high school teacher that her students have some gender stereotypes about certain professions. To combat this stereotyping, the teacher could do which of the following?

   A. Use the opposite of the stereotype in all classroom activities.

   B. Require students to write a paper on the first woman elected to Congress.

   C. Invite a woman astronaut to be a guest speaker in the class.

   D. Ask the students why they think women cannot do some jobs.

D The item above measures Competency 002: The teacher understands student diversity and knows how to plan learning experiences and design assessments that are responsive to differences among students and that promote all students' learning.

Here's How to Crack It
Step 1: Identify the scenario.

   • Age range: high school

   • Goal: combat gender stereotypes

Step 2: Use POE to narrow down the answer choices.

   A. Maybe. Constant reinforcement of the opposite stereotype might work.

   B. No. If anything, this will only cause resentment.

   C. No. That's only one example and could be seen as an anomaly.

   D. Maybe. Confronting the stereotype might work.

Step 3: Make a final decision.
Choices A and D are both plausible. But because the situation involves high school students, the students are old enough to apply critical thinking skills to the examination of their own stereotypes. Choice D is therefore the best answer.

46. Which of the following situations should most concern a teacher?

    A.   Matthew suffers from anxiety in situations such as testing.

    B.   Aaron has memorized all of his math formulas but does not understand how to apply them.

    C.   Lynn doesn't like science and often does not complete her science homework.

    D.   Mary is typically the last student in her class to understand difficult concepts.

B   The item above measures Competency 010: The teacher monitors student performance and achievement; provides students with timely, high-quality feedback; and responds flexibly to promote learning for all students.

Here's How to Crack It

Step 1: Identify the scenario.

- Age range: none given

- Goal: identify the most serious problem

Step 2: Use POE to narrow down the answer choices.

    A.   That's a common problem, and shouldn't be a major cause for concern. Cross it out.

    B.   Maybe. That suggests a cognitive problem.

    C.   No. That's also a common problem.

    D.   Maybe.

Step 3: Make a final decision.

Choices B and D are both worrisome, but at least Mary understands the concepts, although she may be slow. B is the best answer.

47. Which of the following behaviors should lead to Travis's being permanently removed from class?

    A.   falling asleep in class

    B.   starting a fight with another student who had never been in trouble before

    C.   interrupting the class to such a degree that all required subjects are not able to be covered

    D.   continually using foul language toward the teacher and other students

C The item above measures Competency 013: The teacher understands and adheres to legal and ethical requirements for educators and is knowledgeable of the structure of education in Texas.

Here's How to Crack It

Step 1: Identify the scenario.

- Age range: none given

- Goal: identify expulsion-worthy behavior

Step 2: Use POE to narrow down the answer choices.

A. No. We'd have all been expelled at one time or another.

B. No. Starting a fight isn't worthy of expulsion.

C. Yes. This interferes with the rest of the class.

D. No. That's a problem, but not in and of itself worthy of expulsion.

Step 3: Make a final decision.
The wording of choice C makes it clear that Travis is preventing others from learning. Under that circumstance, he should be permanently removed from class. The best answer is C.

48. Which of the following would be the most efficient tool a teacher could provide to a deaf interpreter working with one of her students?

    A. copies of all textbooks that will be used in the classroom

    B. a list of required content for the course

    C. a daily copy of the teacher's lesson plan

    D. a permanent small area in the classroom

C The item above measures Competency 012: The teacher enhances professional knowledge and skills by effectively interacting with other members of the educational community and participating in various types of professional activities.

Here's How to Crack It

Step 1: Identify the scenario.

- Age range: none given

- Goal: efficiently help a deaf interpreter

Step 2: Use POE to narrow down the answer choices.

Let's see what we have:

    A.   No. Textbooks can be read by the student with no help.

    B.   Maybe. This would provide the interpreter with an idea of the course content, but not necessarily day-to-day lessons.

    C.   Maybe. This would help the interpreter follow what was going on in the class on a daily basis.

    D.   No. The student should be integrated into the class as much as possible.

Step 3: Make a final decision.

The question asks for the most efficient tool. A daily copy of the lesson plan would help prepare the interpreter for the immediate task at hand; a list of required content wouldn't tell the interpreter what information was going to be covered next. Choice C is more efficient, and is therefore the correct answer.

49.   A French teacher could most effectively instill in students a sense appreciation of French culture through which of the following methods?

    A.   teaching students about French celebrations

    B.   discussing what foods Americans eat that are French in origin

    C.   showing students a French movie

    D.   celebrating French holidays or celebrations in the classroom

    D   The item above measures Competency 002: The teacher understands student diversity and knows how to plan learning experiences and design assessments that are responsive to differences among students and that promote all students' learning.

Here's How to Crack It

Step 1: Identify the scenario.

- Age range: none given

- Goal: effectively instill appreciation of French culture

Step 2: Use POE to narrow down the answer choices.

    A.   Maybe. Keep it for now.

    B.   Maybe. Keep it for now.

    C.   No. That's worse than the first two. Cross it out.

    D.   Maybe.

Step 3: Make a final decision.
Choice D is preferable to choice A because it involves active student participation. Cross out A. B instills appreciation for French culture only insofar as it influences American culture. D is the best answer.

50. A special education student who is transferring from another state will be joining a ninth-grade classroom. The teacher is concerned about how the other students will receive this new student. Which of the following would most help to ease this transition for everyone?

   A. Encourage the students to treat this student the same way they do everyone else.

   B. Always demonstrate patience and acceptance when problems arise during the transition.

   C. Assign students a research project about special education needs.

   D. Establish clear rules for the other students to follow before the new student arrives about how to treat this new student.

B   The item above measures Competency 005: The teacher knows how to establish a classroom climate that fosters learning, equity, and excellence and uses this knowledge to create a physical and emotional environment that is safe and productive.

Here's How to Crack It

Step 1: Identify the scenario.

   • Age range: ninth grade

   • Goal: ease entry of a special education student

Step 2: Use POE to narrow down the answer choices.
Clearly, the teacher should prepare students for differences, yet not draw embarrassing attention to the new student. Let's see what we've got:

   A. No. There are differences that students should be aware of. Cross out A.

   B. Maybe. That's always good advice.

   C. No. A classroom discussion would suffice.

   D. No. The teacher and students should remain flexible, because it's impossible to prepare for every possible scenario.

Step 3: Make a final decision.
Choice B is a very general answer, but it's the best choice of the four.

51. High school students are more likely to respond to constructive criticism when it is offered:

    A.   one-on-one.

    B.   during a meeting the student has scheduled about a different topic.

    C.   equally to each student in a small group of students.

    D.   anonymously.

A   The item above measures Competency 010: The teacher monitors student performance and achievement; provides students with timely, high-quality feedback; and responds flexibly to promote learning for all students.

Here's How to Crack It

Step 1: Identify the scenario.

- Age range: high school

- Goal: determine the best forum for presenting constructive criticism

Step 2: Use POE to narrow down the answer choices.
High school students don't like being singled out in front of their peers. Let's see what we have.

    A.   Maybe. That singles the student out, but not in front of his peers. Keep it.

    B.   No. No one likes feeling ambushed.

    C.   No. That's in front of the student's peers.

    D.   No. How much credence would you give anonymous criticism?

Step 3: Make a final decision.
A is the only answer left.

52. What must a teacher do if he or she hears a rumor about a student who may have brought a weapon to the school campus?

    A.   Call the police immediately.

    B.   Try to determine the source of the rumor.

    C.   Try to establish if there is in fact a weapon.

    D.   Notify other teachers.

A   The item above measures Competency 013: The teacher understands and adheres to legal and ethical requirements for educators and is knowledgeable of the structure of education in Texas.

Here's How to Crack It

Step 1: Identify the scenario.

- Age range: none given

- Goal: determine teacher action following a gun rumor

Step 2: Use POE to narrow down the answer choices.
You should know this one, because it's a legal requirement.

    A. Yes. The teacher must do this.

    B. No. That's not a legal requirement.

    C. No. That's not the teacher's responsibility.

    D. No. That's not a legal requirement.

Step 3: Make a final decision.
The only answer remaining is A.

> 53. Mrs. Peters has been asked how effective her new classroom policies have been. Measuring the success of these new policies requires:
>
>   A.   an unbiased observer's opinion.
>
>   B.   students to give their opinions through a survey.
>
>   C.   a veteran teacher to observe the classroom.
>
>   D.   a comparison between the classroom before and after the new policies were established.

D   The item above measures Competency 003: The teacher understands procedures for designing effective and coherent instruction and assessment based on appropriate learning goals and objectives.

Here's How to Crack It

Step 1: Identify the scenario.

- Age range: none given

- Goal: measure the success of a new classroom policy

Step 2: Use POE to narrow down the answer choices.
Notice the question asks what the measurement requires. Let's see what we've got:

    A. No. There could be other mechanisms, such as counting the number of rule infractions.

    B. No. There could be other ways to measure effectiveness as well.

C. No. Again, there could be other ways.

D. Yes. In order for there to be measurement, there must be a benchmark.

Step 3: Make a final decision.
With the understanding that we're looking for a requirement, D is the best answer.

> 54. A high school art teacher will soon begin to study
> contemporary art with her students. She would like to
> take her students on a field trip to the Contemporary
> Art Museum to see a special display there on interac-
> tive art. The purpose of this field trip is most likely to:
>
> A. develop students' interest in contemporary art.
>
> B. reward students with a field trip.
>
> C. show students a type of art they are not familiar
> with.
>
> D. experience a change of scenery.

A The item above measures Competency 004: The teacher understands learning processes and factors that impact student learning and demonstrates this knowledge by planning effective, engaging instruction and appropriate assessments.

Here's How to Crack It

Step 1: Identify the scenario.

- Age range: none given

- Goal: identify the purpose of a field trip

Step 2: Use POE to narrow down the answer choices.
In general, the purpose of a field trip is to enhance understanding in a way that can't be appreciated in a classroom setting. Let's see what we've got:

A. Maybe. Keep it for now.

B. No. Field trips shouldn't be considered a reward.

C. Maybe. Keep it for now.

D. No. There should be a better reason for a field trip than that.

Step 3: Make a final decision.
Both choices A and C are possible, because a field trip should provide an experience that students couldn't have in a classroom. We have no evidence to suggest that students are unfamiliar with contemporary art, so we choose A as the best answer.

55. A teacher with over 20 years of teaching experience is returning to teaching after several years outside the profession. He is concerned about his lack of computer experience. He would benefit the most from which of the following options?

    A. relying on help from other teachers in his field.

    B. enrolling in a community college computer course.

    C. attending a computer workshop at a teachers' convention.

    D. reading about new computer trends in a professional publication.

C The item above measures Competency 012: The teacher enhances professional knowledge and skills by effectively interacting with other members of the educational community and participating in various types of professional activities.

Here's How to Crack It

Step 1: Identify the scenario.

- Age range: none given

- Goal: enhance one's computer experience

Step 2: Use POE to narrow down the answer choices.
Let's see what we've got:

    A. No. He needs more help than that.

    B. Maybe. Let's keep it.

    C. Maybe. Let's keep that, too.

    D. No. You need to work with a computer to fully understand it.

Step 3: Make a final decision.
We're down to choices B and C. Because choice C specifically addresses the use of computers in teaching, it's a better answer than B.

56. Which of the following tools would most effectively compute grades that are weighted differently?

    A. a grade book

    B. a calculator

    C. a computer spreadsheet

    D. a ledger

C The item above measures Competency 009: The teacher incorporates the effective use of technology to plan, organize, deliver, and evaluate instruction for all students.

Here's How to Crack It

Step 1: Identify the scenario.

- Age range: none given

- Goal: identify the means to efficiently calculate weighted grades.

Step 2: Use POE to narrow down the answer choices.

A. No. A grade book can't calculate.

B. Maybe, but it would be awfully slow.

C. Yes. That would be effective.

D. No. A ledger can't calculate.

Step 3: Make a final decision.
Choice C is the best answer.

57. Maria asks to speak to her teacher, Ms. Voss. During the conversation Maria expresses concerns about her best friend. She claims that her best friend has confided in her that her father is molesting her. What is Ms. Voss required to do?

A. Report the incident to the police for investigation.

B. Determine if there is enough truth in Maria's story to contact authorities.

C. Speak to Maria's best friend before contacting any authorities.

D. Report the accusation to all involved parties.

A The item above measures Competency 013: The teacher understands and adheres to legal and ethical requirements for educators and is knowledgeable of the structure of education in Texas.

Here's How to Crack It

Step 1: Identify the scenario.

- Age range: none given

- Goal: identify a legal requirement

Step 2: Use POE to narrow down the answer choices.
You should know this one: she must report the suspicion.

    A. Yes.

    B. No. That's not Ms. Voss's responsibility.

    C. No. Again, it is not Ms. Voss's responsibility to confirm or disprove information.

    D. No. This is not the correct course of action and could do more harm than good.

Step 3: Make a final decision.
A is the best answer.

58.   Before leaving on a field trip, the teacher must:

    A.   count the number of students on each bus.

    B.   arrange for eating lunch off campus.

    C.   verify that all medical information is on file for the students.

    D.   have written permission from each student's parent/guardian.

D   The item above measures Competency 013: The teacher understands and adheres to legal and ethical requirements for educators and is knowledgeable of the structure of education in Texas.

Here's How to Crack It

Step 1: Identify the scenario.

- Age range: none given

- Goal: identify a legal requirement

Step 2: Use POE to narrow down the answer choices.
You know this question deals with a legal requirement because is uses the word *must*. You should know the answer to this one already:

    A. No. The teacher might do this, but it is not a legal prerequisite for the trip.

    B. No. This may be done, but it is not a legal requirement for taking a field trip.

    C. No. This is a good idea, but is not a legal requirement for conducting a field trip.

    D. Yes. That's a legal requirement.

Step 3: Make a final decision.
D is the only answer remaining.

59. Giving students a picture and asking them all to discuss what they each see in the picture is an example of:

    A. convergent thinking

    B. divergent thinking

    C. memory recall

    D. brainstorming

B The item above measures Competency 007: The teacher understands and applies principles and strategies for communicating effectively in varied teaching and learning contexts.

Here's How to Crack It

Step 1: Identify the scenario.

- Age range: none given

- Goal: identify the type of thinking

Step 2: Use POE to narrow down the answer choices.

    A. No. That's determining one best approach from many possible approaches.

    B. Maybe. That's coming up with multiple solutions to a problem.

    C. No. That's just repeating memorized information.

    D. Maybe. That's coming up with ideas without stopping to evaluate correctness.

Step 3: Make a final decision.
Because students are using the picture as a starting point and asked to be creative, B is the best answer.

60. A science teacher is planning a lesson on weather phenomena. The class could best be prepared for this lesson by first:

    A. talking about the weather patterns of the area.

    B. discussing the types of weather phenomena that they already know about.

    C. watching the weather on the TV news.

    D. measuring rainfall.

B The item above measures Competency 004: The teacher understands learning processes and factors that impact student learning and demonstrates this knowledge by planning effective, engaging instruction and appropriate assessments.

Here's How to Crack It

Step 1: Identify the scenario.

- Age range: none given

- Goal: best prepare a class for a new lesson

Step 2: Use POE to narrow down the answer choices.

A good teacher introduces new material in the context of the old. Let's see what we have:

A. Maybe. Let's keep it for now.

B. Maybe.

C. No. That doesn't help put new information into context.

D. No. That's too detailed to start with.

Step 3: Make a final decision.

Both A and B are good choices, but B explicitly mentions putting information in the context of previously understood information, so it is the best answer.

61. To motivate his tenth-grade government class, Mr. Bernard should consider:

A. requiring students who do not participate in class to attend detention after school.

B. assigning failing grades to students who do not participate in class.

C. distributing small prizes to students who participate fully in class discussions.

D. rewarding students who participate or have high grade averages by allowing them to skip a test.

D The item above measures Competency 008: The teacher provides appropriate instruction that actively engages students in the learning process.

Here's How to Crack It

Step 1: Identify the scenario.

- Age range: tenth grade

- Goal: motivate a government class

Step 2: Use POE to narrow down the answer choices.
Ideally, motivation should be internal. Let's see what we have:

    A.   No. That's a negative motivation.

    B.   No. That's also a negative motivation.

    C.   Maybe. Keep it in.

    D.   Maybe. Keep it in.

Step 3: Make a final decision.
Neither of the remaining answer choices is an internal motivation. Of choices C and D, D is a better motivator for a tenth-grade class, because grades are more important to them than small prizes. The best answer is D.

62.   An eighth-grade teacher is taking her class on a guided tour at the state capitol building. The teacher must make special arrangements for a boy in her class who is still learning English and may not be able to understand everything the guide will say. What should the teacher do to accommodate the needs of this student?

    A.   Make arrangements for the boy to spend the day at the school with another eighth-grade class.

    B.   Contact the guide service ahead of time to arrange for a tour on tape in the student's language.

    C.   Pair the student with a friend during the tour who can help him follow what the tour guide is saying.

    D.   Ask the student's parents to accompany their son on the field trip.

B   The item above measures Competency 002: The teacher understands student diversity and knows how to plan learning experiences and design assessments that are responsive to differences among students and that promote all students' learning.

Here's How to Crack It

Step 1: Identify the scenario.

- Age range: eighth grade

- Goal: accommodate a student's needs

Step 2: Use POE to narrow down the answer choices.

    A. No. A teacher must accommodate a language difference.

    B. Yes. This is a reasonable accommodation.

    C. No. It's not the friend's responsibility.

    D. No. There's no guarantee that the parents speak better English than the student.

Step 3: Make a final decision.
Choice B is the best answer.

    63.   A tenth-grade teacher has a student, Tammy, who has recently started performing poorly in class and also seems uninterested in school. Tammy's teacher is concerned that she may be using drugs. What is the first step Tammy's teacher should take?

        A.   Talk with the school counselor.

        B.   Talk with the parents.

        C.   Talk with Tammy.

        D.   Talk with Tammy's friends.

    C   The item above measures Competency 010: The teacher monitors student performance and achievement; provides students with timely, high-quality feedback; and responds flexibly to promote learning for all students.

Here's How to Crack It

Step 1: Identify the scenario.

- Age range: tenth grade

- Goal: address the concern that a student may be using drugs

Step 2: Use POE to narrow down the answer choices.
There are no laws governing this area, so approaching the issue directly is a good idea. Let's see what we have:

    A. No. It's inappropriate to get others involved at this stage.

    B. No. That could upset the parents without cause, if Tammy is not using drugs.

    C. Yes. That's approaching the problem directly.

    D. No. That's inappropriate behavior for the teacher.

Step 3: Make a final decision.
We're only left with one; C is the best answer.

64. During the school's open house, the music teacher asks parents who play an instrument to come and volunteer a bit of time to play for the students during music class. The music teacher's motivation for this is:

A. to expose students to types of music they would not hear outside of school.

B. to allow parents the opportunity to see their children in a classroom setting while they are volunteering.

C. to meaningfully include parents in their children's formal education.

D. to allow parents to see what resources the school has in contrast to what is needed.

C   The item above measures Competency 011: The teacher understands the importance of family involvement in children's education and knows how to interact and communicate effectively with families.

Here's How to Crack It

Step 1: Identify the scenario.

- Age range: none given

- Goal: determine the motivation for the teacher's invitation

Step 2: Use POE to narrow down the answer choices.

Parents and teachers should be viewed as equal partners in a child's education. Let's see what the choices are:

A. No. Students may hear all kinds of music outside of school.

B. Maybe. Keep it in.

C. Maybe.

D. No. That's an inappropriate way to address this issue.

Step 3: Make a final decision.

Of choices B and C, choice C better conveys the idea of parents and teachers being equal partners. The best answer is C.

65. Critical thinking is an important skill for students to develop. Which of the following exercises would be best to have the students do in order to help them develop their critical thinking ability?

    A.   Identify the tone of a newspaper article.

    B.   Research the meaning of unfamiliar words found in a story.

    C.   Imagine what might occur after the end of a story.

    D.   Identify the main idea and conclusion of an article.

A   The above item measures Competency 007: The teacher understands and applies principles and strategies for communicating effectively in varied teaching and learning contexts.

Here's How to Crack It

Step 1: Identify the scenario.

- Age range: none given

- Goal: best develop critical thinking skills

Step 2: Use POE to narrow down the answer choices.

    A.   Maybe. That's certainly not a rote skill.

    B.   No. That doesn't involve higher-order thinking.

    C.   Maybe. That's not a rote skill.

    D.   No. That's a rote skill.

Step 3: Make a final decision.

Both choices A and C are plausible. Identifying the tone of an article would require interpretation of statements in the article. Imagining what might occur after the end of a story could incorporate interpretation and higher-order thinking skills, but it wouldn't have to. A is the best answer.

66. Which of the following math exercises requires higher-order thinking than the others?

    A.   converting fractions to decimals

    B.   reducing a fraction

    C.   recognizing a shape as a larger version of a 5-12-13 triangle

    D.   converting a decimal to a percentage

C   The above item measures Competency 004: The teacher understands learning processes and factors that impact student learning and demonstrates this knowledge by planning effective, engaging instruction and appropriate assessments.

Here's How to Crack It

Step 1: Identify the scenario.

- Age range: none given

- Goal: identify the problem requiring higher-order thinking skills

Step 2: Use POE to narrow down the answer choices.

A. No. That's a rote, algorithmic exercise.

B. No. That's also a rote exercise.

C. Yes. That requires higher-level pattern recognition.

D. No. That's a rote exercise.

Step 3: Make a final decision.
C is the best answer.

67. Ms. Delta believes Tony is not living up to his potential. What is the best way for her to communicate her higher expectations for Tony?

    A. Praise Tony's work in front of others.

    B. Challenge Tony and let him know she believes he is capable.

    C. Have Tony work with students who have routinely challenged themselves.

    D. Remove the emphasis on tasks that would be challenging for Tony.

B The item above measures Competency 005: The teacher knows how to establish a classroom climate that fosters learning, equity, and excellence and uses this knowledge to create a physical and emotional environment that is safe and productive.

Here's How to Crack It

Step 1: Identify the scenario.

- Age range: none given

- Goal: communicate high expectations

Step 2: Use POE to narrow down the answer choices.

A. No. If Tony is not working up to his potential, he does not yet merit praise.

B. Yes. Students respond to appropriate challenges.

C. Maybe.

D. No. Students need challenges.

Step 3: Make a final decision.
Choices B and C are both viable, but choice B is more directly stated and is more likely to achieve the desired result than is choice C. B is the best answer.

68. The parents of a high school senior are concerned that their daughter's science classes are not preparing her well enough for college. What is the most appropriate response from the teacher?

   A. Try to reassure the parents by listing the teacher's credentials and experience.

   B. Listen to the parents' concern and explain how the curriculum does meet requirements.

   C. Solicit the parents' ideas as to how the curriculum could be improved.

   D. Suggest the parents meet with a college science professor to learn what is really expected.

B The item above measures Competency 011: The teacher understands the importance of family involvement in children's education and knows how to interact and communicate effectively with families.

Here's How to Crack It

Step 1: Identify the scenario.

- Age range: none given

- Goal: respond to parents' concerns

Step 2: Use POE to narrow down the answer choices.
As always, the teacher should address the concern without upsetting the parents.

   A. No. This makes the teacher appear defensive and doesn't address the parents' concern.

   B. Yes. This is what we're looking for.

   C. No. That's not the parents' job.

   D. No. That sounds as though the teacher is passing the responsibility back to the parents, which might upset them.

Step 3: Make a final decision.
B is the best answer.

69. Allowing students to grade their own essays based on specific criteria would provide the teacher with:

   A. specific information about which students worked the hardest.

   B. no real usable information.

   C. a glimpse into what criteria are more important to the student than others.

   D. information about how the students perceive their own work.

D   The above item measures Competency 001: The teacher understands human developmental processes and applies this knowledge to plan instruction and ongoing assessment that motivate students and are responsive to their developmental characteristics and needs.

Here's How to Crack It

Step 1: Identify the scenario.

- Age range: none given

- Goal: determine what allowing students to grade their own essays would provide the teacher

Step 2: Use POE to narrow down the answer choices.

   A. No. A teacher wouldn't be able to determine that from self-evaluation.

   B. Unlikely. That's an extreme answer choice.

   C. No. The students wouldn't necessarily provide that information.

   D. Yes. A teacher would be able to determine that.

Step 3: Make a final decision.
D is the best answer.

70. Two students, Jack and Conner, often resort to fighting physically with each other. Their teacher's primary goal should be to do what?

   A. Separate the boys from each other in as many activities as possible.

   B. Involve school administrators in the situation as additional resources.

   C. Determine if there is a pattern of aggressive behavior by one of the students.

   D. Teach the students how to work through their problems without becoming physical.

D   The above item measures Competency 006: The teacher understands strategies for creating an organized and productive learning environment and for managing student behavior.

Here's How to Crack It

Step 1: Identify the scenario.

- Age range: none given

- Goal: determine the teacher's primary goal

Step 2: Use POE to narrow down the answer choices.
One goal should be for the teacher to keep the students from fighting. Let's see what the choices are:

   A. No. That's not a good long-term solution.

   B. No. Teachers should be able to solve their own problems.

   C. No. That's not the teacher's primary goal.

   D. Yes. Fundamentally, that will stop the fighting and teach the students not to fight in the future.

Step 3: Make a final decision.
D is the best answer.

71. A history teacher is preparing to start a section about D-Day. To best prepare, the teacher should:

   A. try to find out if the students have a family member who served in WWII.

   B. have students map the invasion on an atlas.

   C. study the history that led up to D-Day.

   D. have a class discussion about D-Day and encourage students to share stories they might know from that day.

D   The item above measures Competency 004: The teacher understands learning processes and factors that impact student learning and demonstrates this knowledge by planning effective, engaging instruction and appropriate assessments.

Here's How to Crack It

Step 1: Identify the scenario.

- Age range: none given

- Goal: prepare a class for a lesson

Step 2: Use POE to narrow down the answer choices.
New knowledge should build on old knowledge. Let's see what the choices are:

    A. No. That doesn't build on old knowledge.

    B. No. That doesn't build on old knowledge.

    C. Maybe. Keep it for now.

    D. Yes. This draws on old knowledge.

Step 3: Make a final decision.
Choice D specifically mentions the idea of bringing in previous knowledge and is therefore the best answer.

72. A teacher must call the parents of a student. Their daughter has been caught skipping school. The teacher should start the conversation by:

    A. explaining the attendance policy of the school.

    B. informing the parents of the consequences of this action.

    C. putting the parents at ease by saying something positive.

    D. assuring the parents of the validity of the charge against the student.

    C   The item above measures Competency 011: The teacher understands the importance of family involvement in children's education and knows how to interact and communicate effectively with families.

Here's How to Crack It

Step 1: Identify the scenario.

- Age range: none given

- Goal: start an unpleasant conversation with parents

Step 2: Use POE to narrow down the answer choices.
Notice the question asks how the teacher should start the conversation. Let's see what we've got:

    A. No. That's not a good way to start.

    B. No. That should come later.

    C. Maybe. It might be best to start with something good.

    D. No. That should come later.

Step 3: Make a final decision.
C is the best answer.

73. Josh's parents have decided to get divorced. As a result, Josh is now shuttled back and forth between two homes, often forgets needed school items at the other parent's house, and has become distracted at school. The best response from Josh's teacher would be to:

    A.   send Josh to visit the school counselor.

    B.   let Josh's friends know he needs their support.

    C.   speak with the parents about making a stronger effort to help their son.

    D.   provide a regular, stable school environment and be supportive.

D   The item above measures Competency 002: The teacher understands student diversity and knows how to plan learning experiences and design assessments that are responsive to differences among students and that promote all students' learning.

Here's How to Crack It

Step 1: Identify the scenario.

- Age range: not given

- Goal: best respond to Josh's situation

Step 2: Use POE to narrow down the answer choices.

    A.   No. This isn't warranted and could make Josh resent his teacher.

    B.   No. It's inappropriate for a teacher to approach Josh's friends in that way.

    C.   No. A conference might be warranted, but not with that as its topic.

    D.   Yes. Josh will benefit from a stable and supportive school environment.

Step 3: Make a final decision.
D is the best answer.

74. Mrs. Laurel spends the first few days of class getting to know her students. This practice has:

    A.   allowed students to feel free to talk during class time.

    B.   helped develop students' communication skills.

    C.   increased students' participation and interest in the class.

    D.   let students learn more about Mrs. Laurel.

C The item above measures Competency 008: The teacher provides appropriate instruction that actively engages students in the learning process.

Here's How to Crack It

Step 1: Identify the scenario.

- Age range: none given

- Goal: determine the benefit of getting to know one's students

Step 2: Use POE to narrow down the answer choices.
Getting to know her students will probably allow Mrs. Laurel to make better choices about her teaching methods. Let's see what we've got:

A. No. That's not a logical outcome.

B. Maybe.

C. Maybe.

D. No. We aren't given facts to support that answer.

Step 3: Make a final decision.
None of the answers is what we're looking for. We don't know how Mrs. Laurel has gotten to know her students, so it's difficult to support choice B. Choice C is the best answer only because the others are indefensible.

75. At the end of each school day, Ms. Lee has her students write one new thing learned that day in their journals. This benefits the students because it:

A. aids Ms. Lee in grading the students' comprehension.

B. helps cement new knowledge the students have just acquired.

C. allows the teacher to see what the students are able to recall.

D. is a tool for the students as well as the parents.

B The item above measures Competency 004: The teacher understands learning processes and factors that impact student learning and demonstrates this knowledge by planning effective, engaging instruction and appropriate assessments.

Here's How to Crack It

Step 1: Identify the scenario.

- Age range: none given

- Goal: determine benefit of journal writing

Step 2: Use POE to narrow down the answer choices.

    A.   No. That's not a benefit for the students.

    B.   Maybe.

    C.   No. That's not a benefit for the students.

    D.   No. That's not a benefit for the students.

Step 3: Make a final decision.
Choice B is the only choice that provides a benefit for the students. The best answer is B.

> 76. Teachers in the math department work together to ensure that students learn the needed skills in one class before advancing to the next. This is an example of:
>
>   A.   communication between all involved parties.
>
>   B.   tracking students from grade level to grade level.
>
>   C.   teachers working together for the best results for their students.
>
>   D.   the math department's strict policies for advancement.

    C   The item above measures Competency 012: The teacher enhances professional knowledge and skills by effectively interacting with other members of the educational community and participating in various types of professional activities.

Here's How to Crack It

Step 1: Identify the scenario.

- Age range: none given

- Goal: identify cooperation among teachers

Step 2: Use POE to narrow down the answer choices.

    A.   No. Not all involved parties are working together, because there's no mention of the students.

    B.   Maybe, but the question seems to be focusing on the collaboration.

    C.   Maybe.

    D.   No. We don't know how strict the policies are.

Step 3: Make a final decision.
This is a vaguely worded question, but choice C does the best job of emphasizing the collaboration. The best answer is C.

77. A teacher borrows a VCR from the library after the librarian has left for the day. He uses the VCR that night at home to tape something he plans to discuss in class. His actions are:

A. ethical because he used the VCR for school purposes.

B. ethical because he returned the VCR before the librarian missed it.

C. unethical because school property should not be removed from the school.

D. unethical because the librarian did not have knowledge of what he did.

A The item above measures Competency 013: The teacher understands and adheres to legal and ethical requirements for educators and is knowledgeable of the structure of education in Texas.

Here's How to Crack It

Step 1: Identify the scenario.

- Age range: none given

- Goal: determine whether a teacher's actions are ethical

Step 2: Use POE to narrow down the answer choices.

A. Maybe.

B. No. That's not grounds for determining ethical behavior.

C. No. The teacher may take equipment home if it's not used for personal purposes.

D. No. There's no ethical requirement to inform the librarian.

Step 3: Make a final decision.
A is the best answer.

78. Mrs. Kobbs has assigned her government students a report on the impact of the Supreme Court case of *Brown v. the Board of Education*. Students will be allowed to research the topic at the school library or at home via the Internet. Allowing students to make use of different resources is most important because it:

A. enables a number of students to search for resources simultaneously.

B. makes it more difficult for students who are not as comfortable using computers.

C. provides different options for students to research their topic.

D. puts a great deal of pressure on the librarian.

C The item above measures Competency 003: The teacher understands procedures for designing effective and coherent instruction and assessment based on appropriate learning goals and objectives.

Here's How to Crack It

Step 1: Identify the scenario.

- Age range: none given

- Goal: determine the importance of providing a wide variety of resources.

Step 2: Use POE to narrow down the answer choices.

A. Maybe.

B. No. That would be a detriment, even if it were true.

C. Maybe.

D. No. That would also be a detriment.

Step 3: Make a final decision.

We're looking for the most important reason. Because choice C has a direct impact on students' learning, it's the best answer.

79. The most important advantage gained by a veteran teacher from subscribing to professional teachers' journals is:

    A.   being able to have access to such a resource at any time.

    B.   remaining apprised of the activities of the professional organization.

    C.   staying current on trends in education and technology.

    D.   building a resource center for new teachers to use.

C   The item above measures Competency 012: The teacher enhances professional knowledge and skills by effectively interacting with other members of the educational community and participating in various types of professional activities.

Here's How to Crack It

Step 1: Identify the scenario.

- Age range: none given

- Goal: determine the benefit of a journal subscription

Step 2: Use POE to narrow down the answer choices.

    A.   No. That's not a very important advantage.

    B.   Maybe.

    C.   Maybe.

    D.   No. That's not an advantage for the veteran teacher.

Step 3: Make a final decision.
Although choices C and D are both advantages, staying current is more important than learning about activities. The best answer is C.

80. A new teacher has been invited to sit in on the class of a fellow English teacher. While observing, the new teacher sees several things she would like to try in her own classroom. After the class ends, the two teachers talk about some of these new ideas. This is an example of:

    A. peer interaction.

    B. professional mentoring.

    C. on-the-job training.

    D. informal mentoring.

D The item above measures Competency 012: The teacher enhances professional knowledge and skills by effectively interacting with other members of the educational community and participating in various types of professional activities.

Here's How to Crack It

Step 1: Identify the scenario.

- Age range: none given

- Goal: identify the teacher interaction

Step 2: Use POE to narrow down the answer choices.

    A. No. The teachers have different levels of experience and that is crucial to the problem.

    B. Maybe.

    C. No.

    D. Maybe.

Step 3: Make a final decision.
Is this formal or informal mentoring? A formal process might involve scheduled appointments and observation of the new teacher by the old teacher. This is less formal. The best answer is D.

81. Eastville High School's dropout rate due to teen-age pregnancies has tripled in the past ten years. To combat this, the school has decided to show a movie depicting the consequences of having a baby as a teen-ager. This type of education is important because:

   A. students don't want to be lectured by adults who might have had similar teenage behavior.

   B. many teenagers don't think about the consequences of their actions.

   C. there are many false rumors about how to avoid becoming pregnant.

   D. many students have been given incorrect information about teenage pregnancy.

B   The item above measures Competency 001: The teacher understands human developmental processes and applies this knowledge to plan instruction and ongoing assessment that motivate students and are responsive to their developmental characteristics and needs.

Here's How to Crack It

Step 1: Identify the scenario.

- Age range: high school

- Goal: determine why the showing of a movie is important

Step 2: Use POE to narrow down the answer choices.
Note that the movie depicts the consequences of having a baby as a teenager. Let's see what our choices are:

   A. Unlikely, but let's see what else is there.

   B. Maybe.

   C. No. That wouldn't be addressed by a movie showing the consequences of being a teenage mother.

   D. No. That also wouldn't be addressed by a movie showing the consequences of being a teenage mother.

Step 3: Make a final decision.
Choice B specifically addresses the issue of consequences and is therefore the correct answer.

82. Mrs. Evans has learned that the uncle of one of her students, Terrell, has died. Which of the following could Mrs. Evans do to help Terrell the most?

    A. Provide a safe, caring and predictable classroom environment for the student.

    B. Suggest to Terrell's mother that he take some time away from school.

    C. Insist Terrell meet with the school counselor.

    D. Monitor Terrell's behavior with his friends and in the classroom.

A The item above measures Competency 010: The teacher monitors student performance and achievement; provides students with timely, high-quality feedback; and responds flexibly to promote learning for all students.

Here's How to Crack It

Step 1: Identify the scenario.

- Age range: none given

- Goal: help Terrell

Step 2: Use POE to narrow down the answer choices.

    A. Yes. Stability is important.

    B. No. That would be a further disruption.

    C. No. That's not warranted at this point.

    D. Maybe.

Step 3: Make a final decision.
Choices D and A are both plausible, but monitoring Terrell's behavior wouldn't help him. Providing a stable environment would. The best choice is A.

83. A teacher is concerned when she hears some students making fun of a male student who has elected to take a cooking class populated almost exclusively by female students. The teacher should react to this situation by doing which of the following?

    A.   Invite male chefs to the next career day event at the school.

    B.   Express disappointment over their behavior and explain how their words can affect others.

    C.   Assign the offending students an essay on famous male chefs as punishment.

    D.   Talk to the home economics teacher about the incident.

B   The item above measures Competency 002: The teacher understands student diversity and knows how to plan learning experiences and design assessments that are responsive to differences among students and that promote all students' learning.

Here's How to Crack It

Step 1: Identify the scenario.

- Age range: none given

- Goal: respond to teasing of a student

Step 2: Use POE to narrow down the answer choices.

    A. No. That does nothing to address the teasing.

    B. Maybe. This directly addresses the teasing.

    C. Maybe. This, like B, addresses the teasing.

    D. No. The teacher should address the problem with those who did the teasing.

Step 3: Make a final decision.

Choice C seems a little punitive. Unless there is a recurring problem, choice B is the best answer.

84. A teacher realizes that students are not enjoying her lecture during their world history class. What can the teacher do to increase students' interest in the content?

    A.   Create a game out of the information the students must learn.

    B.   Allow students who participate to leave class early.

    C.   Deduct points for lack of enthusiasm.

    D.   Postpone the lecture until another day.

A The item above measures Competency 008: The teacher provides appropriate instruction that actively engages students in the learning process.

Here's How to Crack It

Step 1: Identify the scenario.

- Age range: none given

- Goal: increase students' attention

Step 2: Use POE to narrow down the answer choices.

A. Maybe. This sounds like a creative way to reframe the lesson.

B. No. It's inappropriate to allow students to leave class early.

C. No. That's unnecessarily punitive.

D. Maybe.

Step 3: Make a final decision.

Although the teacher could postpone the lesson, there's no guarantee that this would solve the problem in the future. Choice A suggests that the teacher try an alternate teaching style, which has a better chance of solving the problem. The best choice is A.

85. A computer teacher should provide her students with which of the following types of software to keep their daily computer journals?

    A. simulation

    B. word processing

    C. database

    D. design

B The item above measures Competency 009: The teacher incorporates the effective use of technology to plan, organize, deliver, and evaluate instruction for all students.

Here's How to Crack It

Step 1: Identify the scenario.

- Age range: none given

- Goal: identify the most appropriate software

Step 2: Use POE to narrow down the answer choices.
Word processing seems like a good choice for journal writing. Let's see what the options are:

    A.   No. This is useful for demonstrating tasks, procedures, experiments, and the like.

    B.   Yes. This is it.

    C.   No. This is best for storing and sorting information.

    D.   No. This is best for art and design projects.

Step 3: Make a final decision.
B is the best choice.

    86.   Which of the following best describes a situation in which students have different ideas but come together in a compromise that they all agree upon?

        A.   convergent thinking

        B.   divergent thinking

        C.   brainstorming

        D.   objective thinking

A   The item above measures Competency 007: The teacher understands and applies principles and strategies for communicating effectively in varied teaching and learning contexts.

Here's How to Crack It

Step 1: Identify the scenario.

- Age range: none given

- Goal: identify the situation

Step 2: Use POE to narrow down the answer choices.
This sounds like convergent thinking.

    A.   Yes. This is it.

    B.   No. This is when you come up with lots of different ideas.

    C.   No. That could be used to generate the ideas, but not to agree on the best one.

    D.   No. This is unbiased or scientific thinking.

Step 3: Make a final decision.
A is the best answer.

87. When choosing which supplemental materials the students will work with for the upcoming school year, the teacher should give primary importance to which of the following?

   A.   materials used in previous years

   B.   the content that the teacher intends to cover with the materials

   C.   the durability of the materials

   D.   the cost of the materials

B   The item above measures Competency 005: The teacher knows how to establish a classroom climate that fosters learning, equity, and excellence and uses this knowledge to create a physical and emotional environment that is safe and productive.

Here's How to Crack It

Step 1: Identify the scenario.

- Age range: None given

- Goal: what to consider when choosing materials

Step 2: Use POE to narrow down the answer choices.
Let's see what we've got.

   A.   Maybe, you might want to consider what worked in the past.

   B.   Yes, that's definitely important.

   C.   No. That doesn't seem as important as their educational value.

   D.   Maybe but not as important as B.

Step 3: Make a final decision.
B is the best answer. Material that is chosen based on the content of the class will be most effective.

88. A teacher has noticed that Danny often carelessly rushes through his classwork so that he can spend the rest of the class time drawing in his notebook. How should the teacher deal with this problem?

   A.   Move Danny away from his friends.

   B.   Take Danny's notebook away from him.

   C.   Encourage Danny to double-check his work before moving on.

   D.   Suggest to Danny's mother that she enroll Danny in art classes.

C The item above measures Competency 006: The teacher understands strategies for creating an organized and productive learning environment and for managing student behavior.

Here's How to Crack It

Step 1: Identify the scenario.

- Age range: none given

- Goal: get Danny to spend more time on his classwork

Step 2: Use POE to narrow down the answer choices.

A. No. His friends aren't the problem.

B. No. That's punitive, and there are better ways to solve the problem.

C. Maybe.

D. No. That won't solve the problem.

Step 3: Make a final decision.
Choice C is the best answer.

89. Mrs. Davidson's English class partnered with a kindergarten class at a school nearby and answered their letters to Santa. The principal at the school then wrote a thank-you letter to Mrs. Davidson's students, which Mrs. Davidson displayed in her classroom and which she read to her students. Her likely educational purpose is to:

    A. show students a new letter-writing style.

    B. have students recognize the value of establishing long-term relationships.

    C. allow the students to feel proud of their accomplishment.

    D. have students learn socially acceptable behavior.

D The item above measures Competency 001: The teacher understands human developmental processes and applies this knowledge to plan instruction and ongoing assessment that motivate students and are responsive to their developmental characteristics and needs.

Here's How to Crack It

Step 1: Identify the scenario.

- Age range: none given

- Goal: determine an educational purpose

Step 2: Use POE to narrow down the answer choices.

    A. Maybe, but it doesn't say the style was new.

    B. No. There were no long-term relationships discussed.

    C. Maybe, but it's unlikely that pride was the educational purpose.

    D. Maybe.

Step 3: Make a final decision.
The best answer as far as an educational purpose goes is D.

90. Several parents have agreed to help chaperone the senior field trip to Washington, D.C. The teacher and students will be accompanied by several parents who will serve as group leaders. To ensure the success of the field trip, the teacher should make sure to:

    A. share the goals of the field trip with the group leaders/parents.

    B. ask the parents to sign waivers for the field trip.

    C. inform the group leaders of the daily schedules ahead of time.

    D. balance the small groups with equal numbers of boys and girls.

A   The item above measures Competency 011: The teacher understands the importance of family involvement in children's education and knows how to interact and communicate effectively with families.

Here's How to Crack It

Step 1: Identify the scenario.

- Age range: none given

- Goal: ensure the field trip's success

Step 2: Use POE to narrow down the answer choices.

    A. Maybe. It would help for the chaperones to understand the goals.

    B. No. That's unrelated to the educational success of the trip.

    C. Maybe.

    D. No. There's no great advantage to that, and it seems unrelated to the problem as stated.

Step 3: Make a final decision.
Choices A and C would both help. In the absence of any additional information, assume that the educational success of the trip is more important than the mechanical success. A is therefore the best answer.

91. Before allowing students to use the new computers in the computer lab, the teacher must first:

    A.   learn to use them herself.

    B.   install student protection software.

    C.   catalog the ID numbers of the computers with the administration.

    D.   load email software onto each machine.

B   The item above measures Competency 009: The teacher incorporates the effective use of technology to plan, organize, deliver, and evaluate instruction for all students.

Here's How to Crack It

Step 1: Identify the scenario.

- Age range: none given

- Goal: identify something the teacher must do

Step 2: Use POE to narrow down the answer choices.
The question says "must," so we should be looking for a legal requirement.

    A.   No. That doesn't sound like a legal requirement.

    B.   Yes. That sounds like a legal requirement.

    C.   No. That doesn't sound like a legal requirement.

    D.   No. That's not a legal requirement.

Step 3: Make a final decision.
The best answer is B.

92. Which of the following assignments would likely require higher-order thinking than the others?

    A.   memorizing the elements on the periodic table

    B.   reading a passage

    C.   composing a letter

    D.   interpreting a graph

D The item above measures Competency 004: The teacher understands learning processes and factors that impact student learning and demonstrates this knowledge by planning effective, engaging instruction and appropriate assessments.

Here's How to Crack It

Step 1: Identify the scenario.

- Age range: none given

- Goal: identify higher-order thinking

Step 2: Use POE to narrow down the answer choices.

A. No. That's just rote memorization.

B. No. Simply reading the passage doesn't involve higher-order thinking.

C. No. Simply writing doesn't necessarily involve higher-order thinking skills.

D. Yes. Interpretation requires higher-order thinking.

Step 3: Make a final decision.
D is the best answer.

93. Introducing a new chapter by asking students what they already know about the general topic:

    A. helps the students process the new information more efficiently.

    B. allows the students to recognize the pattern of learning.

    C. brings the community into the classroom.

    D. helps the students develop critical reading skills.

A The item above measures Competency 007: The teacher understands and applies principles and strategies for communicating effectively in varied teaching and learning contexts.

Here's How to Crack It

Step 1: Identify the scenario.

- Age range: none given

- Goal: determine why you should ask students what they already know

Step 2: Use POE to narrow down the answer choices.
You should know this one: new knowledge should build on old knowledge.

    A. Yes. This is it.

    B. No. That doesn't mention new knowledge building on old knowledge.

    C. No. That's not relevant.

    D. No. That's also not relevant.

Step 3: Make a final decision.
A is the best answer.

> 94. Which of the following is an example of divergent thinking?
>
>   A. singing in the school choir
>
>   B. playing the flute in the school orchestra
>
>   C. composing a new song
>
>   D. interpreting sheet music in a new manner

D   The item above measures Competency 007: The teacher understands and applies principles and strategies for communicating effectively in varied teaching and learning contexts.

Here's How to Crack It

Step 1: Identify the scenario.

- Age range: none given

- Goal: identify divergent thinking

Step 2: Use POE to narrow down the answer choices.

    A. Doubtful. This is not looking a problem in a new way.

    B. Similar to choice A, so we can cross them both out.

    C. Maybe.

    D. Maybe.

Step 3: Make a final decision.
Divergent thinking can be defined as looking at problems in new ways, so D is a better answer.

95. A group of girlfriends are arguing in the hallway. The teacher is able to sort out that one of the girls has had her feelings hurt by her friend. The teacher's primary goal in having the two girls sit down together to talk about what was said was to help the girls:

   A. understand this is not how they should solve disagreements.

   B. communicate better in the future.

   C. discuss the problem without feedback from others.

   D. see the consequences that their actions have on others.

B The item above measures Competency 006: The teacher understands strategies for creating an organized and productive learning environment and for managing student behavior.

Here's How to Crack It

Step 1: Identify the scenario.

- Age range: none given

- Goal: determine why the teacher had the girls talk to each other.

Step 2: Use POE to narrow down the answer choices.

   A. Maybe. Understanding alternate ways to solve disagreements is important.

   B. Maybe. Promoting better communication is a likely goal.

   C. No. The teacher is providing feedback.

   D. Maybe. Identifying consequences of their actions might be a goal.

Step 3: Make a final decision.

None of the answers seems great, but a teacher's goal should be to give the students the tools to solve problems on their own, so B is the best choice.

ABOUT THE AUTHOR

Fritz Stewart has been working for The Princeton Review in a variety of capacities since 1988. A former high school teacher, he holds a Master's Degree in Computer Science from Stanford University and a Master's Degree in Orchestral Conducting from the University of Cincinnati College-Conservatory of Music.

NOTES

NOTES

NOTES

NOTES

NOTES

NOTES

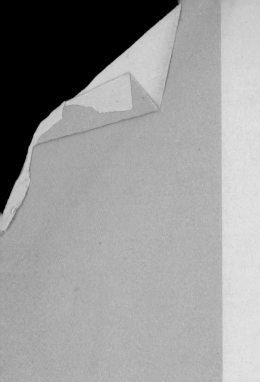

Need More?

If grad school is in your future, you're in the right place. Our expertise extends far beyond the TExES, and we've helped countless students get into their top-choice grad schools.

One way to increase the number of acceptance letters you get is to raise your test scores. So, if you're experiencing some trepidation, The Princeton Review can help.

We consistently improve prospective grad school students' scores through our books, classroom courses, private tutoring, and online courses. Call 800-2Review or visit *PrincetonReview.com* for details.

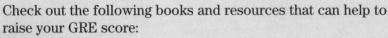

Check out the following books and resources that can help to raise your GRE score:

- *Cracking the GRE*
- *Math Workout for the GRE*
- *Verbal Workout for the GRE*
- *GRE Classroom Courses*
- *GRE Online Courses*
- *GRE Private Tutoring*